ADDITIONAL PRAISE FOR
Smart Women Finish Rich

"*Finally* a book for women that talks about money in a way that makes sense. David Bach is not just an expert in managing money—he's the ultimate motivational coach for women. I can't recommend this book enough. It's a must-read!"

—Barbara DeAngelis, Ph.D., bestselling author of *Real Moments*

"David Bach both educates and enlightens his readers through his sound investment advice and humor. I highly recommend this book!"

—Marci Shimoff, coauthor of *Chicken Soup for the Woman's Soul*

"[David] Bach gets across some complicated stuff: how to organize a portfolio, keep the taxman at bay, invest in yourself, and earn more, all of which make this book one of the best overall."

—*Working Woman*

"Straight-shooting, action-oriented tips for getting a handle on [your] spending and saving habits . . . presented in a straightforward, nonintimidating manner perfect for the personal finance newbie."

—ABC News.com

"I love this book! It's more like a motivational seminar than a financial primer. Following David's insightful steps, you will not only increase your net worth, you will change your life. Everyone, not just women, should read this book—at least once!"

—Barbara Stanley, author of *Prince Charming Isn't Coming*

"Finally, a financial planning guide that addresses the unique issues that women face today. But what I like the most is that David starts with the most important principle: aligning your money with your values."

—Harry S. Dent, Jr., bestselling author of *The Roaring 2000s*

"In this book, David Bach lays out a simple but effective pathway that any woman can follow to reduce spending, start saving, and plan for a rich future while enjoying life along the way. The book is filled with practical suggestions to help women achieve strong financial plans for their security."

—*Business Life*

"If I had to identify one fundamental career skill that most workers lack, it would be how to manage their money so their salary goes further."

—*San Francisco Chronicle*

PRAISE FOR *Smart Couples Finish Rich*

"I know how hard it is to make a personal-finance book user-friendly. Bach has done it. *Smart Couples Finish Rich* picks up where *Smart Women Finish Rich* left off . . . This is an easy, lively read filled with tips that made me smile and at least once made me laugh."

—*USA Weekend*

"David Bach offers a prescription both to avoid money conflicts and to plan a harmonious future together. Bach's new book offers some valuable new nuggets. The bottom line is action, and Bach's chatty writing style helps motivate you to that end."

—*BusinessWeek*

"Bach does a great job convincing couples to think about money, talk about money, get a financial plan in order—and yes, spend less and save more."

—*American Way*

"*Smart Couples Finish Rich* teaches women and men to work together as a team when it comes to money. Bach's nine steps are powerful, yet easy to understand and fun to implement. The entire family can benefit from this great book."

—Robert T. Kiyosaki, author of *Rich Dad, Poor Dad*

"My husband and I read this book and found it easy to understand, compassionate, and full of simple financial tools that we could use together. *Smart Couples Finish Rich* takes the guesswork out of the complicated realm of joint finances and leads you down the path of true success."

—Chérie Carter-Scott, author of *If Life Is a Game, These Are the Rules* and *If Success Is a Game, These Are the Rules*

"[David Bach's] advice is heartfelt and worthy. For most couples struggling to make their financial lives smoother, this is a good place to get the dialogue rolling."

—*USA Today*

"[Bach] specializes in commonsense advice and a clear-cut path for engaging your partner in fruitful discussions about your shared financial future . . . His advice serves to free you and your beloved from the stress of never being quite sure of exactly where you stand financially. You'll probably be surprised by how big a difference Bach's strategy can make in your relationship."

—*Better Investing*

"*Smart Couples Finish Rich* is a must-read for couples. Bach is a great financial coach . . . he knows how to bring couples together on a topic that often divides them."
　　　　—John Gray, author of *Men Are from Mars, Women Are from Venus*

"*Smart Couples Finish Rich* will help not just couples but financial advisors who work with couples. Bach's approach of looking at your values first and your 'stuff' second is right on the money."
　　　　—Harry S. Dent, Jr., author of *The Roaring 2000s Investor*

"David Bach brilliantly acknowledged the true economic power of women in his EVEolutionary first book, *Smart Women Finish Rich*. He smartly follows up with *Smart Couples Finish Rich*, believing in the importance of women, recognizing that traditional roles are changing and that incorporating a woman's financial needs will move a couple into their best future."
　　　　—Faith Popcorn, futurist author of *EVEolution:*
　　　　The Eight Truths of Marketing to Women

"David Bach is a financial genius with a passion for coaching couples on how to reach their financial dreams! His program will quickly empower you to make smart choices with your money. I especially like the way he teaches couples to dream-plan together and spend money based on their values."
　　　　—Marcia Wieder, author of *Making Your Dreams Come True*

"*Smart Couples Finish Rich* hits the perfect balance, and goes above and beyond to be a reference book and counselor. Bach has seen a lot, between couples coming into his office, students at his seminars, letters from readers of his previous book, and his own marriage. All of this knowledge is incorporated into steps that are useful and doable. [The book's] flexibility makes it a perfect reference guide as life changes. The clear and concise information is written conversationally. The format really makes it feel as though your finances have been reviewed by a professional. More important, you and your partner do it together, which ideally gets you talking."
　　　　—*Pacific Coast Business Times*

SMART WOMEN FINISH RICH

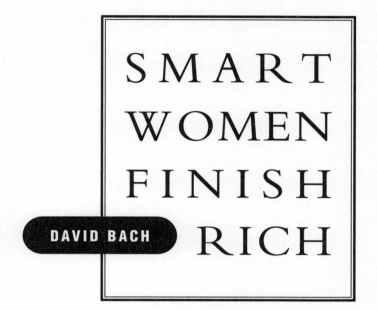

SMART WOMEN FINISH RICH

DAVID BACH

9 STEPS TO ACHIEVING FINANCIAL SECURITY

AND FUNDING YOUR DREAMS

Canadian Edition

DOUBLEDAY CANADA

National Library of Canada Cataloguing in Publication

Bach, David

  Smart women finish rich : 9 steps to achieving financial security and funding your dreams / David Bach. — Canadian ed.

ISBN 0-385-65967-9

  1. Women—Finance, Personal. 2. Investments. 3. Financial security.
I. Title.

| HG179.B323 2003 | 332.024'042 | C2002-904162-7 |

The U.S. edition of this book was published by Broadway Books.

Smart Women Finish Rich, Smart Couples Finish Rich, Purpose-Focused Financial Plan, FinishRich Inventory Planner, FinishRich File Folder System, The Latté Factor, and *Seven-Day Financial Challenge* are trademarks of FinishRich, Inc.

This book is designed to provide accurate and authoritative information on the subject of personal finances. While all of the stories and anecdotes described in the book are based on true experiences, most of the names are pseudonyms, and some situations have been changed slightly to protect each individual's privacy. It is sold with the understanding that neither the author nor the publisher is engaged in rendering legal, accounting, or other professional services by publishing this book. As each individual situation is unique, questions relevant to personal finances and specific to the individual should be addressed to an appropriate professional to ensure that the situation has been evaluated carefully and appropriately. The author and publisher specifically disclaim any liability, loss, or risk which is incurred as a consequence, directly or indirectly, of the use and application of any of the contents of this work.

The diagram on page 159 is reprinted with the permission of Successful Money Management Seminars, Inc.

Printed and bound in Canada

Published in Canada by
Doubleday Canada, a division of
Random House of Canada Limited

Visit Random House of Canada Limited's website: www.randomhouse.ca

TRANS   10   9

To my beloved grandmother Rose Bach,

who taught me the importance of living life to its fullest.

You will forever be with me in thought and spirit.

I miss you.

Contents

Acknowledgements   xiii

Introduction to the Canadian Edition   xvii

INTRODUCTION
   WHY SMART WOMEN ARE TAKING CONTROL
   OF THEIR FINANCIAL FUTURES   1

STEP ONE
   LEARN THE FACTS—AND MYTHS—
   ABOUT YOUR MONEY   15

STEP TWO
   PUT YOUR MONEY WHERE YOUR VALUES ARE   38

STEP THREE
   FIGURE OUT WHERE YOU STAND FINANCIALLY
   . . . AND WHERE YOU WANT TO GO   56

STEP FOUR
   USE THE POWER OF THE LATTÉ FACTOR . . .
   HOW TO CREATE MASSIVE WEALTH ON JUST
   A FEW DOLLARS A WEEK!   87

STEP FIVE
PRACTISE GRANDMA'S THREE-BASKET APPROACH
TO FINANCIAL SECURITY   106

STEP SIX
LEARN THE 10 BIGGEST MISTAKES INVESTORS MAKE
AND HOW TO AVOID THEM   185

STEP SEVEN
RAISING SMART KIDS TO FINISH RICH   208

STEP EIGHT
FOLLOW THE 12 COMMANDMENTS OF
ATTRACTING GREATER WEALTH   228

STEP NINE
FINISHRICH SUCCESS STORIES—BE INSPIRED   252

Appendix 1
WHERE DOES YOUR MONEY *REALLY* GO?   271

Appendix 2
FINISHRICH INVENTORY PLANNER   275

Suggested Programs and Readings   281

Index   285

Acknowledgements

Grandmother Bach once told me that the key to having a fulfilling life was to understand that life's greatest fruit was always at the end of the branch and that you had to be willing to fall out of the tree to get it. The key, I was told, was to have people around you who could catch you should you fall. I have been blessed to have an incredible group of people around me as I go about taking risks to grab the fruit of life. Only because of these people who have supported me am I where I am today.

First and foremost, to the readers of the original edition of *Smart Women Finish Rich*, thank you, thank you, thank you. I will be forever grateful for having heard from so many of you about how *Smart Women Finish Rich* changed your life. It is your letters and e-mails that made the process of revising and updating the book so motivating. The knowledge that I have reached so many of you has made all the travel, hard work, and tight deadlines worth it. It is you who inspire me to want to help even more. I hope this new edition of *Smart Women Finish Rich* tailored specifically for Canada answers your questions and meets your expectations.

Thank you also to the thousands of financial advisors throughout North America who now teach my Smart Women Finish Rich™

seminars and Smart Couples Finish Rich™ seminars. Thank you for bringing my message to so many people in your local communities.

To my new readers and friends in Canada a huge "thank you" for all your requests to have a Canadian edition of these books. It was your letters, e-mails and support that helped convince Doubleday Canada to publish these books. To Maya Mavjee, publisher at Doubleday Canada, thank you for recognizing the great potential for these books in the Canadian market. To my wonderful editor in Canada, Meg Taylor, thank you for caring about the message of these books and for working so hard to bring it to Canada. To Bruce McDougall, thank you for working closely with me to adapt the American text to be specific to Canada. You have both done an out-standing job. To the Doubleday Canada team that I know will work tirelessly to help us reach and help Canadian women—thank you!

Smart Women Finish Rich would never have happened if I hadn't found a superstar agent. To Jan Miller, my "go-to gal," I will be for-ever grateful for our friendship and your belief in me and my vision. You make things happen, and I love it! To Jan's right hand, Shannon Miser-Marven—thank you for all your help with my contracts and scheduling.

To Allan Mayer, my collaborator on the original *Smart Women Finish Rich*—as well as on *Smart Couples Finish Rich*—thank you, thank you, thank you for making these books what they are. From the beginning to the end, you have been a true professional and a delight to work with.

To Vicki St. George, thank you for being the angel who tapped me on the shoulder at "Date with Destiny" and told me you could help me make my dream come true. It is because of your help on my book proposal that I was able to have my pick of agents. I will be for-ever grateful to you and your partner, Karen Risch, at Just Write for being the first experts to believe in and see my vision.

To my incredible team at Broadway Books, I loved you guys from the minute I met you. To my editor, Suzanne Oaks, you are absolutely amazing. Your insight and ideas on this book have been invaluable. I am thrilled to have now worked with you on three books. To David Drake, thank you for your consistently outstanding publicity effort. I am eternally grateful to your wisdom and efforts in helping me get my message out. To Claire Johnson, thank you for keeping me on track with deadlines and for your outstanding assistance. To Harry Cornelius, thank you for helping me take my FinishRich™ seminars national. Your ability as my agent in my financial service deals has been invaluable. Here's to many more life-changing opportunities. A very special thank you goes out to my incredible sponsors and team at Van Kampen Investments. As a result of our efforts, we have so far reached nearly a half million people with Smart Women Finish Rich and Smart Couples Finish Rich seminars. To Jack Zimmerman, Dave Swanson, Dominic Martellaro, Lisa Kueng, Scott West, Gary DeMoss: thank you for believing in me and the power of this project.

Thank you to my world-class team in the office at The Bach Group. To Kathy Price, Emily Bach, Tom Moglia, Jeff Borges, and my father, Marty Bach—thank you for keeping the office running so smoothly and our clients happy. Thank you also for understanding my desire to spend more of my time and efforts writing, speaking, and educating people about money.

To my many mentors, I owe both thanks and recognition. To my teacher and mentor Anthony Robbins, your friendship, teaching, and seminars have shaped my life since 1990, and for that I am eternally grateful. To Bill Bachrach, your book *Values-Based Financial Planning*, your TAC program, and your friendship have changed my life forever. Thank you for teaching me how to help others tap into their values about money. To Dan Sullivan, your "Strategic Coach" program already has had a major impact on both my life and my teachings. Thank you for showing me the power of focus and simplicity. To my personal coach, Shirley Anderson, "Bravo, bravo, bravo." I applaud your greatness in coaching, and I feel blessed to have found you.

To my good friend Jeff Odiorne, who suggested over dinner, "Why don't you just take a day off work each week and write your book?" Gosh, that was obvious. Thanks for coming up with it! To my close friends who have both listened to me talk about this book and supported me emotionally throughout the process, I thank you for your love and friendship.

To my many clients and students, with whom I have grown and from whom I have learned along the way, thank you for allowing me to make a wonderful living doing something I love.

To my incredible mother, Bobbi Bach, thank you for raising me to believe I could accomplish anything. You gave me the greatest gift a mother could give: the gift of love, security, and confidence.

To my successful sister, Emily Bach, you epitomize today's Smart Woman who is living smart and finishing rich. I am very proud of you. I know the transition of me leaving my financial planning business and you running The Bach Group will go flawlessly.

To my father, Marty Bach, I never realized how much work it took to get to the level of success you have achieved. Now I do. You always have been there for me, and I love you for it. Thank you for brainwashing me into the investment business and supporting me in everything I've done. This book would not have been possible without your support.

And finally to my wife, Michelle: You are without question the most wonderful woman I have ever met. Thank you for your fantastic input on this book, for always bringing a smile to my face, for helping me to run our company, and for being my safe island in the storm. Most important, thank you for believing in me. Each year our life together gets more exciting and our journey more adventurous.

I love you all with all my heart.

INTRODUCTION

TO THE

CANADIAN

EDITION

A Personal Message

from David Bach

It's hard for me to believe that five years have passed since I began writing the original *Smart Women Finish Rich*. Back in 1997, I had a simple goal: I wanted to write a book that a million women could use to take charge of their financial future quickly and easily. At the time, I thought this was an extremely challenging goal. What I didn't understand then was the power of word of mouth.

Smart Women Finish Rich came out in the U.S. in January of 1999, and in less than a month it was a bestseller. Before long, it had made not only the *New York Times* and *Wall Street Journal* Business bestseller lists but also the *BusinessWeek*, *San Francisco Chronicle*, *Boston Globe*, and *Washington Post* bestseller lists. *BusinessWeek* called it one of the top financial books of 2000. The book's success also led to a PBS special—called, naturally enough, "Smart Women Finish Rich"—and eventually to my Smart Women Finish Rich seminars going national, and now global. What I began as a small workshop in San Francisco, California, with a few dozen women is now a program taught by thousands of financial advisors in more than 1,500 cities. Indeed, in any given month, you can find thousands of women attending Smart Women Finish Rich seminars throughout North America, learning the strategies laid out in this book in a fun and supportive environment. (If you would like to find a list of classes in Canada, please visit our website at *www.finishrich.com*.)

And now we're reaching out across the globe. *Smart Women Finish Rich* is currently published in six languages and is being distributed in a growing list of countries that includes Australia, Canada, Taiwan, Spain, and Korea.

What's made all this possible is you, the reader. The reason *Smart Women Finish Rich* has reached so many women is that readers have shared its message with friends and loved ones. If it were not for this word of mouth, *Smart Women Finish Rich* would have gone nowhere.

If I've learned one thing in the last five years about women and money, it is this: Once a woman learns how to take charge of her finances, she will never go back. The growing financial empowerment of women is not a fad. It is a new reality in the households of North America, and it is going to change our destiny.

So, given all this, if the book has had such an amazing impact, why update it and create a special *Canadian Edition*?

The answer is simple. **In Canada you have entirely different tax laws, regulations, retirement planning strategies, investment opportunities, and resources.** You deserve to have financial books that are written specifically to your needs. And that is exactly where this special edition comes in. This edition of *Smart Women Finish Rich* and its companion book *Smart Couples Finish Rich* are now completely tailored to Canada.

You will find everything you need to know about Canadian retirement planning, including tax laws and how they affect your ability to fund your retirement. You'll learn how to use Canada's retirement planning tools to their full advantage and where to invest. Specifically, in this book you'll get information on Registered Pension Plans (RPPs), Registered Retirement Savings Plans (RRSPs), and defined-benefit plans. We'll also cover everything you need to know about how to invest your retirement savings and what resources to go to in Canada to get the appropriate help.

Another reason for this new edition is the Internet. Compared to what's out there now, it barely existed when I wrote the original book. Today, the Internet is the most powerful tool I know for taking charge of your finances. Reflecting this fact, when I suggest a strategy in this edition of *Smart Women Finish Rich*, I accompany the suggestion with a web address where you can take immediate action to implement the strategy, and I recommend Canadian resources and websites.

Moreover, since I wrote the first edition, I have developed some additional financial strategies that I want to share with you. The best part about publishing *Smart Women Finish Rich* was the incredible response it generated from readers. Literally thousands of women took the time to let me know how my book helped them take charge of their financial lives. Your letters and e-mails have had a profound impact on me, and I am deeply grateful for them. Your stories make me realize how lucky I am to be in a position to serve as a financial coach to so many. At the same time, many of your questions came as a challenge, making me realize that there is so much more to teach and explain.

Largely in response to readers' stories about increasing their income after reading my original "12 Commandments of Attracting Greater Wealth," I have rewritten this chapter to include more specifics on how you can grow your income in a difficult job market. For similar reasons, I also have updated the section on how to hire a financial professional, providing a source of referral systems to help you locate one in Canada.

Perhaps most noticeably, I've added two powerful new steps to what was originally a seven-step journey to achieving financial security and independence. Our new Step Seven is called "Raising Smart Kids to Finish Rich," and I wrote it in response to a huge outpouring from mothers who asked me to include a chapter about kids. This transforming chapter is designed to help you make the step from student to teacher. It is my conviction that our children need to be taught about money and they need to be taught now. Because we often don't teach our kids about money in school, we are raising a nation of financial illiterates. Until our school systems in North America make financial education a mandatory part of the curriculum, we've got no choice but to teach our kids at home. This chapter is meant to show you how. In addition to explaining how to teach your kids about money, it also covers how to pay for university or college, including details on Registered Education Savings Plans (RESPs) and the Canadian Education Savings Grant.

Finally, there is our new Step Nine: "FinishRich Success Stories . . . Be Inspired." This is my favourite step because it came from readers sharing with me how the original edition of this book helped them change their lives. The material in this chapter is taken from the thousands of stories I received from women like you who succeeded by taking action after they read *Smart Women Finish Rich*. Because I found their letters so moving—and because I believe that other people's success stories can be a huge motivator when it comes to taking action in your own life—I convinced the publisher to let me share some of them with you. One thing that has not changed in this new edition is the book's primary goal. *Smart Women Finish Rich* is still about the simple idea that if you take the right kind of action now, you can easily live and finish rich. As I have said time and time again, you deserve to live and finish rich, and I know you can do it. So let's get started.

I hope you enjoy this revised edition custom tailored to Canada. If you have any suggestions for a future edition—whether they concern something I may have missed or something I didn't explain fully enough—please let me know. You can contact us by visiting our website at *www.finishrich.com*.

And, again, to all those of you who helped make *Smart Women Finish Rich* the success it's been, THANK YOU!

Live Rich!

SMART

WOMEN

FINISH

RICH

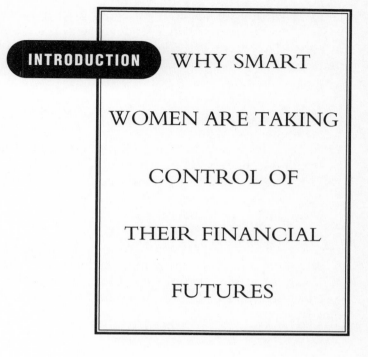

WHY SMART WOMEN ARE TAKING CONTROL OF THEIR FINANCIAL FUTURES

I'll never forget the moment I asked my mom, "What really makes the world go round—money or love?" I was only about five at the time. She looked me straight in the eyes and said, "David, love is what makes life special, but without money you are in deep trouble!"

Actually, "deep trouble" are my words. What my mom really said can't be repeated. I had never heard my mom use an "adult" swear word before, so even at age five I knew then and there that not having money could be really painful. The obvious next question that came to my five-year-old mind was, "Are we rich, Mom?" That question took a little longer for her to answer (I think she eventually made me go play with my toys), but the thought of money has stayed with me ever since. If not having money is so bad, why don't more people figure out how to get and keep it? It can't be that hard. Or can it?

More than 25 years later, I'm privileged to make my living teaching thousands of people—mostly women—how to invest and manage their money. And I'm happy to report that, when you strip away all the baloney, learning how to handle your own finances turns out to be relatively easy. Indeed, through my Smart Women Finish Rich seminars, I've already helped hundreds of thousands of women travel the same road to financial independence as you are going to take in this book. They have learned—as you will—the three keys to smart money management that enable a woman to gain control over her own financial destiny and, yes, finish rich:

- How to use both your head and your heart in making financial decisions.
- How what I call "the Latté Factor" can transform even the most modest wage earner into a significant investor.
- How my "three-basket" approach to financial planning can assure you not only long-term security but the ability to realize your lifelong dreams.

As you will discover, my approach to personal money management involves some powerful and exciting techniques. And all of them are pretty easy to master. Before we get started, however, it might be a good idea for me to address a question that often comes up at this point—namely . . .

WHO AM I TO HELP
YOU FINISH RICH?

One way to answer this question is to tell you that prior to founding FinishRich, Inc., for nearly a decade I was a Senior Vice President and financial advisor for a major New York Stock Exchange firm and a partner in The Bach Group, which managed during my tenure over half a billion dollars for individual investors. Most of my hundreds of clients are women who have come to me after attending one of my investment seminars or through referrals from other women.

But what you probably really want to know is why a man (and yes, I admit it—I can't hide the fact that I am a man) is so driven to teach and empower women to take control of their finances. Well, the answer has mainly to do with my grandmother. Her name was Rose Bach, and she was unlike any other grandmother I ever met.

My Grandma, the Investor

The head buyer for wigs at Gimbel's (back when Gimbel's was one of America's leading department stores), Grandma Bach was a working woman at a time when most women weren't. Now, my grandparents were never wealthy; in fact, they never even owned their own home. Nonetheless, my grandmother decided at a very early age that she wanted to be an investor. Acting on her own, she took her earnings and put as much as she could afford into stocks and bonds. Over time, and without any advice from her husband, she built up a high-quality portfolio. When she passed away recently, at the age of 86, her investments were worth close to $1 million—this from a woman whose first job paid only $10 a week!

There were many things my Grandma Bach taught me, but for our purposes, there's one lesson that deserves to be singled out:

You don't have to be rich to be an investor!

Of course, by becoming an investor, if you do it wisely like my Grandma Bach, you will almost certainly get rich!

It was Grandma Bach who helped me make my first stock purchase. I was seven years old, and my favourite restaurant in the world was McDonald's. So whenever I spent time with my grandmother, she would take me there for lunch. One day, at her prompting, instead of asking for ketchup for my fries when I marched up to the counter, I looked at the woman on the other side and asked, "Is this company public?"

The counter lady looked back at me as if I were nuts, then called over the manager. Yes, he told me, McDonald's was a publicly traded company. After a little persuasion from Grandma Bach (and a lot of vacuuming and dishwashing), I saved my allowance for three months and managed to accumulate enough money to buy three shares of McDonald's Inc.

That was over 25 years ago. Since then McDonald's stock has gone up in value and split so many times that those original three shares of mine have multiplied into close to 200 shares. If I'd had enough money to purchase 100 shares of the company back then (an investment of around $10,000 at the time), my McDonald's holdings would today be worth close to $500,000! (I often give my parents a hard time for not having lent me the additional money.) And all I had done was go out to lunch with my grandmother when I was a little kid and put my allowance into a company whose hamburgers I liked.

Every Woman Can Be Wealthy

Because Grandma Bach was my biggest inspiration as a child, I grew up thinking every woman was like her—aware of the importance of investing and pretty darn good at it too. So it came as something of a shock to me, when I followed my father into the investment business, to discover that, if anything, the opposite was true. Most women never receive even a basic education in finance until it's too late—which is to say, after they get divorced or widowed and suddenly find themselves forced to deal with everything at the worst possible moment. The result, all too often, is financial devastation.

I wanted to help. I wanted every woman to have the information, the education, and the tools to take care of herself financially no matter what the circumstances. So I designed an investment seminar called "Smart Women Finish Rich!" in which I did two important things. One, I addressed the heart as well as the head, recognizing that financial planning is as much an emotional issue as an intellectual one. And two, I laid out a simple but effective pathway that any woman could follow to achieve financial security and freedom.

The response was immediate and incredible. First dozens, then hundreds of women signed up for my classes, and over the last few years, I've personally done speeches for rooms of hundreds of women to as many as 3,000. Additionally, thousands of financial advisors in over 1,500 cities throughout North America have taught Smart Women Finish Rich seminars from coast to coast with thousands of women attending every month. (To find a seminar in your city, please visit *www.finishrich.com*.) Why the huge response? In a word, necessity. As one student told me, "Growing up, no one taught me about money, not my father, not my mother, not my school—so I realized it was time to teach myself." Explained another student: "Nobody is going to take care of me. I have to take the responsibility myself." Added a third: "We'd be in deep trouble if we left everything up to our husbands. We need to know about our finances so we can be independent and take care of ourselves."

Though my students come from all walks of life—rich, poor, old, young, married, single—virtually all of them believe in the empowering importance of education. As a working mother of two from Walnut Creek, California, put it after taking my course, "Understanding your own finances is as important as knowing about your health. You can't make financial decisions if you're not educated."

What I've learned from my seminars is that women want to be responsible for their financial futures. The problem is, most of them just don't know how to get started. Or if they've taken steps in certain areas, they've neglected others. I can't tell you how gratifying it's been for me to see the thousands of women who've been through my seminars taking control of their financial destiny, making better decisions about their financial future, and feeling great about their financial well-being as a result.

WELCOME TO

THE CLUB!

And now you are going to join their ranks.

Congratulations are in order, for you've just taken a very important step toward achieving financial security and independence. The fact that you've picked up this book shows that you've decided to take control of your financial future. You may not believe it, but in making that decision and acting on it, you've just completed the hardest part of the process.

Congratulations too because your timing couldn't have been better. The fact is, there's never been a better time in the entire history of the planet for women to be taking control of their financial futures. These days not only are women pursuing successful careers, but in many cases, the woman's paycheque contributes substantially to the family's financial stability.

According to Statistics Canada, women make up more than 45 percent of the workforce. Single women in Canada earned an average of almost $31,000 a year in 1999. Almost 65 percent of Canadian households headed by a husband and wife relied on earnings of both individuals. Together, they earned an average of $79,000 a year.

Between 1991 and 1996, the number of self-employed women grew 44.3 percent, and the growth in the number of Canadian unincorporated businesses owned by women has surpassed the U.S. since 1989. In fact, women are starting businesses at *twice* the rate of men, with women starting half of all new businesses in Canada. Women own one-third of small- and medium-sized businesses. In 1997, women created more jobs than Canada's top 100 companies, and women-led businesses were creating employment at four times the average rate for all businesses. Finally, the number of self-employed women under 30 rose an impressive 30 percent between 1991 and 1996, compared to a 4 percent increase in self-employed young men.

In other words, women are earning more money, in more ways, than ever, and many of them are running their own businesses. They deserve to keep as much of their earnings as possible and watch their savings grow.

Something Men May Not Want to Hear . . .

Having worked as a financial planner and advisor with literally thousands of women over the past few years, there's something else I can tell you about women and money: As a rule, women make better investors than men. When women become investors, they generally devise a plan, and then they stick to it. In a word, they "commit." Men, on the other hand . . . well, we've all heard that dreaded phrase "fear of commitment," haven't we? Rather than stay with a great, solid investment, men often get bored and start looking around for the next "hot thing."

My experience is that women simply do not do this. As a rule, women who invest tend to be wary of so-called hot tips. Not many men. Time after time I have had male clients phone me with orders to buy 1,000 shares of stock merely because they heard a "hot tip" at the gym or on the golf course. Often these requests to make a stock purchase involve no research, just brazen bravado.

And this is not just my opinion. U.S. statistics bear me out. According to a study by the University of California, Davis (based on 38,000 accounts), women investors at discount brokerage firms did better than men by 9 percent a year! Just a fluke? Hardly. According to UC National Association of Investors Corporation, women's investment clubs have outperformed men's in *9 out of the last 12 years!* I suspect we'd find similar results in Canada.

Do you find that surprising? Many of us do. That's because we've unthinkingly accepted the stereotype that money management is a man's game—one that women simply aren't suited to play. Why? It may have something to do with the fact that most of us grew up watching our fathers manage the family money. Certainly, many women have told me that was the reason it never dawned on them to take an active role in shaping their financial futures. Whatever the cause, however, far too many women decide early on that, when it comes to money, they'd prefer to stay on the sidelines. They say things like "Well, I'm not good with money," or "I'm not driven by money," or "I'm not materialistic," or "Money doesn't make you happy," or "Why bother—the more you make, the more the government will take," and on and on, trying to justify their fear of dealing with their financial situation.

A "Game" You Just Can't Sit Out

I think that is a mistake. As a woman today, you've got to stop watching and start participating. Even more important, you've got to start calling the shots for yourself. There's no getting around it: This so-called money game (a misnomer if ever there was one) has very real, very serious consequences for all of us. People who say they've decided not to play the money game are only fooling themselves. After all, how we handle our money colours every aspect of our lives—the education of our children, the sort of home we provide our families, the type of contribution we make to our communities (not to mention all those mundane things like the kind of food we eat, the clothing we wear, and the vacations we take).

The fact is, none of us really has a choice: We are all playing the money game whether we want to or not. The only question is: Are we winning?

Most people, unfortunately, are not. Why? Because no one ever taught them the rules. Think about it. How could you possibly ever win a game—or even do well at it—if you didn't know the rules? You couldn't. Maybe every once in a while you'd luck out—but that's all it would be: luck. You couldn't depend on it; you certainly wouldn't want to risk your bank account, your retirement income, or your dream of a brand-new house on it.

So what we need in order to take control of our financial destiny is a copy of the rules. An instruction manual. A road map.

More Good News for Women

That's what this book is: It's a financial road map that will show you how to get from where you are right now to where you want to be. The good news here is that women tend to be pretty good about using road maps. Certainly they're better than most men. Men generally prefer to drive around aimlessly, hoping to spot a familiar landmark, rather than admit they're lost and ask someone for directions. You know what I'm talking about. I'm sure you were once out on a date, or maybe you were in the car with your husband or your father, and suddenly you realized you had been driving for what seemed like an awfully long time with no sign of the Wayne's Kountry Kitchen you were looking for. The conversation probably went something like this.

YOU: Honey, I think we're lost. Maybe we should stop in a gas station or something . . .
HIM: No, we're fine. I know exactly where we are.
YOU: But . . .
HIM: I said we're fine. It's just a ways up here—I'm sure of it.

Of course, what each of you was thinking at the time was something else again.

YOU: He doesn't have a clue where we are. If he'd just pull over and get some directions, we could figure this out and get there!
HIM: I can't believe we're lost! I thought I knew the way. Jeez, where are we? I probably should stop and ask for directions, but if I do that, she'll know I don't know where we are, and so will some stranger. How much of a loser would that make me!

The same thing tends to happen with our money. As a rule, men feel they are supposed to know what they're doing when it comes to personal finance, so even when they don't, they often pretend that they do and resist asking for help. As a result, many men wind up making wrong turns onto bumpy back roads that wind up stranding them (and you) 100 miles from Wayne's Kountry Kitchen.

Women, on the other hand, have relatively few hang-ups about admitting it when they don't know something. That's why they can make better investors than men. It's because they don't have any trouble with the idea that they have to have an education in order to be successful. Women are comfortable not only learning and studying but also asking questions—and by asking questions, of course, they learn more. I see this in my investment seminars all the time. When women take the classes, they study, read, and ask questions. Their goal is to become educated—to learn the techniques of managing their own finances. It's not to prove to everyone else in the class that they're smarter than the instructor. (That role invariably goes to some guy sitting in the back of the room who thinks he has all the answers—but whose money is still sitting in a savings account earning a measly 2 percent interest.)

IT'S TIME FOR YOU
TO TAKE CHARGE

The basic premise of this book is simple. I believe in my heart and soul that no matter what your age, status, or situation—whether you're in your 20s or your 80s; whether you're single, married, divorced, or widowed; whether you're a career woman or a homemaker—you as a woman are more than capable of taking charge of your finances and your financial future. All that's required is that you be given the right tools—which is where this book comes in.

A Journey That Will Change Your Life

In the pages that follow, we are going to embark on a nine-step journey that begins with education and ends with your taking action. By the time it's done, you will have learned the fundamental principles of personal financial management—principles you can use to turn your dreams of freedom, security, and independence into concrete realities.

As you will see, the nine steps that make up our journey to financial security and independence cover a considerable amount of ground. At the same time, however, they are individually quite easy. They are so easy, in fact, that not only will you be able to use them to change your life, you also will be in a position to teach them to the people you care about so they can achieve the same kind of success you have.

Specifically, our nine steps consist of a series of easy-to-understand, practical strategies for taking control of your financial future, which you can begin implementing before you've even finished reading. As you make your way through them, you'll learn not only what your options are but also which options might be best for you—and how to design a customized course of action tailored to your own particular situation.

In the first leg of our journey, you'll find out what you don't know—but should—about your own personal and family financial situation. After that, you'll learn how to identify your own deep-seated attitudes toward money, how to define the personal values those attitudes reflect, and how to create realistic financial goals based on those values. Once you know where you want to go, you'll be shown exactly what you need to do to get organized and how you can start building a nest egg on even the most modest income (just like my Grandma Bach did). This last point is especially important, since so many women seem to think that investing and financial planning make sense only for people with high incomes and lots of money. As you'll see by the time we're finished, it's not how much you make that counts, it's how much you keep!

Finally, our program will lay out a series of simple yet powerful strategies designed to provide you with (1) an effective plan for long-term security, (2) financial protection against the unexpected, and (3) the ability to build the kind of life you've always dreamed about. Along the way, it will explain everything you need to know about tax planning, wills, insurance, the stock market (including the nine big mistakes most investors make), retirement planning, how to buy a house, and how to hire a financial advisor. Finally, our program ends with real-life success stories of women who have already read this book and put the steps into action in their own lives. Proven results from Smart Women who are on the journey to living and finishing rich. *The journey you are about to take.*

In the end, whether you earn $25,000 a year or $25,000 a month, our nine-step journey will dramatically change the way you think about money—and by doing that, it will change your life.

Become One of the Financial Elite

Individually, each of the nine steps in our journey is as powerful as it is simple. Indeed, as I suggest to the women who attend my seminars, if you manage to learn and apply just two or three of the nine steps, I am confident you will wind up in better financial shape than 90 percent of the people in the country. If you do four or five of the steps, I believe you will find yourself in the top 5 percent of the population—financially better off than 95 percent of Canadians. And if you do all nine of the steps, I believe you can elevate yourself to the nation's financial elite—the top 1 percent of the population. What's more, you'll be able to bring your family and loved ones along with you.

And as you acquire the tools you'll need to control your economic destiny, our nine-step program also will help you learn to become comfortable with the idea of taking financial responsibility for yourself.

This is a key point, for the psychological and emotional aspects of financial planning are enormously important. Yet, for some reason, most approaches to the subject ignore them.

The fact is, of course, that nothing brings out emotion like the topic of money. (According to marriage counsellors, it is the leading cause of divorce.) Needless to say, everyone attaches different emotions to the issues of saving and investing. Some people save to create security and provide for their families; others spend to feel free or experience adventure. Whatever the case may be, the emotions we attach to money often determine whether we will live our lives in comfort or poverty. Yet people rarely know what is truly driving them emotionally when it comes to money.

The Bag-Lady Syndrome

Among women, the impact of emotion on their financial lives shows up clearly in what experts call "the bag-lady syndrome," in which women who are materially well off still find themselves living in daily fear of going broke and being forced to live on the street. I can't tell you the number of female clients of mine with investment portfolios worth literally millions of dollars who have sat in my office and asked me, "David, if the market goes down, will I be a bag lady?"

This sort of worry may be baseless, but it is real, and it can't just be dismissed. By showing you how to understand the emotional and psychological needs that affect the way we all think about money, the program in this book will teach you how to overcome the fears that often lead to financial paralysis and, worse, shortsighted decision making. Equally important, you'll learn how to create a meaningful agenda from which you can design a long-term financial plan that will truly reflect what you are really looking for in life.

HOW BEST TO
USE THIS BOOK

Before we begin in earnest, I want to give you some tips on how to read this book. First, please think of this book as a tool. As I put it earlier, it's a kind of road map—your personal road map to a successful financial future. At the same time, I'd like you to think of me as your "money coach," a new friend who can offer some helpful advice on how you can get to where you want to go.

You also should understand that each of the nine steps that make up this book can be followed separately or in conjunction with the others. My recommendation is that you go through them in order, reading each chapter at least twice before you move on to the next one. Why? Because repetition is the secret of all skill, and when we read something for the first time, we don't always catch it all or retain as much as we may like.

Another suggestion: As we progress on our journey together, and as you learn lots of new things about handling money, don't get bogged down by all the stuff you suddenly feel you should have done years ago but didn't. If I bring up something you didn't know or wish you had known sooner, don't get down about it. What you are *not* doing right now is not the issue. The issue is what you *will* be doing with your new-found knowledge once you finish reading this book.

With that in mind, I'd like to share a quick story with you about a young woman who attended one of my seminars.

It's Never Too Late . . . or Too Early!

Lauren stood up in the class looking a little depressed. "David," she said, "I think I'm the youngest woman here and I'm not sure I belong here, but I know I need to get started planning for retirement and I don't know what to do."

As I scanned the class, I realized Lauren was right about one thing. She probably was the youngest of 100 or so women in the room. I smiled at her, then turned to her classmates and asked, "How many of you ladies here wish now that you had taken a class like this 20 years ago?"

Every hand in the room went up. I looked back at Lauren. "It looks to me," I said, "like you're in the right room at the right time."

A few weeks later Lauren came into my office. It turned out she was 28, with a university degree, and was pursuing a career in management consulting. Like many women her age, however, Lauren was not taking advantage of her retirement plan. In fact, even though she was earning more than $50,000 a year, she was living paycheque to paycheque. Employing the same techniques as I will show you in this book, I showed Lauren how she could get her spending under control immediately and start "maxing out" her contributions to her retirement plan. As a result, less than three years later, Lauren now has more than $20,000 in her retirement plan and, at the rate she is saving, she could easily have $2 million to her name by the time she reaches her late 50s! Even more exciting, by using the tools you will learn in this book, Lauren got herself a new job and has doubled her income! Today, at age 31, she is totally in charge of her money and has a brilliant new career that pays her what she is worth.

Now, I'm not going to take credit for all of this. Lauren deserves most of the credit. She attended the class, took the advice, and (most important) acted on it.

And you can too!

Remember, this book is about moving forward and taking control of your life, not giving yourself a hard time for what you didn't know before you picked it up.

Finally, this book *is* meant to be fun. Enjoy yourself. You are about to embark on an exciting journey to the new "you"—a woman in control of her destiny who has learned how to take charge of her own financial future.

Let's get started!

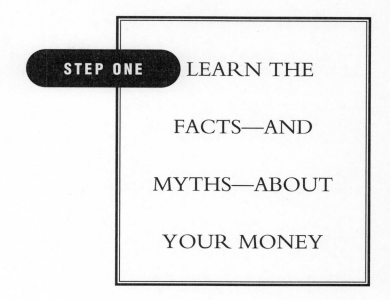

STEP ONE — LEARN THE FACTS—AND MYTHS—ABOUT YOUR MONEY

Wendy sat in my office, perched on the edge of her chair, alert, inquisitive, and a little bit embarrassed. An experienced and highly successful real-estate agent, she had come to me for a financial consultation—and the facts of her situation were hardly reassuring. Although she earned well over $250,000 a year and was able to put two kids through private school at an annual cost of $15,000 each, her personal finances were a mess. A self-employed single parent, she had less than $25,000 saved for retirement, no life or disability insurance, and had never bothered to write a will.

In short, this intelligent, ambitious businesswoman was completely unprotected from the unexpected and utterly unprepared for the future. When I asked Wendy why she had never done any financial planning, she shrugged and offered a response I'd heard countless times before: "I've always been too busy working to focus on what to do with the money I make."

Looking across the restaurant table, I could see the sadness in my mother's eyes. A good friend of hers had just gone through a bitter divorce. Suddenly, after more than three decades of marriage to a wealthy surgeon, the friend now found herself living in a tiny apartment, struggling to make ends meet as a $25,000-a-year secretary. Like many formerly well-off women, she had never paid much attention to her family's finances, and as a result her estranged *husband was able to run rings around her in the settlement talks. It was a terrible thing—all the more so because it could have been prevented so easily—and it made me wonder if my mother was similarly in the dark. So I asked her. "Mom," I said, "do you know where the family money is?"*

I thought it would be an easy question. After all, my father was a successful financial consultant and stockbroker who taught investment classes three nights a week. My mother had to be up to speed on the family finances.

At first, however, she didn't reply. Then she squirmed slightly in her chair. "Of course I know where our money is," she finally said. "Your father manages it."

"But where is it? Do you know where he's got it invested?"

"Well, no, I don't. Your father handles all that."

"But don't you have your own accounts, your own line of credit?"

My mother laughed. "David," she said, "what do I need a line of credit for? I have the best bank in the world—your father."

The reason I've started our journey with these two stories is that I know you are a very special woman—the kind of woman who believes in herself. Specifically, you believe that you possess the abilities and the intelligence to have the kind of life you feel you deserve. (If you didn't, you would have never picked up this book in the first place.) You also believe—correctly—that money is important and that you need to learn more about accumulating and protecting it. Finally, I know that you are someone who recognizes that it takes more than a single burst of enthusiasm to improve yourself and develop new skills; it also takes commitment and education.

That is why the first step of our journey is all about getting motivated to educate yourself now and on an ongoing basis about your money and the role it plays in your life. I believe that no matter what your current situation is—whether you are already wealthy or living paycheque to paycheque—a little education combined with motivated action can go a long, long way.

I also know from working with thousands of women that, sadly, neither Wendy the real-estate agent nor my mother are at all unusual. Yes, women have long owned nearly half of the financial assets in this country. Yes, most women work, and nearly half of them are their family's main income earner. Yes, the statistics about divorce and widowhood are appalling. Yet, despite all this, the sad fact is that shockingly few women know even a fraction of what they should about the state of their own personal and family finances.

By the same token, very few people know all of the fundamental principles about money that you are about to learn. And most important, even when they think they do, they rarely follow the principles on a consistent basis. This last point is a key one, for as you will discover in the course of our journey, it is not what we learn that makes a difference in our lives but what we do with what we learn.

THE FACTS AND MYTHS ABOUT
YOU AND YOUR MONEY

What we're going to do in this chapter is familiarize you with what I call the financial facts of life. By the time you have taken in all the facts, you will understand fully why it's essential that you take charge of your own financial future. Moreover, you will be totally motivated to get started learning how to do it.

The first fact of financial life to understand is that, while planning ahead is important for everyone, it's more important for women. Indeed, though in many ways we live in an age of equality, there is no question that . . .

Fair or not, women need to do more financial planning than men.

As I said in the introduction, compared to previous eras, this is a great time for you to be a woman. In terms of opportunities and resources, you couldn't have picked a better time to begin a journey to a secure financial future. And it's more than just a matter of economics. Because of advances in both technology and public attitudes, women are not only living longer than ever before, they are active longer. In my seminars, I often joke that today's 80-year-old women are drinking green juice and doing aerobics every morning. I know my Grandma Bach was like that. Up to the age of 86, she hiked five miles a day and went dancing three nights a week! In her mid-80s, my grandmother enjoyed a life that was more active, socially and physically, than mine was at 30!

But if the good news is that we live in an age in which the barriers that held women back for so long seem finally to be falling, the bad news is that there are still many obstacles to be overcome. For one thing . . .

Women still typically earn 25 percent less than men.

For another, women are less likely to have a steady income stream over the course of their lifetimes. In some cases, that's due to discrimination, but it's also due to the fact that responsibilities such as child rearing and caring for elderly parents cause women to move in and out of the workforce a lot more than men do. That's why more than twice as many women (28%) than men (11%) work part-time. And this ratio will increase with future population aging. What's more:

Women are the ones hurt most by corporate downsizing.

That's because it takes women longer to find new work, and the replacement jobs women get are often part-time posts that offer less pay and fewer benefits.

As a result of all this, your accumulated pension benefits probably are going to be lower than those of your male counterparts—that is, if you have a pension at all. While one in five Canadian men over 65 lives in poverty and government benefits account for 47 percent of their income . . .

The poverty rate for unattached women
65 years and over is 43.4 percent, and government transfers
account for 65 percent of their income.

But it's not simply that as a woman you'll have fewer benefits to look forward to and rely more heavily on government benefits. It's also that, as a woman, you'll have to make them go further. Specifically, you probably are going to live longer than most of your male counterparts,, which means that you are going to need even more retirement resources than they will. (Life expectancy for Canadian women is now 81.3 years while men's is 75.3 years.) And you'll need those resources not just for yourself, but for others as well, specifically your parents. Because of your longer life expectancy, chances are that the financial burden of caring for elderly parents will fall on your shoulders.

What All This Adds Up to Is One Big Ouch!

This, in a nutshell, is why long-term financial planning is more important for women. Compared to men, you've got to be more far-sighted, start saving earlier, and stick to your plans with more discipline. Fortunately, doing all this is not only possible, it's actually relatively easy. The trick is simply recognizing that it needs to be done—which leads us to the other basic fact of financial life: Ignorance is not bliss. Quite the contrary . . .

It's what you don't know that can hurt you!

A wise woman once said, "It's not what you know that can hurt you but rather what you don't know." I'd like to extend that a bit and suggest that what generally causes the most suffering and pain is *what you don't know that you don't know.*

Think about that for a minute. In our everyday lives, there are really only a few categories of knowledge.

- What you know you know (e.g., how much money you earn each month)
- What you know you don't know (e.g., what the stock market will do next year)
- What you know you should know (e.g., how much it will take for you to be able to retire comfortably)
- What you don't know you don't know (e.g., that in 2001, federal and provincial governments made dozens of amendments to the Income Tax Act and related legislation, many of which could directly affect how much you will earn at retirement and how much you can deduct from your taxable income for expenses such as child care, medical treatment and pension savings).

It's this last category, by the way, that causes the most problems in our lives. Think about it. When you find yourself in a real jam, doesn't it always seem to be the result of something you didn't know that you didn't know? (Consider the "prime" Nova Scotia real estate you bought that actually was in the middle of a swamp.) That's the way life is—especially when it comes to money. Indeed, the reason most people fail financially—and, as a result, never have the kind of life they want—is almost always because of stuff they didn't know that they didn't know.

This concept is incredibly simple, but it's also tremendously powerful. Among other things, it means that, if we can reduce what you don't know that you don't know about money, your chances of becoming financially successful—and, most important, staying financially successful—can be significantly increased. (It also means that the more you realize you don't know as you read this book, the happier you should be, because it shows you are already learning!)

So how do we apply this concept? Well, I think the best way to reduce what you don't know that you don't know about money is to
learn what you need to unlearn. That is, you need to discover what
you may have come to believe about money that isn't really true. Or,
as I like to put it . . .

Don't fall for the most common myths about money.

Whenever I conduct one of my Smart Women Finish Rich seminars I generally begin the class by suggesting that the reason most people—not just women—fail financially is that they have fallen for a
bunch of money myths that are simply not true. As we're learning the
facts, I think it's important to spend a little time exploring these myths
and learning to recognize them for what they are. The reason is simple: By doing this, you lessen the chances that you'll ever be taken in
by them.

> ## MYTH NO. 1:
> ### MAKE MORE MONEY AND YOU'LL BE RICH!

The most commonly held myth about personal finances is that the
most important factor in determining whether you will ever be rich is
how much money you make. To put it another way, ask most women
what it takes to be well off, and they will invariably say, "More money."

It seems logical, right? Make more money and you'll be rich. Now,
you may be thinking, "What's wrong with that? How can it be a myth?"

Well, to me, the phrase "Make more money and you'll be rich"
brings to mind certain late-night TV infomercials, with their enthu-
siastic pitchmen and slick get-rich-quick schemes. My current
favourite is the one in which a guy wearing a gold necklace smiles
into the camera and says you can earn a fortune while lying on the
sofa watching television. Without getting into the question of
whether his particular scheme makes any business sense, let me suggest to you that the basic premise of his pitch—namely, that the key
to wealth is finding some quick and easy way to boost your income—
is simply not true. In fact, what determines your wealth is not how
much you make but how much you keep of what you make.

I'll take that even further. I believe that most Canadians who think
they have an income problem actually don't. You may not believe
that. It's possible you feel you have an income problem yourself.

Perhaps you're thinking right now, *David, I'm sorry. I don't care what you say—with my bills and expenses, I'm telling you I have an income problem.*

Well, I'm not saying that you might not be facing some financial challenges. But I would be willing to bet that if we were to take a good look at your situation, we'd find that the problem really isn't the size of your income. Indeed, if you're at all typical, over the course of your working life you will likely earn a phenomenal amount of money. If you find that hard to believe, take a look at the Earnings Outlook chart (see p. 22).

The numbers don't lie. Over the course of their lifetimes, most Canadians will earn more than $1 million, and many of us will earn more than $3 million!

Based on your monthly income, how much money does it look like you will earn in your lifetime? It's close to seven figures, isn't it? Don't you think you deserve to keep some of that money? I do—and I bet you do too! Unfortunately, most of us don't keep any. In fact, the average Canadian works a total of some 80,000 hours in his or her life—and has nothing to show for it at the end! The typical Canadian saves just 3.2 percent of her disposable income. Meanwhile, the average Canadian carries debts such as a mortgage and consumer loans equivalent to 98 percent of her disposable income. And one in 10 working Canadians say they could not support themselves for more than one month if they and their spouses lost their jobs.

How do we explain that? It's simple, really.

The problem is not our income, it's what we spend!

We'll go into detail on this concept in Step Four. For now, just trust me on this one. It's not the size of your income that will determine your financial well-being over the next 20 or 30 years, it's how you handle the money you earn.

I know that sounds hard to believe, but it's true. Consider the findings in a recent book that I recommend highly to my students. It's called *The Millionaire Next Door,* and it was written by a man named Tom Stanley, who interviewed hundreds of millionaires and came up with some findings that surprised me and probably will surprise you.

There's a phrase Texans use to describe someone who is all show and no substance: "Big hat, no cattle." What Stanley found was that most millionaires are just the opposite. In other words . . .

EARNINGS OUTLOOK

How much money will pass through your hands during your lifetime
and what will you do with it?

Monthly Income	10 Years	20 Years	30 Years	40 Years
$1,000	$120,000	$240,000	$360,000	$480,000
$1,500	180,000	360,000	540,000	720,000
$2,000	240,000	480,000	720,000	960,000
$2,500	300,000	600,000	900,000	1,200,000
$3,000	360,000	720,000	1,080,000	1,440,000
$3,500	420,000	840,000	1,260,000	1,680,000
$4,000	480,000	960,000	1,440,000	1,920,000
$4,500	540,000	1,080,000	1,620,000	2,160,000
$5,000	600,000	1,200,000	1,800,000	2,400,000
$5,500	660,000	1,320,000	1,980,000	2,640,000
$6,000	720,000	1,440,000	2,160,000	2,880,000
$6,500	780,000	1,560,000	2,340,000	3,120,000
$7,000	840,000	1,680,000	2,520,000	3,360,000
$7,500	900,000	1,800,000	2,700,000	3,600,000
$8,000	960,000	1,920,000	2,880,000	3,840,000
$8,500	1,020,000	2,040,000	3,060,000	4,080,000
$9,000	1,080,000	2,160,000	3,240,000	4,320,000
$9,500	1,140,000	2,280,000	3,420,000	4,560,000
$10,000	1,200,000	2,400,000	3,600,000	4,800,000

Source: *The Super Saver: Fundamental Strategies for Building Wealth* by Janet Lowe (Longman Financial Services Publishing)

SMALL HAT, LOTS OF CATTLE

Here are some of Stanley's findings.

- The average net worth of a millionaire is $3.7 million.
- The average millionaire lives in a house that cost $320,000.
- The average millionaire's taxable income is $131,000 a year.
- For the most part, millionaires describe themselves as "tight-wads" who believe that charity begins at home.
- Most millionaires drive older, American cars. Only a minority drive new cars or ever lease their cars.
- Fully half of the millionaires Stanley surveyed never paid more than $399 for a suit.
- Millionaires are dedicated investors—on average, investing nearly 20 percent of their total household income each year.

Stanley based his findings on surveys of U.S. millionaires, but we're not so concerned here with the actual numbers as we are with the underlying behaviour of a typical millionaire. What amazes me about these facts is that a family with a net worth of nearly $4 million (the average net worth that Stanley surveyed) is, by most people's standards, very wealthy. I certainly feel $4 million is a rather comfortable amount to have accumulated, and I'd be willing to guess that you do too. Yet the income these people earn (an average of $131,000 a year) is really not all that high. It's certainly above average, but it is definitely not of the extraordinary magnitude we tend to associate with people who have amassed great wealth.

The fact is, what has allowed most of these people to become millionaires is not how much they've made but how little (relatively speaking) they've spent. To use a sports metaphor, while their offence was probably pretty good, the defence they've played with their money has been nothing short of brilliant.

Unfortunately, most people handle their finances in the opposite way. They are great on offence and lousy on defence. As a financial advisor, I've personally met in my office with many people who make over $100,000 a year and feel wealthy and live wealthy but in fact are not wealthy.

Here's a case in point.

BIG HAT, NO CATTLE

Nora first came to see me after attending a retirement-planning course I taught at the University of California–Berkeley Extension.

The moment she entered my office it was clear I was dealing with a very successful woman. Her clothes were the current year's top of the line, she was wearing a gold Rolex watch worth at least $10,000, and I had seen her drive up in a brand-new $82,000 Mercedes-Benz (which, it turned out, she leased).

A fit and attractive 48-year-old, Nora owned and ran a company that employed 10 people and grossed more than $5 million a year. But though her personal income was more than $200,000 a year, and she had been pulling down a six-figure income for well over a decade, her net worth was almost zero! Nora didn't even have a retirement plan started. She did have about $50,000 in equity in her home, but she also had two mortgages on the house, on which she owed a total of $400,000. To make matters worse, Nora had run up more than $35,000 in credit card debt!

After she filled me in on her situation, I shook my head and said, "Nora, are you planning on working forever?"

She looked at me, confused. "What do you mean?" she asked.

"Well," I said, "were you planning on working for the rest of your life?"

"No," she replied. "I hope to retire by the time I turn 55."

"Really?" I said. "With what?"

Nora blinked at me, not seeing what I was getting at.

"Is your business salable?" I continued.

Nora bit her lip. Her business, she explained, was built mainly on a few good relationships that probably couldn't be transferred to anyone else.

"I see," I said. "Then I suppose you have a wealthy relative who is planning to die in time for you to inherit this money when you turn 55?"

Once again, Nora looked perplexed. "No," she said slowly, "I don't have any inheritance coming."

"Then I'm confused," I said. "How are you going to retire? You don't have any savings. You can't sell your business. The equity in your house is minimal."

Nora shrugged. "I make so much money," she said, "that I thought I could play catch-up."

SPEND MORE THAN YOU MAKE, AND YOU'LL HAVE A SERIOUS PROBLEM!

I'd like to tell you there was a quick fix for Nora, but there wasn't. First of all, Nora had some really bad habits—the worst of which was that she simply spent more than she made, all the time! Second, she didn't really believe me when I told her that she needed to change her ways and change them fast.

It took Nora 18 months to get around to opening a retirement savings plan and making her first contribution. That, however, was four years ago, and these days, fortunately, Nora is a completely different person. Every two weeks now, like clockwork, she sends me a cheque for her retirement fund. With this and other strategies, Nora has managed to save close to $90,000 and, by slightly increasing her monthly mortgage payments, she will have her house fully paid off in 15 years instead of 30, which will save her close to $285,000! (You'll learn how you can do this for yourself in Step Six.) Equally important, she has stopped leasing brand-new luxury cars (instead, she bought a used one), and she has paid off all her credit card debt.

Nora isn't bringing home any more money than she was before. Yet now, for the first time, she is building real wealth. What changed? The answer is her spending habits—and, most important of all, her investment habits. That's the key. Like Tom Stanley's millionaires, she saw through the income myth and learned that it's not how much you make, it's how much you keep.

One important advantage Nora did have going for her was that she realized early on that she had to take care of herself, which is one reason why she started her own business. Instinctively, she understood that one of the most fundamental principles of smart money management is self-reliance—or, as I like to tell my clients . . .

Don't ever put your entire financial fate in someone else's hands.

This brings us to the second biggest myth I see women falling prey to—what I call the Cinderella myth, otherwise known as the "My husband will take care of me" myth (or, even worse, the "Find and marry a wealthy man and everything will be fine" myth).

> **MYTH NO. 2:**
> MY HUSBAND (OR SOME OTHER MAN)
> WILL TAKE CARE OF ME.

Now, before I go into detail on this subject, let me say that I know it is entirely possible that you are happily married or that you have chosen to be happily single. Nonetheless, I have found from experience that this myth is worth spending a little time on, for some version of it affects nearly every woman. Indeed, over the years, hundreds of women have shared with me their painful personal stories of how their lives were nearly destroyed by the belief that some man—if not a husband, then a father, or an employer, or a financial advisor—would take care of them. And when I started to write this book, many more women implored me not to pass over this issue lightly. So here goes.

It's neither safe nor practical to assume that the man in your life can be counted on to take care of your finances.

Why do I say this? Let's look at the facts. If men generally have been in charge of their families' money for the last century or so, then clearly they have not been doing a very good job. Consider these sobering statistics . . .

- About 30 percent of Canadian families of two or more people may not have saved enough money to retire at 65 and receive two-thirds of their current income.
- About 46 percent of unattached Canadians aged 45–64 may not have saved enough.
- About 59 percent of Canadians who do not own a home may not have saved enough.
- And about 41 percent of Canadians with pre-retirement incomes of $75,000 or more may not be able to replace at least two-thirds of their pre-retirement incomes.

But wait, the bad news gets worse. As I noted earlier, women live longer yet tend to earn fewer pension and other retirement benefits than men do. Thus you are likely to be forced to make do with even less.

What all this adds up to at retirement—or, more accurately, does not add up to—is another scary statistic . . .

About 24 percent of women aged 65 and older have incomes below Statistics Canada's low-income cut-off, and another 25 percent are considered poor. That means they spend disproportionate amounts of their income on food, shelter, and clothing.

But, you may ask, what about Canada Pension and Old Age Security? That will help, won't it? Maybe—assuming the system is still around by the time you reach retirement age. (And there's no guarantee it will be.) The fact is, Old Age Security was never intended to be a retirement plan. At most, it was designed to provide an income supplement.

Look at the numbers. In 2002, the average retired woman's Old Age Security benefits totalled $425.56 a month, or slightly more than

$5,000 a year. Additionally, the average Guaranteed Income Supplement was $370.56 a month—about $4,500 a year. And the most anyone can possibly hope to get from Old Age Security and Guaranteed Income Supplement is about $12,600 a year. That may be okay for walking-around money, but you sure wouldn't want to have to live on it. Unfortunately, many women have no choice but to try to do just that. You don't want to be one of them.

That's not to say you should forget about Old Age Security. It's just that you shouldn't count on it to provide more than a small fraction of your retirement income. How small? For the poorest families in Canada, Old Age Security makes up more than 80 percent of their income, and women aged 65 and over derive more of their income than men from Old Age Security.

As it happens, there's a very simple way to find out now what your Old Age Security and Canada Pension Plan cheque ultimately will look like—and I can't emphasize enough the importance of taking advantage of it right away. This is especially crucial for women, since, as I mentioned before, women tend to work less consistently throughout their lifetimes than men—and, as a result, often their Canada Pension Plan benefits turn out to be much smaller than they had been expecting.

As a rule of thumb, the Canada Pension Plan pays a basic monthly amount equal to 25 percent of an individual's average monthly pensionable earnings. Canadian taxpayers automatically receive a statement of contributions every year, which shows how much you've contributed and how much you can expect to receive in CPP income at age 65. You can also contact Human Resources Development Canada (HRDC) to obtain this information.

You should have this information available now. Today. This very minute. And it's really quite easy to get. Just call your local HRDC office (you'll find the number in your local telephone directory under "Federal Government") and tell them you want a copy of your statement of CPP contributions. You can also request the form on-line, by visiting HRDC's website at *www.hrdc-drhc.gc.ca*.

When it comes to divorce, women still end up with the short end of the stick.

Yes, we all want to believe that we can count on our spouses. Unfortunately, the statistics tell a very different story. Fully 50 percent of all marriages these days end in divorce. What about alimony and child support and matrimonial property? The bleak truth is, once her husband is gone, the average divorced woman sees her standard of living plummet. Several studies have shown that women, especially those who gain custody of their children, will experience a drop in income after they divorce, while men will see their incomes increase.

These studies are hardly news. But despite all the attention they've received in recent years, apparently many women remain convinced that they will be the exception to the rule—and they are shocked when they're not. I can't tell you the number of women who've come to me for advice after being absolutely blindsided by the husbands in whose hands they'd trustingly placed their futures. Unfortunately, by then it's usually too late to do more than try to pick up the pieces.

To be fair, there are many good men out there. But even if you're fortunate enough to have wound up with one of them, that's still no guarantee of a happy and secure future. Why? Because no matter how good the man in your life is, sooner or later he is going to die—and whether it's sooner or later, it probably will be before you do. Remember, the average Canadian woman lives six years longer than the average Canadian man. Of course, no one likes to think about this. Indeed, it's terrible how many well-intentioned men who sincerely love their wives and families simply refuse to face up to this inescapable truth. The worst thing about this sort of denial is that it leads otherwise good husbands to put off dealing with disagreeable reminders of their mortality such as life insurance and wills. And that's a prescription for disaster. For try as we might to ignore it . . .

The risk of widowhood increases with age: 30 percent of Canadian women may be widowed at age 65, and 50 percent by age 75. At the age of 65, about 80 percent of men are married vs. 55 percent of women!

Because of our unwillingness to accept this unpleasant reality, we tend to be woefully unprepared to cope with it when it comes to pass. That's why, for a woman, losing a husband is generally as devastating economically as it is emotionally. Indeed, most widows living in poverty were not poor before their husbands died. How did they get that way? Inadequate—or, more likely, nonexistent—planning. How else do you explain the fact that the poverty rate for unattached women 65 years and over is 43.4 percent, compared to 21.3 percent of men aged 65 and over?

When I shared this notion in one of my investment seminars, a woman named Sarah stood up in tears. "David," she told the room, "everything you're saying is true. I'm 57, and my husband was a successful lawyer who owned his own practice. He passed away six months ago and now I'm almost bankrupt."

I asked Sarah how this could have happened. It turned out that though her husband specialized in trusts and wills, he had never bothered to do one for himself!

The entire group was aghast. I could see the question on everyone's face: *You mean a lawyer who wrote wills for a living didn't have a will himself?* But when I asked the class, "How many of you have a will?" less than half the people in the room answered in the affirmative. And when I asked further, "How many of you have reviewed your will in the last five years?" less than 10 percent of them raised their hands. So maybe Sarah's story shouldn't have been surprising after all.

Then I asked Sarah, "If your husband was so successful, why are you almost broke?" She replied that when her husband died she discovered that the $2 million home in which they lived carried a $1.5 million mortgage. With her husband gone and no income of her own, the massive mortgage payments were now way beyond her means. As a result, Sarah found herself forced to put the house up for sale. Unfortunately, this was at a time when the California real estate market was badly depressed, and she couldn't find a buyer. To make matters worse, not only had her husband neglected to make a will, he had never taken out life insurance. And as if that wasn't bad enough, he had used their home as collateral on loans for his law practice— which was now defunct, because his former partners had elected to start a new firm without the obligation of her husband's debts! Sarah was in big trouble, all because she had assumed her husband would take care of her, and he had not prepared for the unforeseen.

Sarah's case was extreme, but it was by no means unusual. In any case, there is an important lesson to be learned from her experience: Don't ever let the "some man will take care of you" myth become your reality. It's a recipe for disaster.

There's one more myth I want to share with you.

MYTH NO. 3:
THE GOVERNMENT FINALLY HAS GOT
INFLATION UNDER CONTROL.

There seems to be an increasingly widespread notion that we no longer need to worry about inflation. This is a particularly dangerous myth not simply because it's untrue, but also because it breeds complacency. Indeed, I can't think of anything more financially self-destructive than the idea that we don't need to worry so much about the future because the government finally has gotten inflation under control.

It certainly would be nice if that were true. Unfortunately, it's not. To the contrary . . .

Inflation is still Public Enemy Number One.

Sometimes when I teach a class, someone will raise a hand and actually try to debate this issue. "But, David," she will say, "it sure looks as if the government has control over inflation. After all, I don't see things costing a lot more today than they used to."

Well, that's not what the statistics say. What the numbers tell us is that a basket of goods and services that would have cost $100 in 1982 would cost $184.77 today, an average rate of inflation of 3.12 percent. Over the last 10 years, it's averaged about 1.8 percent. But it's probably a safe bet to figure that inflation will run at about 2 to 3 percent a year for the foreseeable future.

Now, that may not sound like very much, but it is. After all, when most people retire, they do so on a fixed income. Unfortunately, if you retire on a fixed income and inflation continues at 3 percent a year, you are going to be in deep trouble. Why? Because, at that rate, your purchasing power will be cut nearly in half within 20 years. In other words, the dollar sitting in your purse today will be worth only about 72 cents a decade from now. In 20 years, it will be worth only about 54 cents.

There's nothing new about this phenomenon. When I talk about inflation in my seminars, one of biggest laughs I always get is when I ask, "How many of you drove here tonight in a car that cost more than your first home?" What's amazing is that usually a third of the people in the class raise their hand. That's the power of inflation. Here's another example: The car I drive today cost more than twice what my parents paid for their first home in Oakland, California, and it was a nice five-bedroom house with three bathrooms. If you think I'm exaggerating, take a look at this chart. Granted, these are U.S. figures. But given the close relationship between the economies of the U.S. and Canada, you can be sure that Canadian prices will follow a similar trend, even if the figures aren't exactly the same.

CONSUMER PRICES: STICKER SHOCK SINCE 1970

Typical Prices	1970	1980	Today	Projected in 20 Years
House	$25,600	$64,000	$210,200 [1]	$463,508
Automobile	3,400	6,910	24,450 [2]	89,965
Gasoline (10 Gal.)	3.48	9.68	17.20 [3]	30.81
Stamp	.06	.15	.34 [4]	1.11

Sources
1 U.S. Department of Housing and Urban Development—average price of new homes, 4th quarter 2000
2 National Association of Auto Dealers—1999 average new-vehicle selling price
3 Lundberg Survey—May 2001
4 United States Post Office
5 American Chambers of Commerce Researchers Association—2nd quarter 1997

The point is, there is no denying the lesson these numbers teach us.

The future is going to be expensive.

That's why, despite all the recent talk about how inflation is no longer a problem, I still consider it to be Public Enemy Number One. The good news here is that learning how to keep your nest egg growing faster than inflation isn't all that hard. But if you don't recognize inflation as a problem in the first place, chances are you won't bother to try to do anything about it—and if you don't try to do anything about it, you are going to find yourself in a world of hurt one day. So don't believe the myth about inflation being under control.

Show Me the Money

Now that we have exposed these money myths for what they are and looked at the external realities of what we can expect in our financial futures, let's examine the facts. The place to begin is close to home, with information about your own personal financial situation. Why here? By way of explanation, let me share a personal story with you.

When I was younger, I once asked my father why so many women seemed to be so devastated financially after a divorce or the death of a husband. "David," he said, "women are not typically involved with the family finances. So when it comes time to split up the pie, they don't know how much pie there is to split up, or even where to find it."

That's it? I thought. *Women don't know where the money is?* Could it really be that basic? I doubted it.

Out of curiosity, I took my mother to lunch to see if she agreed with my dad's assessment. What followed was the scene I described at the beginning of this chapter. As I mentioned, a good friend of my mom's had just gone through a brutal and costly divorce. Quite understandably, my mother was very upset about it—not least because her friend was now in financial trouble so serious that she had been forced to take a secretarial job and move to a tiny apartment.

"But, Mom," I said, "they were living in a million-dollar house. Where did all the money go?"

"It turned out her husband had used all the equity in their house to build up his medical practice," my mother explained with a sigh. "And now, with the HMO situation, his practice isn't doing so well."

As much as I hated to admit it, it looked as if my dad was right. The terrible outcome was a result of the woman's lack of knowledge about her family's finances. She had signed papers allowing her husband to take out a second mortgage without knowing or even asking about what she was signing. The result was, for her, a financial disaster. It was scary.

With that in mind, I asked my mom the test question: "Do you know where our family's money is?"

As I said, though I thought this would be an easy one for her to answer, it turned out that she had no idea. All she could tell me about our money was that my dad took care of it. And when I pressed her about her ignorance, she simply laughed at me.

I couldn't believe it. This, from a woman who was president of a million-dollar nonprofit theatre group, involved in numerous charity boards, and published two professional newsletters. This brilliant, beautiful woman was the same person who, when personal computers first appeared on the market, convinced the family that we needed one—and then single-handedly taught herself to master its intricacies so completely that she was able to computerize my father's entire business! Yet she hadn't a clue as to where our money was invested.

I was horrified. If a woman as sharp and successful as my mom could be so in the dark about money, what was happening to the millions of other women in this country who weren't married to men who managed money for a living? In the years since then, of course,

I've seen firsthand how widespread this sort of ignorance is and how much damage it can do. So with that in mind, I ask you now the same question I asked my mother . . .

Do you know what's going on with your money and your family's money?

To help you answer this important question. I've prepared a short quiz. Take a few moments to complete it, answering true or false for each statement. The results should give you a good idea of how knowledgeable you are (or aren't) about your personal finances.

THE "SMART WOMEN FINISH RICH"
FINANCIAL KNOWLEDGE QUIZ

True or False:

[ ]   [ ] I know the current value of my home, including the size of the mortgage and the amount of equity I've built.

[ ]   [ ] I know the length of the mortgage-payment schedule and how much extra it would cost each month to pay down the mortgage in half the time. I also know the interest rate we are paying on the mortgage and if it is competitive in today's market.

[ ]   [ ] I know how much life insurance I [and my spouse, if applicable] carry. I know how much cash value there is in the policy, and I know the rate of return my cash value is earning.

[ ]   [ ] I know the details (including amount of coverage, cost, monthly or yearly payment, etc.) of all other insurance policies carried by myself [and my spouse, if applicable]. This includes health, disability, term life, and so on.

[ ]   [ ] I have reviewed my life insurance policy in the last 12 to 24 months to see if the price I am paying for it is still competitive in today's marketplace.

[ ]   [ ] If I own my own home, I know what kind of homeowner's coverage I have and what the deductibles are.
If I rent, I know the amount of tenant's insurance I have
and what its deductible is. In either case, in the event of
a fire or other catastrophic loss, I know whether my
insurance will reimburse me for the actual cash value of
my property or the cost of replacing it at today's current values.

[ ]   [ ] I have attempted to protect my family's nest egg from
lawsuits by carrying an "umbrella" insurance policy
that includes liability coverage.

[ ]   [ ] I either prepared my own tax return this year or reviewed my tax situation with the person who prepared
my return.

[ ]   [ ] I know the location and amounts of all my or my family's investments, including
  • cash in savings or money market accounts
  • GICs or savings bonds
  • stocks and bonds
  • real-estate investments (mortgages, rental agreements, etc.)
  • collectibles (valuation and where items are)

[ ]   [ ] I know the annualized return generated by each of the
above investments.

[ ]   [ ] If I or my family owns a business, I know the current
valuation of the business, including how much debt it
currently carries and the value of its liquid assets.

[ ]   [ ] I know the value, location, and performance of all my
retirement accounts [and those of my spouse, if appli-
cable], *including RRSPs,* and company pension plans.

[ ]   [ ] I know the percentage of income I am putting away for
retirement and what it's being invested in [and, if applicable, how much my spouse is putting away and what
he is investing in].

[ ]   [ ] I know if I [and my spouse, if applicable] am making
the maximum allowable contribution to my retirement

plan at work, whether my employer is making matching contributions, and what the vesting schedule is.

[ ]   [ ] I know how much money I [and my spouse, if applicable] will be getting from the Canada Pension Plan and Old Age Security and what my [and, if applicable, his] pension benefits will be.

[ ]   [ ] I know whether my [and my spouse's, if applicable] income is protected should I [or my spouse] become disabled, because I own disability insurance. In addition, I know what the exact coverage is, when the benefits would start, and whether the benefits would be taxable.

[ ]   [ ] I [or my family] maintain a safety deposit box, know how to gain access to it, and have reviewed its contents within the last 12 months. If I have the only key, other family members know where to find it if something should happen to me.

Scoring:

Give yourself 1 point for every time you answered "true" and 0 for every time you answered "false."

14 to 17 points: Excellent! You have a good grasp of where your money is.

9 to 13 points: You're not totally in the dark, but there are some areas in which your knowledge is less than adequate.

Under 9 points: Your chances of being hurt financially because of insufficient knowledge are enormous. You need to learn how to protect yourself from future financial disaster.

If you scored well on this test, congratulations! But don't go out and start celebrating just yet. Even among knowledgeable money managers, it's rare to find anyone, male or female, who has a handle on every aspect of her own finances and what she could and should be doing to assure herself a secure future. So even if you scored 12 or above, I guarantee you'll discover many secrets and ideas that will be of enormous value to you in the pages that follow.

WHAT IF I DIDN'T SCORE WELL?

If you didn't score so well, take heart—by the time you've finished this book, you'll know *exactly* what you need to take immediate charge of your financial health and invest wisely for your family's future security.

If you're like most people, you probably knew some of the answers but not all of them—and some of the questions may have struck you as awfully complicated. Trust me, none of it is really that difficult. Before long you'll be surprised by just how easy understanding your finances can be. Indeed, you'll probably wonder why you ever thought any of it was confusing. In the meantime, don't panic because you've just discovered there is all this information about your family finances that you don't know. We'll take care of it all soon enough.

At this point, what's important is simply that you realize that there's a lot you don't know—and, even more important, a lot that you now want to know. If that's how you feel, pat yourself on the back—you've completed Step One. You are motivated to educate yourself about how to take control of your financial future—which is what the "Smart Women Finish Rich" journey is all about.

ENOUGH WITH THE BAD NEWS . . . LET'S GET TO THE GOOD STUFF!

It's possible that some of the myths about money that I've presented to you in this first step have struck you as being overly negative. If so, I apologize. As a rule, I make it a policy to avoid negative people, those dream stealers, as I call them, who seem to enjoy raining on other people's parades. But I started our journey this way for a reason: Because I know you purchased this book to make a positive change in your life, and sometimes change can be difficult. In fact, many people live their lives going nowhere and doing nothing, not because they like where they are but simply because they are afraid of change. Overcoming this fear takes real motivation. It has to hurt so much that finally you can't take it anymore and you say, "Enough is enough! I want my life to be different!"

It's in this spirit that I've offered some cautionary tales and depressing statistics. I simply want you to come to grips with the fact that, if you don't take care of your financial future, no one—not the government, not your employer, not your spouse—is going to do it for you. And it definitely won't take care of itself.

But don't let the negativity get you down. Remember: Those gloomy facts and figures don't have to be your reality!

I often repeat to clients what my Grandmother Bach used to tell me. "You know, David," she would say, "when I was growing up, going to work, starting my career, many people asked me why was I worrying about retirement plans. 'You'll have Social Security,' they'd say. 'You'll have a pension from your company.' But even at a young age, I didn't think it was a good idea to depend on someone else to take care of me—not my employer, not the government, not even your grandfather."

That's why, unlike most of her friends, my grandmother always made a point each time she got a paycheque of putting some money aside and buying some high-quality stocks or bonds. It's also why, unlike most of her friends, when she reached retirement age, she was able to enjoy herself in worry-free comfort.

I hope now that you've accomplished Step One, you're motivated to take control of your financial future by getting educated about your money.

Now it's time to begin Step Two, in which we take a look at what's important to you about money.

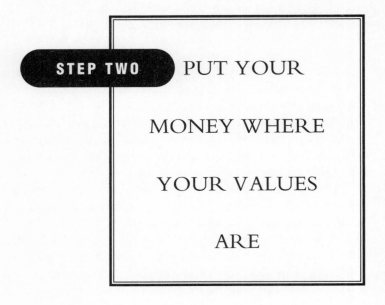

STEP TWO PUT YOUR

MONEY WHERE

YOUR VALUES

ARE

As a financial advisor, I specialize in doing what we call values-based financial planning. What this means is that I help my clients discover (often for the first time) what their true values about money actually are.

Initially at least, talking about personal values often throws people for a loop. It's not the sort of thing most of us expect to be discussing with a financial professional. Most people assume that, when they meet with a financial advisor, the conversation will focus on investments, assets and liabilities, taxes, and how many years they have to go before retirement. Well, all that does need to be talked about, but it's not where I believe the conversation should begin. What needs to be discussed first is what is really driving you when it comes to money.

Think about it. Your attitudes about money are what define everything that matters about your personal financial situation: how much money you need, how hard you are willing to work for it, how you will feel when you finally get it. That's why I can say with total confidence that, once you understand what money really means to you, you will be unstoppable. Indeed, the process I am about to share with you is probably the single most effective tool I know to help people create a life plan that will lead them to the ultimate financial security they want.

A SMART WOMEN FINISH RICH
SEMINAR IN ACTION

I gave a seminar recently in my hometown of San Francisco, but it could have been anywhere. As usual, the room was filled with women of all ages and types—old, young, rich, poor, single, married, you name it. Also as usual, I began with an announcement and a question. "My name is David Bach," I said, "and I'm here to show Smart Women how to finish rich. Would that be okay with any of you?"

Virtually in unison, every woman in the room shouted out, "Yes!"

That's generally the answer I get. I grinned at the crowd and continued. "Well, here's my next question, and it's the most important one I will ask you tonight. But don't worry—it's also the easiest." I looked out at them intently. "When you stop and think about it, what's really important about money to you?"

The room was totally silent. "Come on," I said. "This is easy. Think."

Still, nobody said anything.

"The reason you came here tonight is because you recognize that money is important," I persisted. "But what is really important about it? Most important, what is important about money to you?"

Finally, someone broke the silence. "No more student loans!" a young woman called out.

I turned to the big pad that had been placed on an easel behind me. Pulling out a marker pen, I wrote down what the young woman had said. "Okay," I repeated, "what's important about money to you is 'no more student loans.' What else? Who else wants to tell me what's important about money to them?"

A 60-ish woman sitting a few rows behind the "student loan" woman was the next to answer. "Security," she said. "I want to know that if something should happen to my husband, I won't need to worry."

I nodded and wrote "security" on the pad.

Then another woman spoke up. "Freedom," she said. "What's important about money to me is freedom."

I turned to face this woman. "That's great," I said. "But 'freedom' means different things to different people. What's important about having freedom to you?"

The woman stood up and looked around the room. "I just want to know I can do what I want to do when I want to do it."

Before she could go any further, another woman jumped to her feet. "I've got one," she shouted. "I want to know that my husband can't control what I do. What's important to me is knowing I have choices."

She was joined by yet another woman who said what was important about money to her was "feeling like I can do what the Lord meant for me to do with my life, which is to help others."

Within about 10 minutes, I had filled two entire sheets with different reasons why money was important to one or another of my students. It was incredible. Money clearly meant something different to each and every woman in the room.

Then I started circling some of the words and phrases I had written down. First I circled "security," then "freedom," then "ability to have choices," "happiness," "live a life of meaning," "able to do what God wants me to do," "more time with family," "help others," "feel satisfied," and "feel happy." By the time I was done, about 80 percent of the reasons I had written down were circled. That first answer—"pay off student loans"—wasn't among them, though. Neither was "pay off credit card debt," or "pay off mortgage," or "travel to Hawaii."

Leaving the class to wonder about this for a moment, I looked out at them and shook my head. "Once again," I said, "a group of women has proven to me how much more in touch with yourselves you are than men." I paused for a moment. "Have you noticed what almost all of you did?" I asked. "Take a close look. Every reason I circled has one thing in common."

The sea of faces staring back at me seemed stumped.

"Look closely," I repeated. "Almost all of the reasons you listed were values. Notice how only a few of the reasons I wrote down are goals, like 'pay off school loans' or 'get the mortgage paid off.' Almost everything here is an idea like security, freedom, and happiness. These are values—your values—the most important things in life. They're the stuff you will do just about anything in the world to achieve—because ultimately they are truly who you are!"

Slowly, first on just a few faces, then on more and more of them, I could see a light dawning.

"Guess what, ladies?" I continued. "What you just did was the most important part of taking control of your financial future, and you did it almost effortlessly. You see, as women you have a tremendous advantage over men: You are already in touch with your feelings and your values. For the most part, men don't get this stuff. It takes them way more time." I grinned at the class. "Pretend you're a man right now," I instructed. "What would you say if I asked you what's important about money to you?"

The room erupted. "Cars!" someone shouted. "A big house!" someone else said. "A boat!" "Football!" "Beer!" "Women!" The class couldn't stop. It was hilarious.

I laughed along with them. "Exactly," I shouted over the hubbub. "It's all goals, all stuff. No values."

Then I got serious again. "Without values, goals rarely get accomplished," I said. "Show me someone who is not reaching his full potential, and I'll show you someone who missed the importance of designing his life around his values. Values are the key. When you understand them correctly, they will pull you toward your dreams—which is a lot better than having to push yourself!"

WHAT'S IMPORTANT ABOUT
MONEY TO YOU?

What I've just described is the way I usually start my Smart Women Finish Rich seminars. In the pages that follow, I'm going to take you on the same personal journey as this group of women—and thousands of women like them—have taken in my classes and in my office. That is, we're going to discover what is important about money to you and in turn discover your values.

The process of understanding "what's important about money to you" is absolutely essential. Asking yourself what money means to you, after all, quickly forces you to evaluate what it is you are looking for in life. And understanding what you are looking for in life is the foundation on which all smart financial planning is based.

Think about it. How could you possibly put together an empowering financial plan unless you know what it is you really care about? Let's say what's important about money to you is the security it can provide, but your current state of financial affairs has you living from paycheque to paycheque. Well, then, something is wrong, isn't it? Clearly, your financial behaviour is out of whack with your deepest values. Similarly, let's say what's important about money to you is the freedom it can bring you, but in actuality you are tied to a job working 60 hours a week to pay a mortgage on a large home—wishing all the while that you were travelling more. Once again, your financial life is in conflict with what you are really all about.

Money is not an end in itself. It is merely a tool to help us achieve some particular goal. If the way we handle our money conflicts with our personal values, we are not going to wind up living happy and fulfilled lives.

So how do you figure out what you are looking for in life and how to use money as a tool to get it? Well, fortunately, you don't have to go to Tibet and meet with a guru on a mountaintop. All you need to do is get clear about what your values are. Once you've done that, it will be easy to develop your financial goals (which we will do in Step Three).

What's great about this process is that it is one of the most powerful legs of your journey to financial security as well as one of the least complicated. What makes it so simple is the fact that you already know what your values are. They are not something you have to study for years to learn. The fact is, most of us have a pretty good sense of who we are and what's important about money to us. These things may not be immediately apparent, but with just a little bit of digging some amazing realizations will pop to the surface.

So now let's eavesdrop on some values conversations I've had over the years. By listening in, you should begin to see how the process works. Specifically, what you are about to learn is how to put your values down on paper and build what I call a *values ladder*.★ This simple but highly effective tool will help you clarify what's pulling you toward (or keeping you from) taking control over your own financial situation. Once you understand how the process works, we can apply it to your situation and life and make sure that, from this day forward, your values are clear so that you are pulled only toward your financial goals.

ONE WOMAN'S
VALUES EXERCISE

Here's an example of a conversation that worked really well and helped a client of mine greatly. Jessica was a successful 33-year-old computer salesperson who met with me in my office after taking one

---

★ The values conversation and values ladder are concepts derived from Bill Bachrach/Bachrach & Associates, Inc. *(www.valuesbasedfinancialplanning.com)*, and have been included here with permission.

of my investment classes. She was married (to her college sweetheart) and had an eight-year-old daughter and a dog named Teddy.

Jessica seemed very focused the day she came to see me, and we got right down to business. Having already attended my seminar, she knew exactly what I was trying to get at when I asked her to tell me what was most important to her about money.

"Well, David," she said, "I guess when I think about money what's really important to me is security."

"That's great," I said. "Of course, security means different things to different people. Help me to understand what's important about security to you."

Jessica didn't hesitate. "Having security lets me feel that I'm free to do what I want, when I want," she replied.

"And what does that feeling of being able to do what you want mean to you?" I asked.

"I guess it means having a sense of freedom. Not feeling constrained by the duties of life."

"I see. So what would not having these constraints in your life and having this freedom mean to you?"

Jessica thought for a moment. "It would mean that I'd have more time to be with my daughter, who is growing up so fast that she's going to be in college before I know it," she said. "And I could spend more time with my husband and my friends, who I rarely see now because I'm always so busy."

"Okay," I nodded. "Let's assume for a moment that you have security, and that as a result you have the freedom to spend more time with your daughter and your husband and your friends. What's important about being in that position to you?"

"Well, I guess it would make me feel calmer and happier," Jessica responded. "Definitely happier. Right now I feel burned out all the time. I'd like to not be tired for a change."

"And what's important to you about that?" I asked her.

Jessica smiled wearily. "I just spend so much time rushing around now trying to do everything—working, being a wife and a mother, keeping the house and bills in order—that I don't feel like I have a life. Some days I don't even remember what it feels like to not be exhausted."

"So it's important for you to not rush around and to feel you have a life again," I said.

Once again Jessica did not hesitate. "Yes, definitely," she said firmly. "I want my life back."

When I asked Jessica what she would do if she had her life back, she said she'd start taking better care of herself, exercising and eating better. When I pressed her on why she wanted to do that, she said her aim was to live longer and be a better example to her daughter.

"Okay," I continued, "so now that you are going to live longer and be an example to your daughter, what else would you do with your life?"

Jessica frowned for a moment, lost in thought. "That's a tough one to answer," she said finally. "I'm not sure."

I wasn't about to let her off the hook. "I know you're not sure," I persisted, "but if you were sure, what do you think you would say?"

"Well," she said slowly, "I guess if I really had my life together the way I wanted it, I would focus on getting more involved with charity groups in my community."

In response to my follow-up questions, Jessica explained that "making a difference and giving something back" was really important to her.

"Is there anything more important to you than making a difference and helping others?" I asked.

Jessica looked me in the eye. "I just want to know that when I go, I'll have lived a full life, loved, been a good example to my daughter and my family, and really made a difference." She blushed self-consciously. "That's all," she said.

That, of course, was a lot—a lot to think about, and a lot to remember when it came time to construct a financial plan. Fortunately, as Jessica and I talked, we kept a record of the values that were important to her, in the order that she had come up with them. On page 46, you'll see Jessica's values ladder. As you can see, at the bottom of the ladder is Jessica's **first value**, security. Above it, each successive rung contains the next value that Jessica told me was important to her.

Take a moment and reread the conversation. Notice how quickly Jessica and I were able to build her values ladder.

Does Your Financial Behaviour Match Your Values?

What Jessica and I learned from our values conversation was that there was nothing more important to her than having more time to devote to her family and community. As things stood, most of her time (and energy) was going to her job. With that in mind, the next thing we did was look at Jessica's financial situation and habits to see how they stacked up against her values ladder.

As a computer salesperson, Jessica earned about $75,000 a year. That's a solid income by any measure, yet for some reason she was still living from paycheque to paycheque. Hence, the pressure she felt to spend so much time at work.

Why was Jessica so strapped for cash? We looked at her spending patterns and found that she was spending a lot of money on what were clearly nonessential items: more than $300 a month on clothes, $100 on a car phone, $350 on restaurants, $150 on dry cleaning, $525 on a leased car, and on and on. In all, she was spending over $2,000 a month—well over half her take-home pay—*on things that had absolutely nothing to do with what was most important to her:* namely, having more time to devote to her family and community.

When I pointed this out to her—that she was spending more than four hours of every eight-hour workday toiling to pay for luxuries that did nothing to give her the life she really wanted—Jessica was shocked. But fortunately, she was also motivated to change her ways. Once she realized how much time and energy she was, in essence, wasting, she worked out a plan under which she was able to start saving money for the first time (and thus stop living from paycheque to paycheque) while slowly cutting back the number of hours she put in at work (thus giving her more time with her family).

The Breakthrough

Jessica got more out of our values conversation than just a new financial plan. She told me later that she also came away with a sense of clarity about her life's purpose that she hadn't really had before. "It made me realize that much of what I was doing with my time had little or nothing to do with my own values about who I am and who I want to be," she said. As a result, she added, "Now when I am doing something, I am much clearer with myself. I always ask myself, 'Is this in line with my values?' If it's not, I try to not do it." Of course, as Jessica acknowledged, there are some things that can't be avoided, but at least she now knows where her focus is supposed to be.

Equally important, the conversation also made Jessica realize that she didn't need nearly as much money as she had thought in order to get what she really wanted out of life. As she told me, "It showed me that, while I've been spending so much time trying to increase my income, I've actually been squandering money on things that have

nothing to do with the values that are important to me. I realized that a new dress, a fancy car, and a car phone were not worth all the weekends I was spending at the office."

Once that became clear, she said, she found it much easier to cut back on unnecessary expenses. "I immediately felt calmer about who I was and where I was going," she reported. "I hadn't had such a sense of inner peace in a long time. It's hard to believe that a question as simple as 'What's important about money to you?' can lead to such an important breakthrough, but it definitely can."

If It's Not About Returns, What *Is* It About?

Values exercises are not just for younger women. Taking a good look inside yourself can be a worthwhile undertaking no matter what your age—especially in this era of economic boom and busts; with record stock prices and record declines, many of us have become so obsessed with growth figures and rates of return that the point of saving and investing sometimes gets forgotten. Looking at your values can help you to focus on meaning in your life rather than the means. This new sense of focus can be life changing.

Take Helen, an older client of mine. Helen was very upset when she came into my office. At first glance, it was hard to see why. A fetching 72-year-old, Helen was a "child of the Great Depression" and, as a result, always had watched her spending and savings very carefully. Ever since her husband had passed away six years earlier, she had been living on Old Age Security and a widow's pension. In addition, she had some $500,000 in guaranteed investment certificates that had been paying her 8 percent annual interest (or $40,000 a year). In short, she had more than enough money to live on.

So what was bothering her? Well, it seemed that her bank had informed her that her GICs were about to mature and, if she wished to roll over her savings into new GICs, the best interest rate she could get now was only 5 percent.

"What am I going to do?" Helen asked me. "These rates are so low, yet I can't afford to take any risk with my money."

When I asked Helen how she spent the $40,000 a year she earned from her GICs, she gave me a look and said she put the money into a savings account at the bank. In other words, she didn't need it to live on.

With that in mind, I asked her what was so important about this $40,000 a year in interest that she was earning but not spending. She said it gave her a sense of security. As we continued what quickly became a full-fledged values conversation, she explained that she wanted to know that she would always be independent; for her, being independent meant never having to be a burden on her family. Her grandchildren, she said, meant the world to her. "I just love them so much," Helen added fervently. "I want to be able to give to them and not need to take."

"And what would you like to give them?" I asked.

Helen's eyes lit up. "You know," she said, "I've always thought it would be so special to take the whole family on a cruise to Alaska." As she told me about this dream trip, she glowed. Her smile disappeared, however, when I asked her why she didn't just do it.

"Oh, David," she said, "it would cost at least ten thousand dollars."

"So?" I replied. "You've been earning more than four times that on your GICs every year." I shook my head. "Helen," I said, "you have your health, you have all these assets, and you have this wonderful dream of taking your family on a trip—and what are you doing? You're sitting in my office worrying about whether your GICs are going to pay you 8 percent or 5 percent. What does it matter what the interest rate is if you're not going to use your money to make your life the way you want it to be?" I then asked Helen the final question on the values ladder: Was there anything more important to her than her family?

As it turned out, there wasn't.

Within a week of our meeting, Helen visited a travel agent and booked the cruise we had discussed. The trip cost her about $12,500. It was the most money she had ever spent on a luxury in her entire life. What was important, however, was not what she spent but what she got—which was the joy of sharing a wonderful experience with her children and grandchildren.

Take a look at Helen's values ladder on page 49, and note how quickly we were able to use that simple question about the importance of money to help her build a future that was exciting for both her and her family.

The point of this story is that values-based financial planning helped Helen use her money the way money is supposed to be used— to make life better. If your money is not helping you make your life better, then something is wrong. Chances are you're not making a connection between your values and the role money plays in your life. The importance of making that connection is the point of this story and the point of this chapter.

CREATE YOUR OWN
VALUES LADDER

Pretend you are arriving at my office. You're going to meet with me, one on one, to create your own personal values ladder to the new you—a woman totally in control of her own financial situation.

You enter my office. In the middle of a round table at which you and I will sit is a piece of paper containing a blank values ladder just like the one that follows. We're going to use it to help you figure out what's important about money to you.

1. Start by relaxing. Take a minute to collect your thoughts. Our objective is for you to give answers that reflect how you really feel—not how you think someone else thinks you should feel. Remember, whatever your values are, they are the right ones for you.

2. Ready? Let's start with the single most important question: Ask yourself: *What's important about money to me?*

3. Write your answer on the bottom rung of the ladder. Remember that we're looking for values (basic aspirations such as *freedom, happiness, security,* and so on) and not goals (which generally involve specific amounts of money or particular acquisitions). If you've just gone through the jolt of a divorce and find yourself on your own with two kids to take care of, for example, your value might be "security." Or maybe you're a single entrepreneur who dreams of travelling around the world, in which case your initial value may be "freedom."

4. Now we need a little more perspective on the values you're listing, because the value you choose means different things to dif-

ferent people. Ask yourself: *What's important about* _____ [your value] *to me?* Write your answer on the next rung up the ladder.

5. Let's assume for a moment that _____ [your second value] has become a reality for you. Ask yourself: *What's important about* _____ [your second value] *to me?* Write your answer on the third rung of the ladder.

6. Continue climbing the ladder, filling in your answers as you go up. Don't cheat yourself. The biggest mistake people make when they conduct a values conversation on their own (and even sometimes in my office) is not taking the process deep enough. It's important to keep digging, because only rarely will the values you hold most important be among the first ones you list. Just keep asking yourself: *What's important about* _____ [the last value you gave] *to me?* You'll know you're done when you can't think of anything more important than the last value you mentioned.

Tapping into Your Values

For those of you who may be having trouble figuring out what is a value vs. what is a goal—and many people do—I've listed some examples in the boxes that follow. By studying the lists, you'll get a better idea of the difference between the two. Don't cheat, though, and

---

SOME EXAMPLES OF VALUES

Freedom	Connection with others
Security	Independence
Happiness	Fulfillment
Peace of mind	Confidence
Power	Being the best
Helping others	Making a difference
Helping family	Fun
Realizing my true potential (self-actualization)	Growing
Greater spirituality	Adventure

Your Values Ladder

(ALWAYS START WITH)
"What's important about money to you?"

borrow some values from my list just because they sound good and you're having trouble filling out your ladder. If the values you write down don't truly reflect what you feel in your heart, then they won't work to motivate you.

What follows are examples of goals that people come up with when they do the values-ladder exercise. Remember, we are not looking for goals. We are looking for values. (We'll get to goals in Step Three.)

SOME EXAMPLES OF GOALS

Pay down debt

Have $1 million

Not run out of money

Pay for college

Buy a house

Travel *(Travel is a goal; what travelling does for you is the value. I bring this up because travel is mentioned quite often in values conversations.)*

Get a new car

Redecorate

Retire rich

Donate money

Tithing *(As with travel the reason you give to charity is a value; what or how much you give is the goal.)*

Put money in my retirement account

Not work

Start my own business

Put my child through college

Get divorced

Get married

Stay married *(Money affects marriages—no question about it. But contrary to what many people believe, it's not how much money you have that matters. It's how you communicate and make decisions about your money that determines whether financial issues will bring you together as a family or drive you apart.)*

What If I Can't Come Up with Enough Values?

This almost never happens. Everyone has lots of values—more than you might think at first. Give yourself some time for them to occur to you. But don't turn it into a marathon. The whole exercise should not take more than 15 minutes! In my office, the average values conversation lasts less than 10.

Also, there are no right or wrong answers here. The only mistake you can make is to be less than honest. In my classes, I always jokingly tell the audience, "Don't look at your neighbour's paper. Those are her values, not yours."

Go All the Way!

The reason our values ladder is designed to elicit at least six personal values is that we are trying to get you to look deep within yourself—so deep that you will come away with a really intense awareness of what is most important to you. Understanding this, you should be able to stop wasting your time, energy, and money on things that don't really matter to you—and begin focusing your resources on the things that do!

As should be clear by now, although we are focusing on the question of money, what we really are getting at in our values conversation is the essence of what matters to you about life in general. That's what makes the technique so powerful. It enables you not only to lay out your values but also to define who you are and what direction you want to take your life.

Don't Think You Can Skip This Step

Don't be like some students who take my classes and try to skip this step in the mistaken belief that the values-based approach is nothing more than "New Age feel-good stuff." There's nothing New Age about getting in touch with your values. The Greek philosopher Socrates was talking about that sort of thing back in 400 B.C. The key to human advancement, he taught, could be expressed in two simple words: "Know thyself." So don't get sidetracked.

As you will see as we continue through our journey, the nine-step approach builds on itself. If you don't complete this step, you'll find the next one much harder than it needs to be. That's because doing Step Two gives you a certain momentum that makes Step Three really easy.

Congratulations! You Have Completed Step Two!

The thing to remember about this step is that we had you look closely at your values for a very practical reason: Knowing "what's important about money to you" not only makes it possible to plan your future intelligently, but also makes it easier to stick to your plan. Once they know what their values are, people will do more to protect them than just about anything else in the world. Values are not tasks or resolutions, like "eat less," "save more," or "keep the house clean." Values are not things we get bored with. Values are what we believe in; they are what motivate and shape us.

Now that you have constructed your own values ladder, keep it handy. We're going to use it in Step Three when we start defining your specific financial goals. But there's one more thing you've got to do before you're ready to design that road map to your financial future. *You need to figure out where you stand today financially.*

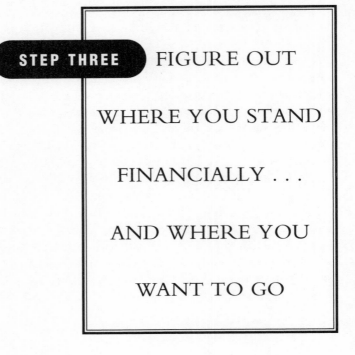

STEP THREE FIGURE OUT WHERE YOU STAND FINANCIALLY . . . AND WHERE YOU WANT TO GO

Imagine that after working late seven consecutive nights, your boss tells you that as a reward for your extra effort he's decided to send you to Paris for a week, all expenses paid. The only catch is, you must be there by the end of the day tomorrow and you must make the arrangements yourself.

No problem, you say, and immediately call up a travel agent. It's after hours, so you get the answering machine. "I need a flight to Paris," you tell the machine, "arriving no later than tomorrow evening." Then you leave your name and phone number and hang up.

The next morning you get a frantic call from the travel agent. "We couldn't book your flight," she tells you.

"Oh, no!" you complain. "Now I'm not going to get to go!" You begin to yell at the travel agent, questioning her competence, but she quickly cuts you off. It's not her fault she couldn't book the flight, she says, it's yours.

"My fault?" you say indignantly. "How is it my fault?"

"You told us where you wanted to go," the travel agent replies, "but you didn't tell us where you are now. How can we get you a flight if we don't know where you're leaving from?"

When it comes to planning a trip, chances are you'd never make such an elementary mistake. But you'd be surprised how many people slip up in precisely the same way when it comes to planning their finances. They plunge into all sorts of detail about what they want to accomplish, what investment they should buy, and where they want to be, without first making sure they know where they stand now.

DO YOU KNOW WHERE
YOUR MONEY IS?

If I asked you about your current financial status, could you, right now, list on a blank piece of paper all your assets and liabilities, including your investments, bank accounts, mortgages, and credit card debts? Do you have an organized filing system in which all your financial documents can be found easily? Or have you left all that stuff to your husband or your accountant? If you're working, do you know how the money in your company pension plan is invested?

You might want to turn back to Step One at this point and take a look at how you did on that quiz about your family's money. If you're like most people, you probably scored lower than you'd like. That's okay. This is where we start to fix the problems you found back there.

Knowing Where Your Money Is Sounds Obvious,
but Trust Me—Most People Don't Have a Clue

Having been a financial coach for hundreds of clients, I can tell you from firsthand experience that most people really don't know where they spend their money and where their money is invested. I've had clients come into my office with shopping bags filled with mutual fund statements, bank statements, RRSP records, you name it. Take Karen and Tom, a successful couple in their 50s. They came into my office one day, dumped the contents of a bulging department-store shopping bag onto my desk, and announced ruefully, "David, we're the people you talk about in your seminars!" We started going through their statements together, and you know what? Even though

Karen and Tom had been organized enough to save the statements they'd been sent, most of the envelopes had never been opened! They hadn't looked at their accounts for months.

Now, I'm sure that you're not like this, but I'll bet many of your friends are.

Six RRSPs, Five Bank Accounts, Four Insurance Plans . . .

After two hours of going through Karen and Tom's stuff, we managed to figure out where all their money was: It was stashed in 12 separate mutual funds, six different RRSPs, five bank accounts, an RESP, two Deferred Profit Sharing Plans, and four separate insurance policies.

Unbelievable, right? Wrong. Karen and Tom are typical of many successful people. As Karen explained it, somewhat defensively, "Tom puts all the responsibility of managing the money in my hands, but with a career and three kids I don't have time to keep track of it all. I really don't know how others find the time."

"You're right, Karen," I said, "No one has the time to monitor what they have, unless they are professional money managers. And I know a lot of professionals who don't take care of their own money because they're so busy taking care of other people's!"

Make Getting Your Financial House in Order Now a Priority!

Old or young, rich or poor, married or single, it doesn't matter— one of the first things we do at The Bach Group after discussing our clients' values is to figure out their current financial condition.

To accomplish this, I have my clients fill out what we call a FinishRich Inventory Planner™. You'll find a copy in Appendix 2.

> **NOTE:** *Don't complete the worksheet until after you've finished reading this book! Why? Sad but true, most people never get past the first few chapters of books like this one if they have to stop reading and fill out a form. So wait until you've gotten through the whole book before you start in on the worksheet.*

If you are like most people, you probably already have all your financial information totally organized. In fact, I'm sure that all of your financial documents are right now sitting in an easy-to-use filing system with brightly coloured folders and neatly typed labels. And because all your financial documents are so well organized and easy for you to review, completing the worksheet in the back of the book shouldn't take you more than 30 minutes, right?

Obviously, I'm being a bit facetious here. Usually when I discuss filling out the FinishRich Inventory Planner in my investment classes, I call this project a "homework assignment." And when I get to the part about most people having all their financial information in colour-coded files, the women in the room either laugh or groan. At that point, I say, "For those of you who use the shopping-bag approach to filing, it may take a little longer."

To be honest, I have had some clients who've told me that this "homework" took them only about 15 minutes (usually because they had everything on a financial software program like Quicken or Microsoft Money). But for most people, it generally takes at least an hour or two.

And don't worry if it takes you even longer than that. Some people find the assignment requires an entire weekend. If you're one of them, don't be daunted. It simply means that you really need to do it!

Getting Organized Is One of the Keys to Financial Security

Admittedly, getting organized sometimes can be a painful experience. I've had some clients who thought they were financially secure, only to discover, after listing all their assets and liabilities, that they weren't doing as well as they had imagined. Then again, I've had plenty of others who completed the worksheet and found they were much closer to financial independence than they realized. Either way, they were much better off knowing the truth about their financial situation.

Take Betsy and Victor, two clients of mine who got a lot out of the process. Their story is quite typical, and I hope it will inspire you to emulate their example.

BETSY'S STORY: LEARNING WHERE YOU STAND

"When I first took David's investment class, I got really excited about the opportunity to become involved in my family's finances. I have to admit, however, that the homework assignment of 'getting my financial house in order' did seem a bit intimidating.

"The thing I liked best about the FinishRich Inventory Planner was that it was something that produced immediate results. I knew my family's financial documents were totally disorganized. I also knew that my husband, Victor, probably didn't know what our net worth was.

"The other thing I really liked about this step was that it gave me an easy way to approach my husband about getting involved with our finances. I basically came home from the class and said, 'Victor, I've got a huge homework assignment and I know I'm going to need your help. Do you think we could work together on it this weekend, because I'm not sure I can do it without you?'

"That approach really worked with Victor, since it wasn't like I was accusing him of anything or trying to take control of the finances. And when I showed him what the assignment was, he readily admitted it was something that we should have done years ago. As Victor put it, he had always wanted to get our financial documents organized, but it was a lot like cleaning out the garage—easy to put off.

"In the end, it wound up taking us almost the entire day to do—a lot longer than the 30 minutes David had promised. But as David said, the fact that it took so much longer meant we really needed to do it.

"When we were through, I could really see for the first time just where our family stood financially. I realized for the first time that we were actually doing a pretty good job of saving money. We had very little debt and our retirement accounts were really starting to add up. Seeing this all on paper got me excited about looking at what else I could do to improve our financial situation."

VICTOR'S STORY: A WEIGHT OFF HIS SHOULDERS

"When Betsy came home with this homework assignment to get our financial house in order, quite frankly I was embarrassed. I knew I had taken on the responsibility of managing the family's money, and I felt I had been doing an okay job—but I also knew there was a lot of stuff all over the place, not well organized.

"I have to admit it really felt good when we finished filling out the FinishRich Inventory Planner that weekend. For the first time in years, Betsy and I really discussed where our financial life was. By getting all of our assets and liabilities down on paper, we were finally able to see in black and white where we actually stood and how much our family was worth. While I always sort of had a running total in my head, filling out the inventory worksheet made it clearer and easier to deal with. I have to say—it's quite a weight off my shoulders to have Betsy involved with our money now. It takes some of the pressure off me."

FROM MY POINT OF VIEW . . .

When I met with Betsy and Victor in my office after their weekend financial housecleaning session, we had a great time. They really had enjoyed getting their finances organized and were excited to talk about where they stood.

Because they had done such a thorough job filling out the worksheet, my job actually was quite easy. One of the first things I noticed was that they had both been maintaining individual Registered Retirement Savings Plans (RRSPs) at several different banks for nearly eight years. They had done this because they thought that's how you get the best return on your money—and also because they had heard that diversifying was important, and they believed that going to a lot of different banks was how you diversified.

Actually, what they really were doing was letting their retirement dollars lay dormant at a measly 5 percent annual rate, which didn't even keep up with inflation. I was able to help them consolidate all their accounts into two self-directed RRSPs and then reposition the money they had invested into more appropriate growth investments. I will explain how we did this—and how you can too—in Step Five, when we discuss your Retirement Basket. For now, what matters is that by getting organized, Betsy and Victor were able to see where they stood and what they needed to do to achieve their goals.

DO YOUR HOMEWORK

The way we work at my office is simple. We send prospective clients the FinishRich Inventory Planner and ask them to fill it out completely before they come in. Nonetheless, some clients show up without having filled out their sheets. Often I'll kid them and ask if they were the kind of students who never did their homework on time. Joking aside, however, there's no getting around the fundamental reality: Until you get your finances organized, you can't get started creating financial security—and ultimately your financial dreams.

So no excuses. When you finish this book, you must fill out the FinishRich Inventory Planner in Appendix 2. It's the best way to start getting organized and involved in your finances and, most important, determine your net worth. (This is key, since if you don't know what you are worth, you won't know where you are starting from.) By the time you are done, you will have a better grasp of your financial situation than the vast majority of Canadians. You will know not only your personal net worth but also where you spend your money and how your new-found wealth is going to be built. You—not someone else—will be in charge of your financial destiny.

Your First Job: Find Your Stuff

Completing the FinishRich Inventory Planner is probably the most crucial homework assignment you'll get in the course of this book. But don't start working on it yet. At this point, all I want you to do is begin finding your stuff. To make this easier, I'm going to share with you an incredibly simple yet powerful way to organize your stuff at home. If you do this now, you'll find it much easier to fill out your worksheet later. So let's get going.

THE FINISHRICH FILE FOLDER SYSTEM™

So here's what I want you to do. First, I want you to get yourself a dozen or so hanging folders and a box of at least 50 file folders to put inside them. Then I want you to label the hanging folders as follows:

☐ 1) Label the first one **"Tax Returns."** In it, put eight file folders, one for each of the last seven years plus one for this year. Mark the year on each folder's tab and put into it all of that year's important tax documents, such as T-4 slips, medical and charitable receipts, and (most important) a copy of all the tax returns you filed for that year. Ideally, you've at least saved your old tax returns. If you haven't but used a professional tax preparer in the past, call him or her and ask for back copies. As a rule, you should keep old tax records for at least seven years, because that's how far back the law allows the Canada Customs and Revenue Agency (CCRA) to go when it wants to audit you. I recommend hanging on to them even longer, but that's up to you.

☐ 2) Label the second hanging folder **"Retirement Accounts."** This is where you're going to keep all of your retirement-account statements. You should create a file for each retirement account you have. If you have three RRSPs, then you should have a separate file for each. The most important thing to keep in these folders are the monthly statements. You don't need to keep the prospectuses that the mutual fund companies mail you each quarter. However, if you have a company retirement account, you should definitely keep the sign-up package because it tells you what investment options you have—something you should review annually.

☐ 3) Label the third hanging folder **"Canada Pension Plan/Old Age Security."** You should put your most recent CPP statement in this folder. If you haven't received one in the mail, get online and go to *www.hrdc-drhc.gc.ca* to request one. If you don't have Internet access, telephone your local Human Resources Development Canada office (the number is listed in phone books under "Federal Government").

☐ 4) Label the fourth hanging folder **"Investment Accounts."** In this folder you put files for each investment account you have that is not a retirement account. If you own mutual funds, maintain a brokerage account, or own individual stocks, each and every statement you receive that is related to these investments should go in a particular folder.

☐ 5) Label the fifth hanging folder **"Savings and Chequing Accounts."** If you have more than one bank account, create a separate file for each one. Keep your monthly bank statements here.

☐ 6) Label the sixth hanging folder **"Household Accounts."** If you own your own home, this one should contain the following file folders: "House Title," into which you'll put all your title information (if you can't find this stuff, call your real estate agent or lawyer); "Home Improvements," where you'll keep all your receipts for any home-improvement work you do (since home-improvement expenses can be added to the cost basis of your house when you sell it, you should keep these receipts for as long as you own your house); and "Home Mortgage," for all your mortgage statements (which you should check regularly, since mortgage companies often DON'T CREDIT YOU PROPERLY). If you're a tenant, this folder should contain your lease, the receipt for your security deposit, and the receipts for your rental payments.

☐ 7) Label the seventh hanging folder **"Credit Card DEBT."** Make sure you capitalize the word "DEBT" so it stands out and bothers you every time you see it. I'm not kidding. I'll explain later how to deal with credit card debt. For the time being, my hope is that this won't be one of your larger hanging folders. You should create a separate file for each credit card account you have. For many women, this folder may contain more than a dozen files. I've actually met some women with as many as 30. However many files you have, keep all your monthly statements in them. And hang on to them. As with tax returns, I keep all my credit card records for at least seven years in case of an audit.

☐ 8) Label the eighth hanging folder **"Other Liabilities."** In here go all of your records dealing with debts other than your mortgage and your credit card accounts. These would include college loans, car loans, personal loans, etc. Each debt should have its own file, which should contain the loan note and your payment records.

☐ 9) Label the ninth hanging folder **"Insurance."** It will contain separate folders for each of your insurance policies, including health, life, car, homeowner's, tenant's, disability, long-term care, etc. In these folders put the appropriate policy and all the related payment records.

☐ 10) Label the tenth hanging folder **"Family Will or Trust."** This should have a copy of your most recent will or living trust and powers of attorney, along with the business card of the lawyer who set them up.

☐ 11) If you have children, put together a folder labelled **"Children's Accounts."** It should hold all statements and other records pertaining to Registered Educational Savings Plans (RESPs), university savings accounts or other investments that you have made for your kids.

☐ 12) Finally, create a folder called **"FinishRich Inventory Planner."** Here's where you're going to put the worksheet found in Appendix 2 after you've filled it out. This folder will also contain a file in which you keep a running semiannual total of your net worth—a vital record that will help you keep track of your financial progress.

That's it. You're done. A dozen folders—eleven if you don't have children. Not so bad, is it?

As you dig into this assignment, you may realize that you don't have all of these documents. In some cases, you may have lost them or thrown them away. In others, you may never have had them in the first place. For example, chances are you've never bothered to order your Canada Pension Plan statements from the CCRA. Or maybe you don't have disability insurance. Whatever the case, it does not matter at this point. All I want you to do now is create the abovementioned files, whether you have anything to put in them or not. It shouldn't take very long. After all, there are only 12 of them.

Once you're done, put the folders in a file cabinet and feel good about yourself. You are already more organized than you were when you first picked up this book and are better prepared to complete the FinishRich Inventory Planner.

If You're Part of a Couple . . .

If you are married (or are in some similarly committed relationship), you definitely should try to get your significant other involved in this project. But be diplomatic. After all, while you've been getting excited about getting organized, your mate has been innocently going about his day with no idea that you are planning to clean house financially. A word of advice: Don't suddenly start jumping all over your partner for being disorganized. Remember—he hasn't read this book. (At least not yet.)

As I tell the women who take my seminars, it's probably not a good idea to run home and tell your husband, "Honey, there's this financial advisor named David Bach and he says that as a man you are more than likely doing a really terrible job managing our finances, so from now on I'm going to be in charge of our money. Now, show me where it is!" Nor should you announce, "I just learned that you probably will die before me. And if you don't drop dead soon, I'll still need to protect myself in case you meet some bimbo and decide to divorce me. So show me where all the money is!"

Now, obviously, I'm exaggerating a little bit. I doubt you would ever be so blatant. But I also know that it is very easy to get excited by a set of new ideas.

And I do want you to get excited. That's the whole point of this book—to get you excited enough to make drastic changes in your life. Still, I don't want a bunch of angry men out there looking for my head. More important, I don't want you to be met with an immediate wall of defensiveness and negative feedback.

My grandmother taught me that you can accomplish anything in life if your approach is right. In this case, the right approach involves recognizing that if you are part of a couple (and this goes for same-sex relationships as well), money issues should be handled jointly. Chances are, at this point yours are not.

That's one of the great things about this financial housecleaning process. Not only does it show you where you stand financially, but also, as Betsy pointed out, it's a very proactive way for couples to start working on their finances together. In filling out the worksheet, nobody is judging or criticizing anyone. All you are doing is getting your stuff organized. If your husband or significant other says, "It's taken care of, honey—don't worry about it," you simply reply, "Great. Show me how it's taken care of and let's discuss it together." If he continues to balk, explain to him how important it is to you to get involved with the family's finances and that knowing where everything is simply a fundamental part of the process.

What If the Man in Your Life Won't Cooperate?

For most of you, this process of discussing your finances with your husband or significant other is not going to be a big deal. My experience is that most men really do want their mates to be involved with the family's finances. I can't tell you how many men have said to me over the years, "I'm so glad my wife is taking an interest in this stuff. She never seemed to care before, and I always worried about how she would cope if something were to happen to me. Having her involved is a real relief."

The point is, someone who really loves you should not be threatened by your wanting to know where the family money is. The key is how you present it. Some men have fragile egos. What can I say? We like to think we are in charge and that we know what we are doing. Of course, for the most part you know that we are not in charge and that you are. That's fine—just don't let us know that you know it.

FIVE-STAR TIP: *If you're concerned that your husband or boyfriend won't read a book entitled* Smart Women Finish Rich, *consider getting the Canadian edition of* Smart Couples Finish Rich *and using it as a guide to plan your financial future as a team. You can visit our website at* www.finishrich.com *and read a few chapters of the book for free.*

In the event your family already has someone who helps to manage your money (a financial advisor or an accountant), then I strongly suggest that you make an appointment to meet with that person. Most likely, he or she does not know exactly where you stand, and completing the Finish Rich Inventory Planner really will help the person to better help you. The initial phone call can be as simple as this: "I'm making an effort to get involved in handling the family's financial decisions. I understand you have been working with my husband [or whomever] and I would like to meet with you to discuss where we stand financially."

When you make the appointment, I strongly suggest that you and your significant other go to this meeting—and all future meetings—together. I can't stress this enough: Financial planning should involve both of you equally. The biggest mistake I see couples make is not handling it together. In our office, if a man calls to make an appointment and tells us that his wife does not need to come with him because he's "in charge of the money," we won't take the meeting. That's how strongly we feel about the importance of doing financial planning as a couple.

HEADING IN THE
RIGHT DIRECTION

Microsoft, which in my opinion is one of the smartest companies in the world today, used to run what I thought was one of the world's smartest advertising campaigns. The campaign wasn't about software but rather about our lives and where they might be headed. Their television commercials asked the question straight out: "Where do you want to go today?" (with the idea obviously being that Microsoft could get you there).

As a Smart Woman, the challenge you face now is to answer that question for yourself—to take the foundational work we have just done (including looking at your values and getting your family finances organized)—and use it to create a compelling future that inspires and excites you.

So where do you start? Well, here's a hint . . .

Success leaves clues.

Have you ever noticed that some people seem to have it all? Their lives always seem to be going in the direction that they want. They always seem to be moving forward, never pushed off course by life's daily demands and challenges. No matter what happens to them, they come out on top.

Don't you just hate those people?

I threw that in just to see if you were paying attention. Of course, you don't really hate them. But doesn't it make you wonder? Why is it that some people can be so successful, have so much fun, and make it seem so easy?

The answer, I believe, lies in the fact that for the most part successful people have specific goals. For her book *The Eleven Commandments of Wildly Successful Women,* author Pamela Gilberd interviewed 125 women who achieved extraordinary success in both their work and their personal lives. What she found was that most of these women had one thing in common: They all knew where they wanted to go. They had goals. They created their own plans, and they focused on making them happen.

The master motivator Napoleon Hill, who wrote the renowned book *Think and Grow Rich,* phrased it differently, but it amounted to the same thing. According to Hill, to achieve your dreams you have to focus on what you want your life to be about. He called this developing "Definiteness of Purpose." After studying the most successful people of his time, Hill concluded that individuals who had this "definiteness of purpose" found it easier to prioritize their time, effort, and money—and, ultimately, to reach their dreams.

Now, "developing definiteness of purpose" is nothing more than a fancy way of saying "setting yourself specific goals." And what Hill teaches us is that successful people do just that. When you ask them, they can tell you where it is they want their life to end up and what they are doing to make sure they get there.

Getting Beyond "Shoulda, Coulda, Woulda"

It's been said many times that if you want to be successful, you should do what successful people do. I wholeheartedly subscribe to this belief. (This is what I was getting at before when I said that success leaves clues.) In other words, if successful people set specific goals for themselves, maybe that's something you should be doing too.

With that in mind, let's spend a moment talking about what a goal is . . . and what it is not. The dictionary defines a goal as the purpose toward which an endeavour is directed. That's clear enough, but it's only part of the story. The fact is, not just any purpose will do. In order to empower us, a goal must be specific. Otherwise, we will treat it as nothing more than a wish—what I call the "shoulda, coulda, woulda" phenomenon.

You know what I'm talking about. It's possible that at times you have succumbed to this phenomenon yourself. I certainly have. As you will learn in Step Four, I used to be a raging shopper. I'd get home from a shopping spree and think, *I really should have left those credit cards home* or *I should have bought less stuff.* My point here is that, back when I was shopping too much, spending less was for me a wish, not a goal. Spending less didn't become a real goal for me until I took a piece of paper and a pen and wrote down the words: "I will not buy anything with my credit cards anymore. I will use only cash."

Achieving Your Goals Isn't
Something That Just Happens

If goals were easy to achieve, then the entire world would be successful. But that's okay. You didn't buy this book because you expect life to be easy. Rather, you are a woman who knows that, to make things happen in life, you have to get involved. But let me ask you something: Do you have written goals right now? Is there a piece of paper somewhere in your home or office on which you have written down what it is you are striving for?

More than likely the answer is no. In fact, studies show that less than 1 percent of Canadians write down specific goals for themselves each year. That's a shame, because writing down your goals is powerful.

In a study done at Harvard University more than 40 years ago, researchers polled the graduating class of 1953 to find out how many students actually had clearly written, specific goals and a plan for achieving them. This being a class of highly intelligent people at one of the world's most renowned universities, you'd expect the answer to be most of them, right?

Not even close. In fact, only 3 percent of the class had taken the time to write down their goals.

Now here comes the really interesting part. Some 20 years later, researchers polled this same group of graduates to see how they had fared in life. It turned out that the 3 percent who had written down their goals had accumulated more wealth than the other 97 percent of their class combined! Researchers reported that these people also seemed to be healthier and happier than their classmates.

I was in college when I first heard about this study, and I wondered if achieving your goals could really be that easy. "Put in writing what you want and focus on it daily"? Well, it may not be easy, but over the years I definitely have seen it work.

Writing a $10 Million Cheque . . . to Yourself!

One of my favourite stories about the power of writing down your goals involves someone we both know. Actually, we may not know him personally, but it definitely feels like we do because these days it seems like he's everywhere. I'm talking about Jim Carrey, the star of such hit movies as *The Mask, Batman Forever, The Truman Show,* and *Me, Myself, and Irene.*

In the late 1980s, after Carrey had moved to Hollywood from Canada, his career started to stall. He had managed to get a few small TV jobs but seemed nowhere near to realizing his dreams of major stardom. It was at this point in his life, when he was struggling to the top, that he went for a drive in the Hollywood Hills and visualized what it would be like to be rich and famous. Carrey did more than just dream, however. He parked his car, pulled out his chequebook, and wrote himself a cheque for $10 million. He dated it: "Thanksgiving Day, 1995."

For the next several years, Carrey kept that cheque in his wallet. When times got tough, he would take it out and stare at it, thinking about what his life would someday be like when his talents and efforts finally were rewarded.

The rest, of course, is history. Carrey got noticed on the TV series *In Living Color,* and his first two movies, *Ace Ventura* and *The Mask,* were huge hits. Late in November 1995, he was offered $10 million to star in *Mask 2.* The following year, with *The Cable Guy,* his price went up to $20 million a picture!

Now, you can be a skeptic like many people and say, "Oh, that was just dumb luck." Or you can focus on the fact that Jim Carrey had Napoleon Hill's "Definiteness of Purpose." He didn't "shoulda, coulda, woulda" his goals into wishes that fade away. He put them in writing, and by making them specific, he was able to make them happen.

See, Hear, Feel, and Smell
Your Way to Your Dreams

In my seminars, when we get to talking about creating goals, I often tell a story about two women. One is named Jill and the other is named Jane. Jill and Jane both want to have successful financial futures, and both believe in keeping a written list of their financial goals. As it happens, they have at least one goal in common: They both want to own a vacation home. But while Jill writes down her goal as "Buy vacation home," Jane is a lot more specific. "I will own a vacation home by January 1, 2005," she writes. "It will be a three-bedroom house with two baths located on the west side of Lake

Muskoka. The mortgage will range between $350,000 and $400,000. I will take out a 30-year mortgage but make extra payments to pay it off in 18 years. I will save $65,000 over the next 36 months to make my down payment."

Now let me ask you the question I ask the students who attend my seminars: Which of these two women do you think is more likely to reach her goal of owning a second home?

The answer, obviously, is Jane. The reason: Jane has been incredibly specific about what she wants and how she intends to get it. Indeed, she has been so specific that she practically can see, hear, feel, and smell that lakeside home. And that's the key. Specificity transforms a vague dream into a concrete, achievable goal. If you can practically see, hear, feel, and smell a goal, the chances are excellent that you'll not only know what's required to make it real, you'll actually do what's required to make it real.

The challenge facing you is to create goals that are equally specific and empowering.

THE SMART WOMEN FINISH RICH

QUANTUM LEAP SYSTEM

Let's say for a moment that you buy what I'm saying. Let's say you accept that you should have goals and that you believe they should be in writing and you want to make them as specific as possible. Now I want to show you a way to formulate a series of goals that will allow you to take a quantum leap toward your dreams in the years ahead. I promise you—if you follow the rules I'm going to lay out, your life just 12 months from now will both surprise and delight you.

> ### RULE NO. 1
> UNTIL IT'S WRITTEN DOWN, IT'S NOT A GOAL
> —IT'S JUST A SLOGAN.

If you don't put what you want in writing, then you might as well not even waste your time thinking about it. You are kidding yourself. Your goals must be written down. Think about it. How many times have you had a "great idea" that you thought could make you a fortune, only to forget what it was a week later? Why? Because you didn't write it down. If your goals are worth focusing your effort and time on, then they must be worth recording—and if you don't record them, who will?

In a nutshell, writing down your goals makes them real and easy to focus on. So from now on, you must commit yourself to recording all your goals on paper. No excuses.

RULE NO. 2
GOALS MUST BE SPECIFIC, MEASURABLE, AND PROVABLE.

Even if it's in writing, if you are not specific about what it is you want to attain—or if you've written down something that really can't be measured or proven—then once again, what you've got isn't a goal, it's a wish.

For instance, there is no point in writing down "I want to be wealthy in the year 2010." That is useless. What you should be writing down is something much more specific—something like "I will put aside 10 percent of my gross income every month for the next 36 months, at which time I will have a minimum of $48,000 in a retirement plan." Similarly, you shouldn't write down, "I will be debt free." Rather, you should write something like "I will pay off my VISA bill over the next 12 months. I will pay cash for all purchases until my credit card debt is completely gone, and I will never spend over $100 on an item without leaving the store and giving myself 48 hours to consider whether I really need that item."

The point is that a goal is very difficult to attain if it's vague. You have to be able to show someone (the most important someone being yourself) exactly where the finish line is. After all, if you don't know precisely what your goal is, how will you be able to tell whether you've attained it or not?

RULE NO. 3
TAKE SOME IMMEDIATE ACTION WITHIN THE NEXT 48
HOURS TO START MOVING TOWARD YOUR GOAL.

Let's say that, like Jill and Jane, your goal is to be able to purchase a vacation home on Lake Muskoka. Now, that's a long-term goal; realistically, you don't expect to accomplish it for at least five years. But that doesn't mean there isn't anything you can do right now, in the next 48 hours, to move toward that goal. You could, for example, call the Muskoka Chamber of Commerce and ask for a list of reputable real estate agents. You could then telephone some of those agencies and ask for information about available houses that fit your price range and interest. You could take out a subscription to the local Muskoka newspaper in order to keep abreast of what is happening in the community.

There are many things you could do. The key is to do something. Take an action—any action—that will make the goal you have written down feel more real and specific!

> **RULE NO. 4**
> ONCE YOU HAVE WRITTEN DOWN YOUR GOALS, PUT THEM SOMEPLACE WHERE YOU CAN SEE THEM EVERY DAY.

I keep my list of goals in my PalmPilot and on a piece of paper posted above my computer where I see it every day. Some people I know tape theirs on the mirror in their bathroom. The point is that you should read your goals every day. By seeing your goals each day (preferably in the morning when you first wake up), you reaffirm to yourself what you are focusing your life on. As a result, you will find yourself subconsciously seeking out information and contacts that can help you attain your goals. In addition, reviewing your goals every day helps to make them clear and, ultimately, very personal and real to you.

> **RULE NO. 5**
> SHARE YOUR GOALS WITH SOMEONE YOU LOVE AND TRUST.

I have heard it said time and time again that you should keep your goals and dreams to yourself, because "other people will try to talk you out of them or squash them." Well, that's total nonsense!

I can't tell you how mad it makes me to think of all the years I wasted keeping my goals and dreams to myself because of bad advice like that. The fact is, the best way to reach your goals is to get help. But if you don't share them with anyone, how are your friends or coworkers going to be able to offer you support and assistance?

I first learned the power of this rule at one of Tony Robbins's "Date with Destiny" seminars. Tony was doing a session on goal setting, and he told the group, "If you keep your goals inside you, you are missing out on the world that wants to help you." Well, I didn't really believe that the world wanted to help me. Then again, this was Tony Robbins, one of the greatest motivational experts in the world, so I figured, "What the heck, it can't hurt to try."

At that point, Tony broke us up into groups and told us to share our biggest dream or goal for the year. Once my group formed up, I hesitatingly announced, "I want to write a book for women on investing called *Smart Women Finish Rich*." Everyone nodded and said that sounded great. Ten minutes later, after the group had dispersed, an incredible woman named Vicki St. George tapped me on the shoulder. "I heard you want to write an investment book for women," she said. "I've worked with Tony for 10 years and now I run my own writing company called Just Write. I'd love to work with you to help you make your book a reality."

I ended up hiring Vicki about three months later, and the book proposal she helped me create was instrumental in getting me one of the top literary agents in the country.

ONLY YOU KNOW WHAT YOU CAN DO

If you share your goal with someone you love and he or she says, "Oh, you can't do that" or "No, that won't work," remember—that person really doesn't know what you can or cannot do. He or she knows only what he or she can or cannot do. Many well-intentioned people will tell you that you can't do something simply because it's beyond their own capabilities. Ignore these people; their negative beliefs are their problems, not yours. Keep sharing your goals until you find someone who will support you.

And here is something else to think about: If your friends really don't support you and your goals, maybe you need a new set of friends. I consider myself very fortunate because I am surrounded by incredible friends. When I originally told them I wanted to write a book, each and every one of them said, "That's great, go for it, I can't wait to read it." And periodically after that, they would ask me how my book was coming along. This inspired me even more. It also put a little pressure on me to keep focusing on my goal. Both the support and the pressure really helped me get the job done.

The key point here is that few things affect how successful you will be as much as the people with whom you surround yourself. If becoming financially independent is really important to you right now but you don't have any close friends to whom you feel you can turn for support, then go out and make some new friends. Join a women's investment club in your area. Take some evening classes on retirement planning. Do something that forces you to get out of your immediate comfort zone and meet some new people. There are many organizations you can join to get help and learn new skills. Take advantage of them.

RULE NO. 6
DEVELOP GOALS THAT FIT YOUR VALUES.

In Step Two, we went through a process specifically designed to help you get in touch with your values about money. Use what you discovered about yourself and what you are looking for in life to create goals that will make your dreams a reality.

For instance, if the phrase at the top of your values ladder is "spend more time with my family," then write that down on your goal list. But remember, you must make the goal measurable and specific. So be sure to indicate how you want to spend time with your family—what you want to do and when you will do it. And involve your family; enlist their ideas and opinions. Tell them, "I've determined that one of my most important values is to spend more quality time with you, and I'd like to plan some special family time together." Get them to suggest specifics, and then, together, write them all down on paper.

If you do this, not only will your goals be written and specific, but your family will be your support team, as well, because you've gotten them involved in your new-found spirit.

RULE NO. 7
REVIEW YOUR GOALS AT LEAST ONCE EVERY 12 MONTHS.

At an absolute minimum, you should review your goals and redo this process once each year. Ideally, I recommend you carry out this review process the last week in December so you can start the new year with total passion and renewed enthusiasm. I go through this process each December myself. In addition, every three months I spend an entire day reviewing both how I am doing and where I want to go. In this way, I am forced to recommit emotionally to my written goals, which in turn helps me refocus my efforts to make them become a reality. If I find I can't recommit to all my goals, that's a major sign it's time to rethink—and probably rewrite—what's on my list.

Remember, this is your list and your life. You should be in charge of what is and what is not important to you. And don't consider a change of heart to be a failure on your part. Your goal list is not a "to do" list. It is much more important. It is your life-planning process!

LET'S GET
STARTED!

Both in my office and in my class, I always ask my clients and students the same question to elicit their goals.

"In a perfect world, if you and I were sitting together three years from today, what would have to happen for you to feel you have made not just good, but GREAT financial progress with your life?"

The point of this question is quite simple. Before you get into investment strategies, you need to be clear about exactly what you want and feel you need to become financially secure.

Think back to Step Two, in which you worked out what was important to you about money. The point of writing down your values then was to make it easier for you now to articulate a series of goals that can help you put your values into practice.

So based on what you said in Step Two and how you feel now, what is it that you would like to see happen in your life over the next three years that will require money? Do you want to see yourself get out of credit card debt? Do you want to own a home? Is your goal to be able to afford to retire in three years? Maybe you would like to move to Paris and study art. Or start your own business. Or expand a business that you already own. Whatever the case may be, use the values you came up with in Step Two and write down, on the chart that follows, what would have to happen for you to feel three years from now that you have made successful progress.

Do it now.

GOALS
Designing a Proactive Life!

THERE ARE TWO PARTS TO THIS EXERCISE:
- Ten blanks for writing down your goals between now and three years from now
- A form in which you specify your five most important goals over the next three years

STEPS:
- On this page, below, fill in the 10 blanks with as many goals as possible that you want to accomplish during the next three years.
- On the next page, specify:
    1. Five Most Important Goals
    2. Make Specific, Measurable, and Provable (i.e., How much will it cost?)
    3. Immediate Action in the Next 48 Hours
    4. With Whom Will You Share Your Goals?
    5. What Values Does It Help You Accomplish?
    6. What Challenges Will You Face?
    7. Strategies to Overcome Anticipated Challenges

1.   6.

2.   7.

3.   8.

4.   9.

5.   10.

FIVE MOST IMPORTANT GOALS	MAKE SPECIFIC, MEASURABLE, AND PROVABLE	IMMEDIATE ACTION IN THE NEXT 48 HOURS	WITH WHOM WILL YOU SHARE YOUR GOALS?	WHAT VALUES DOES IT HELP YOU ACCOMPLISH?	WHAT CHALLENGES WILL YOU FACE?	STRATEGIES TO OVERCOME ANTICIPATED CHALLENGES
1						
2						
3						
4						
5						

Figuring Out Where You Want to Be

Many people call what we have just done together goal setting. I call it *Designing a Proactive Life!* However you label it, one thing is inarguable: If you can't figure out where you want to be in three years, how are you ever going to be able to plan out your life 10 to 20 years from now? Equally important, how will you know how much money you are going to need to reach your goals? The answer is, you won't and you can't.

Why three years? Three years is a very useful amount of time to work with. You can accomplish a tremendous amount in three years. In fact, you can change your life.

Consider the story of Lucy, a woman who used this question to make massive changes in her life. Lucy took my Smart Women Finish Rich seminar a few years ago, but unlike many of my students, she didn't come to my office to review her finances when the class was over. In fact, I didn't hear from her almost an entire year.

When we finally sat down together, my first question to Lucy was why she had waited so long to come see me.

"Well, David," she began, "when you asked us in class where we wanted our lives to be in three years, I realized that I had some serious decisions to make."

Indeed, it turned out that my question had led Lucy to transform her life totally.

LUCY'S STORY: TURNING OFF THE AUTOMATIC PILOT

"What I realized after thinking about that question of David's was that, after 32 years of marriage, I was not happy. I was living a loveless life. I also realized that more money was not going to make my marriage any better—not then or in three years. So for me the question was: Do I have enough money to get divorced? If I don't want to be married, can I afford to be single?

"The more I thought about this, the more I realized it wasn't simply an issue of money. I truly did not want to go on with my life the way it was. My kids were grown, I was just starting the 'fun' phase of my life, as David had put it in the class, and I realized that the time was now to make a decision. So I made one.

"On the worksheet I had received in class, I wrote down, 'Get separated and independent of Sam within three years.'

"Once I had written that down, I got to thinking. *Why should this take three years?* I realized it shouldn't. I also realized that I had probably wasted the last 10 years of my life with Sam, because I had never really stopped to ask myself where it was I wanted my life to head. Looking back, I see now that I had let my life get on automatic pilot. Unfortunately, as a result of being on automatic pilot, I had ended up at a destination that did not work for me.

"Now, however, thanks to the three-year question and the technique of writing down your goals, my life has been dramatically changed for the better."

FROM MY POINT OF VIEW . . .

I find Lucy's story incredibly empowering. Less than three years after she took stock of her values and goals, she is a new person. First and foremost, she is divorced. And while I am not an advocate of divorce, in Lucy's case it happened to be necessary. Was it hard for her? You bet it was. But, in fact, both of her children supported her decision. (Indeed, they wanted to know why she had waited so long.)

Second, as a result of the divorce settlement, Lucy has been able to pay off her home mortgage completely, and we have positioned her additional assets to grow for her retirement. With a well-defined plan in place, Lucy can look forward to retiring in 10 years without having to worry about money.

Third, she has upgraded her career from a position in retail sales to office management at a law firm, and she is increasing her job skills on a daily basis.

Finally, and most important of all, Lucy is happier than she has been in years.

IS YOUR LIFE ON AUTOMATIC PILOT?

Letting your life go on automatic pilot has a tendency to lead to disaster. Yet we do it all the time, usually without noticing it.

The best and quickest way I know to protect yourself from this syndrome is to stop, think, and put in writing what it is you specifically want out of life. In addition to formulating these wants in terms of three-year goals, I suggest you also write out intermediate and long-term goals. If you haven't already done so, remember to use the "Designing a Proactive Life!" worksheet on pages 78-79.

Remember to use the seven rules of goal setting I listed earlier. Most important, remember that this is your opportunity to create the future you want. Have fun with this. If you create a really compelling future for yourself, you will find yourself jumping out of bed every morning, knowing you are facing not just another day but a day full of promise that will bring you closer to the future that you want!

Don't Let Challenges Get You Down!

Guess what? It's possible that you could do this entire exercise and still not stay on track and reach your desired goals. Why? Because life is filled with challenges, both financial and personal, and unless you prepare for them, you could get stopped dead in your tracks.

So here is what I want you to do. After you write down your goals, I want you to list in detail all the potential challenges that could derail you from attaining them. Notice I don't call them problems. I want you to wipe that word out of your vocabulary. Short of death (which is the only permanent problem I know of), there are no problems. There are only challenges.

Now, with that in mind, I want you to put down on paper everything you can think of that possibly could prevent you from achieving your goals. You may be thinking that I'm being pessimistic, but trust me on this—I'm not being pessimistic, I'm being realistic. By highlighting all the potential challenges on paper, you are acknowledging two very important realities: that there are challenges, and that you can come up with ways to overcome them.

In fact, that is the next step. Once you've listed all the challenges you can come up with (and I'll bet that right now without realizing it you are thinking subconsciously of all the reasons why you might not be able to make your goal a reality), I want you to write down a specific solution for each of them. And don't despair—all challenges have solutions.

I call this process drafting your "Personal Plan for Success." An example of a Personal Plan for Success that I used with a client when discussing retirement planning follows. Take a look at it and then create one for yourself and your number-one goal.

A Personal Plan for Success
Designing a Specific Plan to Overcome Your Challenges

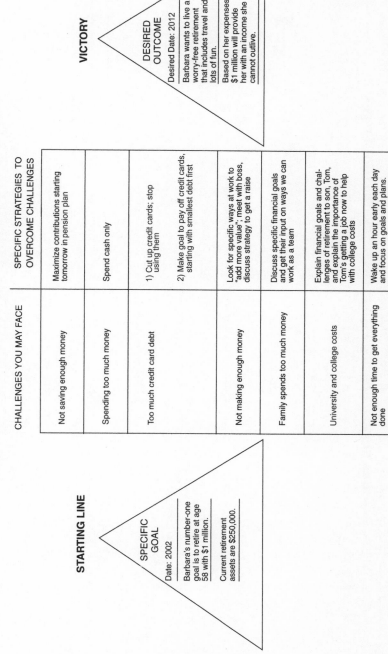

STARTING LINE

SPECIFIC GOAL

Date: 2002

Barbara's number-one goal is to retire at age 58 with $1 million.

Current retirement assets are $250,000.

CHALLENGES YOU MAY FACE	SPECIFIC STRATEGIES TO OVERCOME CHALLENGES
Not saving enough money	Maximize contributions starting tomorrow in pension plan
Spending too much money	Spend cash only
Too much credit card debt	1) Cut up credit cards; stop using them 2) Make goal to pay off credit cards, starting with smallest debt first
Not making enough money	Look for specific ways at work to "add more value"; meet with boss, discuss strategy to get a raise
Family spends too much money	Discuss specific financial goals and get their input on ways we can work as a team
University and college costs	Explain financial goals and challenges of retirement to son, Tom, and explain the importance of Tom's getting a job now to help with college costs
Not enough time to get everything done	Wake up an hour early each day and focus on goals and plans.

VICTORY

DESIRED OUTCOME

Desired Date: 2012

Barbara wants to live a worry-free retirement that includes travel and lots of fun.

Based on her expenses, $1 million will provide her with an income she cannot outlive.

A Personal Plan for Success
Designing a Specific Plan to Overcome Your Challenges

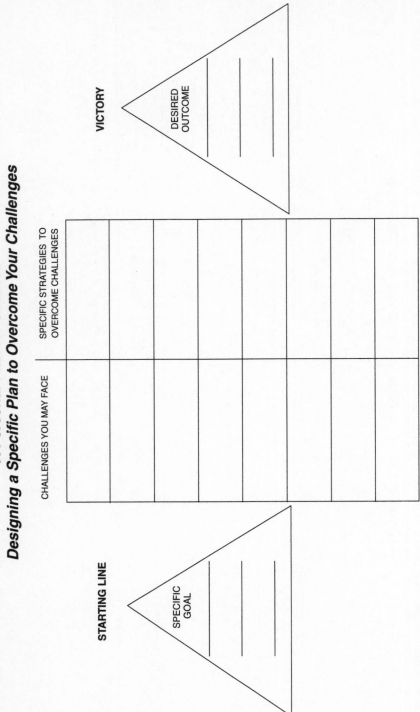

STARTING LINE

SPECIFIC GOAL

CHALLENGES YOU MAY FACE

SPECIFIC STRATEGIES TO OVERCOME CHALLENGES

VICTORY

DESIRED OUTCOME

Challenges Are Your Building Blocks
to the Future You Want!

As you finish Step Three, I want you to think about the following question: When was the last time you did something perfectly the first time you tried it?

The answer is probably never.

Imagine if, when you were a toddler, crawling around on all fours, your parents had berated you for not being born a walker. Imagine if, instead of encouraging you, they criticized and yelled, saying things like "I can't believe you can't walk—you'll never be able to walk." It would have been not only cruel but dumb, as well. The fact is, sensible adults do the exact opposite with their kids. We not only encourage them when they start trying to walk, we run out and buy all sorts of high-tech video equipment to record it all. We take rolls and rolls of film to capture the moment when the child finally takes his or her first step.

So why is it that we start criticizing ourselves for not walking the first time we try to take a step? If this is the first time you have ever put down in writing what you want your life to be about, what your goals for the future are, you should be congratulating yourself—not feeling bad if your initial attempt doesn't turn out perfectly!

Remember, your first attempt to record your goals is not supposed to be perfect. Each time you do this exercise, it will become easier, and you will become better at designing your life. The exciting thing you should realize is that by making the effort to write down your goals, you are saying to yourself, "I am responsible for my future." Nothing could make you more powerful.

By itself, the single act of writing down your goals makes you special. Don't believe me. Test it. Do this entire step, put everything down in writing that I have suggested, then ask your friends and family if they have written goals. Not ideas about where they want their life to go, but actual written goals. Most likely, you will find that you are now a unique woman. In fact, my guess is that when they learn you have put your goals down in writing, your friends and family will begin to hold you in higher esteem. You also may find them deciding that they too should have written goals. So share this chapter with them. You may become the inspiration that your friends and family need to make their lives even better.

Congratulations! You Have Finished Step Three

Now let's take the goals and dreams you have written down and learn about a powerful system that will enable you to achieve them without having suddenly to start earning a lot of money. This system employs something I call **the Latté Factor**™, and it is the most pow-erful and easy way I know of to transform a woman's financial goals and dreams into reality.

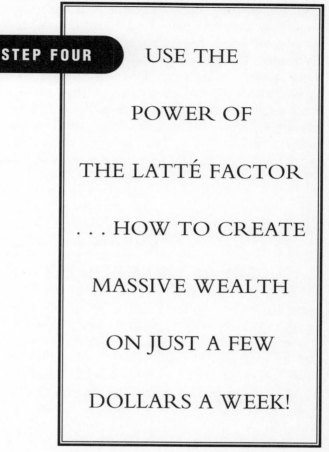

STEP FOUR USE THE

POWER OF

THE LATTÉ FACTOR

. . . HOW TO CREATE

MASSIVE WEALTH

ON JUST A FEW

DOLLARS A WEEK!

Have you ever heard someone say, "If I could only make more money, then I could really start to become a saver, or maybe even an investor"? Perhaps you've even said something like that yourself.

If so, you may have been mistaken. Making more money won't necessarily make you a better saver or investor. Look at the newspapers—virtually every day someone famous, someone you or I might reasonably regard as a huge money earner, declares bankruptcy. Take M. C. Hammer, the hip-hop star. In the early 1990s, Hammer was one of the world's highest-paid performers, earning a reported $35 million in one year. Almost overnight, he had gone from being a bat boy for the Oakland Athletics to a millionaire many times over.

I remember thinking how incredible it must have felt to become so wealthy so quickly. Then one day I saw Hammer on television taking a reporter through the extravagant house he was building in Fremont, California. The place was huge. Though it was only half-finished, it was rumoured to have cost him more than $10 million already.

When I saw how out of control his spending was, I told friends that M. C. Hammer would be bankrupt in five years. I was wrong. It was only about three years later that he declared bankruptcy. Unfortunately for M. C. Hammer, being rich and famous did not lead to financial security. But M. C. Hammer is not alone. . . .

DO YOU RECOGNIZE
ANY OF THESE PEOPLE?

Larry King, Francis Ford Coppola, Debbie Reynolds, Redd Foxx, Dorothy Hamill, Wayne Newton, Susan Powter, Burt Reynolds. Do you know what they all have in common? Aside from being famous, they have all filed for bankruptcy. So did almost 80,000 Canadians in 2001, although they tend to declare bankruptcy less often than Americans. Canadians declared bankruptcy at a rate of 2.2 per thousand people in 2001; Americans at a rate of 5.4 per thousand. Nevertheless, the number of consumers filing for bankruptcy in Canada is almost four times as high as it was in 1980. What accounts for this epidemic of insolvency? Well, among other things, Canadians have become addicted to spending money by using "plastic cash." In 2001, Canadian credit card holders owed an average of $1,269 on their cards, there were more than 68 million credit cards in circulation, and there were 2.9 cards for every Canadian over the age of 18. Only half paid their bill on time, and 40 percent didn't know the interest rate charged on their outstanding balances. Which leads me to suggest . . .

It's time to keep more . . . and spend less.

As I noted back in Step One, the reason most people fail financially is not because their incomes are too small, but because their spending habits are too big. In other words, they spend more money than they make. This may sound awfully basic, but it's true. If you spend more than you make, you always will be in debt, always stressed, rarely happy, and eventually poor or bankrupt.

Controlling your spending, though, isn't all there is to being a Smart Woman and finishing rich. You also must make a point of saving a portion of every dollar you earn. No matter how large your paycheque is, if you don't save, you will never live a life of financial abundance. (Just ask M. C. Hammer.)

Whether you are a highly compensated doctor or lawyer supporting mortgages on two homes or a more modestly paid teacher, office worker, or sales trainee who barely makes the rent each month, the key to financial independence can be summed up in three words . . .

Pay yourself first.

Why in the world would you work 40 (or 50, or 60, or more!) hours a week, and then pay someone else first? Search me, but most Canadians pay *everyone* else before they pay themselves. Most of us pay the government first (through our withholding tax), then our mortgage or our rent, then our utilities, then our car payments, then our VISA or American Express bills, and on and on. If by some miracle there is something left over after all those payments—meaning there have been no "Murphy's law" disasters, like the car breaking down or the washing machine dying—then maybe (and I mean just maybe) we might manage to put away a few dollars for our future.

I call this the "Pay Everyone Else First, You Last" system, and it stinks. It's like having "investor dyslexia"; it's all backward. Among other things, it's why the average Canadian has so little in the bank and so much in credit card debt.

Whatever You Do, Don't Pay Your Taxes First!

Of all the crazy things people do with their money, the one I really can't fathom is paying their taxes before they pay themselves. Not even the government expects you to do that. If the government did expect to get paid first, it wouldn't have enacted laws to that allow us to put part of our earnings into retirement savings plans *before* the tax man takes his cut. This is called "pretax" investing, and it is the single smartest thing you can do to build wealth.

Unfortunately, millions of Canadians don't take advantage of pretax investing. Instead, they let provincial and federal tax authorities funnel off as much as 40 percent of each paycheque—that's 40 cents out of every dollar they earn—before they even get to see it. This is a huge mistake. In Step Five, you'll learn all about pretax retirement accounts. Until then, just remember that the government really does want you to have financial security—so much so that it's willing to give you a break on your taxes if you use part of your earnings to fund a retirement account. Whatever you do, don't pass up this break. You've earned it!

THE 12 PERCENT

SOLUTION

So what does "pay yourself first" mean? It means that whenever you make any money, no matter how much or how little, before you spend any of it on anything else, you should put some of it aside for your future.

Now, when I say, "before you spend any of it on anything else," I mean *anything* else. That includes your rent or mortgage, your credit card bills, even your payroll withholding tax. Ideally, you should pay 12 percent of the gross—meaning your total earnings *before taxes*—into some sort of retirement plan that you will never touch until you actually retire. Of course, it's possible that, because of how much you make or the kind of retirement plan you have, you may not be eligible to put that much into a pretax retirement plan. In that case, you should make up the difference by putting money into an after-tax account.

Why do I suggest putting away 12 percent of your gross income? First, the government allows you to invest up to 18 percent of your gross income or $13,500, whichever is less, into a tax-sheltered retirement plan.

If you're self-employed, you're probably trying to save this much already. If you're employed by a company with a pension plan, you'll find it a challenge to save more than 12 percent of your take-home pay. For years, the financial experts have been suggesting that, to prepare properly for retirement, everyone should be saving at least 10 percent of what he or she makes. Of course, when they say "everyone," the experts are really talking about men—and in this case, at least, what's good enough for men isn't necessarily good enough for women. After all, women live longer than men—and as a result, they need to put away more money for their retirement. How much more? Well, if women's retirements tend to last 20 percent longer than men's—and that's what the statistics tell us—then women's retirement nest eggs need to be

20 percent larger. In other words, if the experts say that men should be putting away 10 percent of their pretax income, then as a woman you should be putting away 12 percent of yours.

Now, I realize that saving 12 percent of your income may sound like a lot. But believe me, it's not as hard as you might think. The trick is not to let the figure overwhelm you. Rome wasn't built in a day, and neither is a new financial future. If you can't imagine saving 12 percent of your income right now, then start with 6 percent and make it a goal to bump up your savings rate by 1 percent a month for the next six months.

If even 6 percent seems like too much, do what I often suggest to clients of mine who really have a problem with the idea of saving. Start off putting away just 1 percent of your income. (I have never met any-one who could look me in the eye and tell me she couldn't save 1 per-cent of her income.) Then increase the amount by 1 percent a month for a year. At the end of a year, you will be saving 12 percent of your income, and you will barely have noticed the difference.

It's a lot like getting in shape to run a marathon. People who train for a marathon don't say to themselves, "Today I think I'll run a marathon" and then go out and run 26 miles. They start off running a block, then two blocks, then a mile, then two miles . . . until one day they are running 26 miles (and are actually enjoying it). Think about your goal of saving 12 percent of your income the same way. Day by day you are striving to become financially stronger. Before you know it you will be in great financial shape!

What About the Real World?

Paying yourself first is one of those concepts that strike a lot of people as sounding great in principle but having very little application in the real world. And I wouldn't be at all surprised if right now you are thinking, *Sure, I'd love to pay myself first. Just tell me where I'm going to get the money.*

Well, I'll let you in on a secret: You already have it.

That's right. No matter how much or how little you earn, you al-ready make enough money to pay yourself first. Your problem—and it's not just *your* problem, it's almost everyone's problem—is not that you don't make enough, but that you spend too much.

Learn to control your spending, and everything else will fall into place.

Spend a Dollar Today and You Lose It Forever

When I was a student at the University of Southern California, my favourite pastime was shopping. Some people get black belts in karate; I had a black belt in shopping. I could go to the mall with my friends and easily spend thousands of dollars in just a few hours. Every week I would come home with bags and bags of clothes. As I often tell my students today, you know you're shopping too much when you can go into your closet and find clothes you don't remember buying. Well, I could. My wardrobe was to die for. Unfortunately, the bills were to die for too—literally! Every month I would close my eyes as I opened my VISA bill.

The truth was that my spending was out of control. It never mattered how much money I made, I always spent more. As soon as my credit card bills were paid, I'd go off on another spending spree.

My life changed when I packed up everything I owned one summer and put it in a storage unit. (At USC, you couldn't leave your possessions in your campus apartment over the summer.) As I was filling up this $50-a-month storage facility under a freeway in L.A., I started thinking, *What if there's an earthquake and this freeway collapses and destroys the warehouse? My clothes would get ruined!*

Suddenly it hit me: I'm looking at a storage unit with "stuff" in it and worrying. Of all the potential consequences of a devastating earthquake, here I am more concerned about *stuff* than about people. Even worse, I'm paying *money* to store stuff that I haven't even paid for yet because it's still on my credit card!

I started laughing so hard I had to sit down. It dawned on me there was an entire industry of storage units around the country filled with people's "stuff." Think about it! How absurd is it to buy so much stuff that you have to pay someone else to store it because you don't have anywhere to put it yourself! The moral seemed clear.

Buy less stuff and you'll be rich!

That insight changed my life. Suddenly I realized that instead of spending money I didn't really have on things I didn't really need, I should be putting my resources into something that mattered. And what could possibly matter more to me than my future? Forget about things; what I really should be concerning myself with was doing whatever I could to ensure myself the kind of life I felt I wanted and deserved. And that's just what I did. From that day on, I stopped

wasting my money on ridiculous shopping sprees and started investing in myself.

Trust me—if a world-class, black-belt shopper like me can cut
back, you can too. It's not easy, but it can be done, and it will change
your life just like it changed mine.

Now, just because you're not buying new clothes every week like
I used to doesn't mean you're not spending money you should be saving. You'd be surprised how easy it is to be wastefully extravagant
without realizing it. The fact is, often the little purchases in life—what
I call the Latté Factor—make the difference between being a millionaire and being broke.

Making the Latté Factor Work for You

In my investment classes, I tell my students that any woman can become an investor—and in the process put herself on the road to financial security—simply by putting aside as little as $50 a month.
Invariably, someone in the audience will raise her hand at this point
and say, "David, I'm living paycheque to paycheque. I'm in debt, and
I'm barely making it. I don't have this $50 a month you keep talking
about."

One day I challenged just such a young woman on her assertion
that she didn't have enough money to invest. Deborah was 23 years
old and worked at an advertising agency. She wasn't being paid a
whole lot, and she insisted there was no way she possibly could put
$50 a month into her retirement plan at work. As she put it, she was
"dead broke and destitute." So I asked her to take me through her average day.

"Well," she began, "I go to work and then I research—"

"Do you start your day with coffee?" I interrupted her.

A friend of Deborah's who was sitting next to her started to laugh.
"Deborah without coffee in the morning is not a good thing," she
said.

Picking up on that, I asked Deborah if she drank the office coffee.

"No way," Deborah replied. "The office coffee is the worst. I go
downstairs and buy a latté every morning."

I asked, "Do you buy a single or double latté?"

"I always buy a double nonfat latté."

"Great," I said. "Now, what does this double nonfat latté cost you every morning?

"Oh, about $2.50."

"Do you just get a latté, or do you also get a muffin or a bagel with that?"

"I usually get a biscotti."

"Do you get the biscotti with chocolate on them?"

"Oh, yes," Deborah enthused. "I love the ones with chocolate."

"Great, Deborah. Now, what does the chocolate biscotti cost?"

"I guess about $1.50."

"So you're spending about $4 a day for latté and biscotti. Interesting."

I let Deborah continue taking me through her day. In the process, we found another $10 in miscellaneous costs—a candy bar here, a Power Bar there, a protein shake in the afternoon, and so on.

When she was done, I pointed out that, just by cutting out her latté, a couple of Diet Cokes, and a candy bar, Deborah could save about $5 a day—and that $5 a day equaled roughly $150 a month, or almost $2,000 a year. This $2,000 could be put into her retirement plan at work, where it could grow tax-free until she retired. If she put in $2,000 every year, and she invested it all in stocks (which have enjoyed an average growth rate of 11 percent a year over the last 50 years), chances are that, by the time she reached 65, she would have more than $2 million sitting in her account. In other words, she would be able to retire a multimillionaire!

By the time I had finished, Deborah's eyes were as big as saucers. "That is so amazing," she said. "I never realized my double nonfat lattés were costing me $2 million!"

So I ask you now . . .

Are you latté-ing away your financial future?

I'm not trying to pick on you if you are a coffee lover. I happen to enjoy a great cup of coffee in the morning myself. I just want to point out a simple fact:

Everyone makes enough money to become rich.

What keeps us living paycheque to paycheque is that we spend more than we make on stuff we don't need. Take the $16 you were going to waste over the next few days on junk food (you'll be healthier without it) and the $9 you were going to throw away on two glossy magazines (you can borrow a friend's copies), and you'll have

$25 this very week that you can devote to savings. Keep this up and you'll soon be putting away 12 percent of what you earn. Before you know it, your life will begin changing dramatically for the better. Once you see the 12 percent solution at work, you automatically will start looking for ways to save even more. The process creates a new habit—one that will make you feel great!

Getting Your Spending Under Control

The hardest part of any undertaking—whether you're preparing for a marathon or trying to contain your spending—is getting started. With that in mind, here are six exercises that should help you get your spending under control . . . and ultimately make it easy for you to pay yourself first.

EXERCISE NO. 1
KNOW WHAT YOU EARN.

This may seem obvious, but in these days of direct-deposit payroll programs and automatic chequing, many of us don't know exactly how much we actually earn, both before and after deductions. Go get your last paycheque. What does it say your monthly gross income is? What's your net? Write down those numbers below. (If you're self-employed or run your own business, you can determine your average monthly pay.)

I currently earn $_____ a month before deductions, and $_____ after deductions.

EXERCISE NO. 2
ESTIMATE WHAT YOU SPEND EACH MONTH.

In Step Three, I asked you to figure out where your money is. Now I want you to figure out where your money goes.

Most people do not have a clue about how much they really spend each month and on what. To be financially healthy, however, you need to have a solid grasp of your spending patterns. Only after you've seen the numbers in black and white can you figure out where you can cut back.

In Appendix 1, you'll find a form with the heading "Where Does Your Money *Really* Go?" Use it to estimate how much you spend each month on everything from food and shelter to lipstick and movie tickets. Then add 10 percent for what I call "Murphy's law expenses"—those unexpected bills for car repairs and plumbing problems that always seem to crop up when you least expect (or can afford) them. To make sure your estimate is in the right ballpark, review your last three months' worth of your cheques, receipts, and credit card bills. Once you're satisfied you have a reasonably accurate figure, write it down.

I currently spend $_____ a month.

Now subtract your monthly spending total from your monthly income after deductions. Is your cash flow positive or negative? Your goal, obviously, is to have a positive cash flow. The next four rules should help you do just that.

I earn a month after deductions		_____
I spend a month approximately	-	_____
Cash flow monthly	=	_____

EXERCISE NO. 3
TRACK WHAT YOU REALLY SPEND.

For the next seven days, I want you to record every single penny you spend. I call this the "Seven-Day Financial Challenge™." Eventually you should do this for a full month, but right now, to get yourself started, I want you to try it for just seven days. Get yourself a note pad, and over the coming week, write down every purchase you make, no matter how big or small. (This means *everything*: highway tolls, candy bars, late fees on videos you forgot to return—everything.)

This seven-day challenge actually can be fun. The trick is to be yourself. That is, don't change your behaviour. Spend money just as you always have. The only thing you should be doing differently is writing everything down. Once you have captured your spending habits on paper, you will quickly see where you are wasting money and you can decide where it makes sense to cut back. (One woman I know found that the simple act of writing down expenditures made her so self-conscious about being extravagant that her excess spending stopped cold. "I just hated the idea of having to write down that I was spending $80 on a sweater I didn't need," she said. "So rather than having to write it down, I didn't buy the sweater.")

EXERCISE NO. 4
START PAYING CASH.

After you have tracked a typical week's expenses and are ready to start changing your ways, the easiest thing you can do to reduce your spending automatically is to start paying for everything with cash. That's right, cash! It's time to start using it again.

When you buy things with credit or debit cards or use cheques, you don't feel the significance of your spending. I dare you to stick $500 in cash in your wallet and try to spend it frivolously on some impulse purchase like a new sweater or a pair of shoes or a stack of new CDs. You won't be able to do it. That's because cash makes you think more about exactly how much you are spending and for what. (As one client of mine told me, a pair of shoes marked down to $160 doesn't seem like that much of a bargain when buying it means taking eight 20s out of your wallet.)

You'd be surprised what a dramatic change this single action can make. I can't tell you how many of my students have told me that when they went to a cash-only system, their spending dropped by 20 percent in a single month!

EXERCISE NO. 5
GIVE YOURSELF A CREDIT CARD HAIRCUT.

Here's an idea that I am sure occurs to you every time you get a large credit card bill: Take a pair of scissors and cut up one of your credit cards. Just one. (I don't expect you to cut them all up—not, at least, on your first attempt.) When you finish reading this chapter, go through all your credit card bills, pull out the biggest one, and then cut that card into about 10 pieces.

The feeling of power you will get from this small token gesture can be tremendous. Just try it. If you think you can handle it, cut up more than one card. Remember, if worse comes to worst, you can always call the credit card company and order a new one.

EXERCISE NO. 6
NEVER SPEND MORE THAN $100 ON ANYTHING WITHOUT TAKING 48 HOURS TO THINK ABOUT IT.

The idea here is simple. Most North Americans spend far too much money on impulse purchases they really don't need to make. It can be a pair of shoes, a new VCR, an expensive dinner. The point is, stores are designed to make sure you get caught up in the excitement of shopping, and before you know what's happened, you've bought something.

So set yourself a ceiling. I suggest $100, but it can be any amount that makes sense to you. Once you've set it, do not permit yourself to buy anything for that amount or more without first leaving the store and giving yourself 48 hours to think about it. By forcing yourself into this cooling-off period, you give yourself a chance to decide rationally whether the purchase really is necessary. If you still feel like buying it two days later, great! Chances are the item in question will still be there—maybe even on sale!

I know how effective this exercise can be from personal experience. As I mentioned earlier, I used to be a world-class shopper. But once I imposed the $100 ceiling on myself, I found that just casually shopping wasn't so much fun anymore. Items I had thought I just had to have no longer seemed so important once I got home and thought about them. Because I was buying less and less, shopping began to feel more and more like a waste of time. Before long I found myself going shopping less often. These days I go shopping once or twice a year, and only with the specific purpose of getting something I need. I'm telling you, these exercises work!

The basic point of getting your spending under control is, of course, to allow you to save more. Ultimately, your goal should be to get your savings rate as high as 20 percent. For now, however, try to start saving at least 6 percent of your gross income and commit to raising that to 12 percent within 12 months.

The Magic of Compound Interest

You may wonder what good it will do to put aside less than an eighth of your income if your income isn't very big to begin with. But remember, even if you earn what seems to you a modest salary, the amount of money that will pass through your hands during your lifetime is truly phenomenal. For a quick reminder of just how phenomenal, go back and review the chart on page 22 in Step One.

Pretty awesome, isn't it? And here's some more good news . . .

The sooner you start saving, the less you will need to put away!

Take a look at the following chart. It shows how quickly the magic of compound interest can help you accumulate a significant amount of assets. To me, "significant" means at least $1 million worth. Now, some skeptics may argue that $1 million doesn't go very far anymore, but regardless of how much it does or doesn't buy these days, wouldn't you rather have $1 million than not? In any case, given that the average Canadian family saved only $1,700 in 2001, let's run with the idea that earning your first million is probably a worthy goal to shoot for.

What the chart illustrates is that simply by putting aside a couple of dollars a day and giving your money a chance to work for you, you can become a millionaire! While it is easy to think "a dollar here, a dollar there" is no big deal, it is a big deal. Depending on how quickly you decide to make your financial future a priority, it can be a *million-dollar deal!*

Stop reading for a second and think about the day you just had. What is your personal Latté Factor? What did you buy today that you could do without tomorrow and thus save a few dollars? Take a few moments right now and think of three things you could cut out of your daily spending tomorrow. What are they? How much money would you save a day? How much would it save you a month? While

$100 a month in savings may not sound like a lot, look at the chart on page 101. Saving $100 a month can add up quickly to a lot of money.

Now, how do you make sure that this money you are now not going to spend on things you don't really need doesn't disappear down some other drain? It's simple, really. The trick to making sure your money goes where it's supposed to go—that is, that your spending matches up with your values—is to arrange things so you don't have any choice in the matter. There's no getting around it. We may like to think of ourselves as being self-disciplined and conscientious, and many of us actually are. But there is only one way to make sure you will consistently pay yourself first, and that is to put yourself on an automatic system. To put it another way . . .

Smart women pay themselves first . . . automatically!

This means that, if you work for a company that offers some sort of contributory retirement program such as a group retirement plan, you should definitely sign up. (We'll discuss this in detail in Step Five.) Under most such plans, after you've signed up, you don't have to do a thing. Every pay period, your employer will take a portion of your gross pay (i.e., *before* taxes are withheld) and put it in a group retirement plan for you. No muss, no fuss, no chance to succumb to temptation.

If you don't have access to this sort of company-sponsored program, then you must set up the appropriate retirement plan on your own. (Again, we'll provide details in Step Five.) You also must arrange your own automatic payroll-deduction system. You may be able to do this through your company payroll department. If not, you can do it on your own by telling your bank to transfer automatically a given amount from your chequing account to your retirement plan on the same day you deposit your paycheque.

The key is to make sure the transfer is done automatically. Otherwise, you probably won't do it consistently. Just as most people can't stick to budgets, most people who promise to pay themselves first don't—unless the money is taken out of their paycheque and put into a retirement account before they have a chance to do anything else with it. If you are married and your husband works, make sure he does this too!

BUILDING A MILLION-DOLLAR NEST EGG

How to Accumulate $1,000,000

Regular Deposits Required to Accumulate $1,000,000
by Age 65 at Stated Rate of Return

$1,000,000
12% Annual Interest Rate

Starting Age	Daily Savings	Monthly Savings	Yearly Savings
20	$ 2.00	$ 61	$ 730
25	$ 3.57	$ 109	$ 1,304
30	$ 6.35	$ 193	$ 2,317
35	$ 11.35	$ 345	$ 4,144
36	$ 12.77	$ 388	$ 4,660
37	$ 14.37	$ 437	$ 5,244
38	$ 16.18	$ 492	$ 5,904
39	$ 18.22	$ 554	$ 6,652
40	$ 20.55	$ 625	$ 7,500
41	$ 23.19	$ 705	$ 8,463
42	$ 26.19	$ 797	$ 9,560
43	$ 29.62	$ 901	$ 10,811
44	$ 33.52	$ 1,020	$ 12,240
45	$ 38.02	$ 1,157	$ 13,879
46	$ 43.19	$ 1,314	$ 15,763
47	$ 49.14	$ 1,495	$ 17,937
48	$ 56.05	$ 1,705	$ 20,457
49	$ 64.08	$ 1,949	$ 23,390
50	$ 73.49	$ 2,235	$ 26,824
51	$ 84.58	$ 2,573	$ 30,971
52	$ 97.75	$ 2,973	$ 35,677
53	$ 113.53	$ 3,453	$ 41,437
54	$ 132.64	$ 4,035	$ 48,415
55	$ 156.12	$ 4,749	$ 56,984

The figures shown above represent the amount of money you would have to save (i.e., daily, monthly, yearly), at the stated interest rate, in order to accumulate $1,000,000 by the time you reach age 65. These figures DO NOT take into account any taxes that may be incurred. Monthly and yearly figures are rounded to the nearest dollar.

Source: *The Wise Investor: Ten Concepts You Need to Know to Achieve Financial Success* by Neil Elmouch (Dunhill & West Publishing)

It's Never Too Late

There's no question that the sooner you get started paying yourself first, the better off you will be. The following chart shows it plainly.

**TO BUILD WEALTH . . . PAY YOURSELF FIRST
AND DO IT MONTHLY**

Your monthly investment	Your age	Total amount of monthly investments through age 65	At a 4% rate of return	At a 7% rate of return	At a 9% rate of return	At a 12% rate of return
$100	25	48,000	118,590	264,012	471,643	1,188,242
	30	42,000	91,678	181,156	296,385	649,527
	40	30,000	51,584	81,480	112,953	189,764
	50	18,000	24,691	31,881	38,124	50,458
$150	25	72,000	177,294	393,722	702,198	1,764,716
	30	63,000	137,060	270,158	441,268	964,644
	40	45,000	77,119	121,511	168,168	281,827
	50	27,000	36,914	47,544	56,761	74,937
$200	25	96,000	237,180	528,025	943,286	2,376,484
	30	84,000	183,355	362,312	592,770	1,299,054
	40	60,000	103,169	162,959	225,906	379,527
	50	36,000	49,382	63,762	76,249	100,915

Incredible, isn't it? But wait. If you study this chart closely, you might come to the conclusion that the key to success is to start young. What if you are older? What if you weren't fortunate enough to start saving when you were in your 20s or 30s? Don't worry. The miracle of compound interest does not depend on how old you are. The only thing that matters is how long your money has been invested and at what rate it is growing.

When students of mine who are in their 40s and 50s insist to me that it's too late for them to start saving, I point out that simply by investing a mere $10 a day in a mutual fund that returns 15 percent a year (and plenty have exceeded this rate), over a period of 25 years they will accumulate well in excess of $1 million!

Remember—the combined power of the Latté Factor and the miracle of compound interest is truly amazing. The only thing that can short-circuit it is the all-too-human tendency to procrastinate. Too many people put off doing what they know they should, and as a result these two powerful tools never get the chance to work for them. Don't make this mistake.

Don't Label Yourself a Procrastinator

Even if everything I've just said makes sense to you intellectually, I know it is still very possible that you simply won't be able to pay yourself first. What many people say is, "I know I should do this, but I'm just a procrastinator." Well, I have never met a real procrastinator. Whenever someone tells me she is a procrastinator, I respond by asking them, "Did you eat this week?" Of course, the person will always answer yes. The fact is, no one procrastinates *all* the time. What you may be is a selective procrastinator—which means that if something is important enough (like eating), you are perfectly capable of taking care of it right away.

So what makes us procrastinate about saving? Most of us do it for one reason: *fear of change.* Why do we fear change? Because we associate change with pain. Saving means reducing your spending. Reducing your spending means changing (however slightly) the way you live. And changing (however slightly) the way you live means . . . who knows what? *Probably something terrible!*

I often run into this when I address employee groups. Many people tell me they know my idea of contributing a portion of their gross pay to a retirement plan makes sense, but they just can't see how they could possibly get by if their take-home were suddenly reduced by 10 percent. I recall one incident in particular. I was at a Fortune 500 company, speaking at a sign-up seminar for the firm's retirement plan, when a gentleman named Dan stood up and challenged my assertion that it was possible to give yourself a pay cut. "David," he said, very agitated, "I don't think you are in touch with reality. Many of us here today are in our mid-40s and 50s. We have expenses, like homes, car payments, and college costs. We are basically living from paycheque to paycheque, and when you are doing that, you can't take a 10 percent pay cut. It's simply not possible."

A murmur of agreement rippled across the room. Clearly many of Dan's co-workers shared his fears. Justified or not, those fears deserved to be addressed.

"What would you do," I asked Dan, "if your boss came into your office tomorrow and told you that because of a corporate restructuring, you had to choose between losing your job or taking a 10 percent pay cut?"

Dan looked startled, then stared at his feet and mumbled, "I'd take the 10 percent pay cut."

"And how would that affect you?" I continued. "Would it make you so depressed that you couldn't get out of bed in the morning?"

Dan looked at me a little strangely. "Of course not," he said. "I'd be bummed, but I'd still be able to get up in the morning."

"Good," I responded. "So we know that being forced to take a 10 percent pay cut wouldn't incapacitate you. Now, what about your house? Would you lose your home if you got a 10 percent pay cut?"

"No," Dan replied. "We'd figure out a way to cut back."

I told him that was good, too. "Now we know that a pay cut will neither incapacitate you nor leave you homeless. What about your wife? Would she leave you if your pay got cut?"

"No, of course not," he answered.

"I didn't think so," I said. I went on to explain to Dan that the point of my questions wasn't to make fun of his concerns. What I was trying to do was show him and everyone else in the room that there are really two options in life: You can be either reactive or proactive to circumstances. And it's a lot more fun and a lot less painful to be proactive—to make decisions about your life before events take control of *you*.

It's Time to Give Yourself That Pay Cut!

If for any reason (a company restructuring, a war, a death, a divorce, whatever), you suddenly found yourself forced to take a pay cut, you'd manage to cope somehow, wouldn't you? So why wait for something to happen and then react to it? Why not take control over your own destiny and create your own future now?

Finally, remember that the key to the Latté Factor is recognizing that small things (like a $2 cup of coffee) can make a big difference. A dollar here, a dollar there, if invested regularly through an automatic pay-yourself-first system, can make you financially secure for life. And quite frankly, you deserve to be!

Congratulations, You've Completed Step Four

You've taken advantage of the Latté Factor to reduce your spending, you've made a commitment to pay yourself first, and you've arranged to put aside a portion of your gross income (ideally, 12 percent) automatically each month. You are now ready to move on to Step Five, in which we'll figure out exactly what to do with all this money you are now paying yourself.

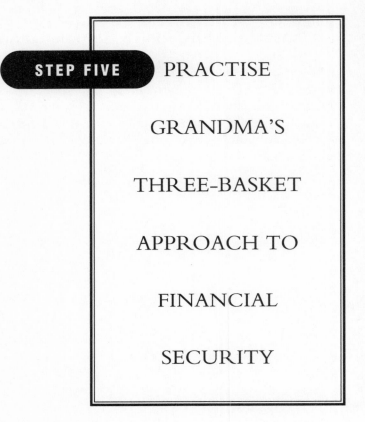

STEP FIVE PRACTISE GRANDMA'S THREE-BASKET APPROACH TO FINANCIAL SECURITY

As I mentioned in the introduction, it was my Grandma Bach who encouraged me to make my first investment—in three shares of McDonald's. I was seven at the time, and the idea of being a stockholder was so exciting to me that as soon as I managed to save up some more money, I bought another share. And then another. And another.

Finally, my grandmother took me aside. "David," she said, "McDonald's is a fine company, but it's not the only one on the stock exchange."

"But I like McDonald's," I protested.

"I know," she replied, "but the sensible thing to do is to spread your money around. Haven't you ever heard the expression 'Don't put all your eggs in one basket'?"

I hadn't—not until then, at any rate. But once my grandmother explained it to me, it made complete sense, and to this day it remains one of the fundamental principles of my approach to financial planning.

Most people assume that financial planning is difficult, complicated, and exhausting. It's not. The fact is, if you do it correctly, actually it's pretty easy. One of the keys is to remember my grandmother's advice: Don't put all your eggs in one basket.

As it happens, there are *three* baskets into which you should put your eggs. I call them **the Security Basket**™, **the Retirement Basket**™, and **the Dream Basket**™. The Security Basket protects you and your family against the unexpected (such as a medical emergency, the death of a loved one, or the loss of a job), the Retirement Basket safeguards your future, and the Dream Basket enables you to fulfill those deeply held desires that make life worthwhile. This three-basket approach may sound simple, but don't let that fool you. If you fill the baskets properly, you can create for yourself a financial life filled with abundance and, most important, security.

The "eggs" we're talking about are, of course, the extra dollars you learned to put aside in Step Four. You are going to use them to fill these three baskets—in some cases by investing the cash directly in money market funds or retirement plans, in other cases by buying things such as insurance policies.

We are going to discuss the Security Basket first—mainly because it involves a bunch of things that you need to take care of immediately. In practice, however, you will be filling up both your Security Basket and your Retirement Basket at the same time. Once you've taken care of your Security and Retirement Baskets, you can start filling your Dream Basket.

We'll get to the details of exactly how retirement saving works in a little while. Right now, let's talk about security.

BASKET ONE:
YOUR SECURITY BASKET

Your Security Basket is meant to protect you and your family in the event of some unexpected financial hardship, such as the loss of a job or some other major income source. It also can help you cope with life's little unplanned surprises, like the car breaking down, the refrigerator needing repair, or the dog eating your child's retainer, which just cost you $496! The Security Basket does this by providing you with a financial cushion—an air bag, if you will—that softens the blow in case of accident. Not only will having this sort of cushion contribute to your peace of mind, but when trouble strikes, it can (quite literally) buy you the time you will need to get back on your feet.

Five Things to Do Right Away for Protection

In order to be properly protected, you must make sure that your Security Basket contains most—if not all—of the following five elements.

> ### SAFEGUARD NO. 1
> YOU MUST HAVE AT LEAST THREE TO 24 MONTHS' WORTH
> OF LIVING EXPENSES SAVED IN CASE OF EMERGENCY.

The goal here is to put away "rainy-day money" to cover expenses in case you lose your income. Exactly how much money you need to put away depends on what you spend each month. (You can figure this out with the help of the "Where Does Your Money *Really* Go?" form in Appendix 1.) I generally recommend to my students and clients that they put away somewhere between three and 24 months' worth of expense money. By this measure, a Smart Woman whose basic spending runs about $2,000 a month should aim to have at least $6,000 in cash in her Security Basket.

That three- to 24-month range covers a lot of ground. What's right for you depends in large part on your particular emotional makeup. Some of my clients simply do not feel safe if they have anything less than two years' worth of cash sitting in a money market fund. I happen to think that's a bit excessive, but if that's what it takes to make you feel comfortable, then by all means make it your goal.

In general, the size of your cushion should depend on how easy it would be to replace your current income. Say you currently earn $75,000 a year. If you suddenly lost your job, how long would it take for you to find a new one paying that much or more? If you are easily employable and are confident that you could land a new $75,000-a-year job relatively quickly, then you probably don't need to have much more than three months' worth of expenses in your Security Basket. If, on the other hand, you think it would take you six months to a year to find another job paying that much, then you should probably have a lot more money—at least six months' to a year's worth of expenses—in your Security Basket.

DON'T LET THE BANKS RIP YOU OFF!

How much you save in your Security Basket is critical. But where you save it is equally important! Many women today keep their rainy-day money in a bank savings account or in a low-earning chequing account. In some cases, it's not earning any interest at all. Please, please don't make this mistake.

As a consumer, you need to protect yourself by shopping around for the best rate of return available in your area. I can't stress enough how important it is that you do this. Indeed, if the only action you take as a result of reading this book is moving your savings from a low-interest account to one that earns competitive money market rates, that alone will earn you back what you paid for this book in a month or so.

Equally important, you should check the fees charged by the financial institution on transactions on your account. Some banks offer as many as 16 different accounts, and the fees range from nothing to $7 per month on a similar package of services. Surprisingly, credit unions don't always charge lower fees than banks, so you should do your homework and not just go with your instincts. (You can compare rates charged on chequing and savings accounts at 16 different financial institutions at a website administered by Industry Canada at *www.strategis.ic.gc.ca*).

Some banks offer high-interest savings accounts that pay rates almost as high as GICs, but give you immediate access to your money if you need it. Also called premium accounts, investor accounts, or cash-performance accounts, they usually require a minimum deposit of $10,000 or more, which you must maintain at all times or forfeit some of the interest.

Most large mutual fund companies offer money market funds that invest primarily in Treasury bills, one of the safest investments available. These funds usually pay a higher rate of interest than a bank savings account, and all the interest earned in the fund accrues to your savings.

These funds are also highly liquid. If you want to take your money back, you can usually have a cheque in your hands within 24 to 48 hours.

Regardless of what you do with your hard-earned savings, make sure you don't leave them in a low-interest or no-interest chequing account. After all, if you have $10,000 sitting in a savings or chequing account earning only 1.0 percent annually when it could be earning 4.5 percent, you're cheating yourself out of $450 a year in interest. The way I see it, that's a plane ticket or a fancy dream night out on the town or more money in your RRSP! In other words, that so-called free chequing account at the bank really isn't. Quite the contrary, it's costing you a fortune.

FIVE-STAR TIP: *Interest rates change daily! To find the current Bank of Canada rate, on which all other rates in Canada are based, check www.bankofcanada.ca.*

SAFEGUARD NO. 2

YOU ABSOLUTELY, POSITIVELY, NO MATTER WHAT, MUST HAVE AN UP-TO-DATE WILL OR LIVING TRUST.

An estimated one out of two Canadians die intestate. That's legal jargon for dying without having written a will or set up a living trust that explains how your assets should be distributed after your death. In Canada, unlike the U.S., the government does not impose estate taxes. However, it does tax capital gains accumulated by assets within an estate. It also taxes RRSPs and RRIFs that are collapsed upon the death of their owner. With this in mind, not taking steps to plan for what happens after you're gone is incredibly irresponsible. In effect, what you are saying to your loved ones is the following:

To those I love—

While I understand that I have the right to determine who will inherit my property when I die, I have decided to let the courts make that decision for me, even though that might mean that people I never knew or never liked could wind up as my heirs.

I also understand that there are perfectly legitimate ways of minimizing the probate fees and complications my loved ones will have to encounter. However, because of the generosity of governments, lawyers, and banks to me throughout my lifetime, I have decided to let them take the biggest bites they can. You get the rest.

In addition, rather than deciding who should take care of my children, I've decided that I'd rather have my family fight about it and then let the courts just go ahead and appoint anyone they feel like.

Finally, I know that as a result of not leaving a will, a significant portion of my assets could be eaten up by lawyers' bills and that all the private details of my financial affairs will be made public.

Now, clearly, that's not what most people want to have happen when they die. Yet millions Canadians have no will or living trust in place.

Please don't make this terrible mistake. Yes, making out a will or setting up a living trust can be difficult; it forces you to consider all sorts of contingencies you'd probably rather not think about. But remember—if you die without a will or living trust in place, it falls to the government to figure out what should be done with the fruits of your life's work. Do you really want the government to decide how your estate should be divided up? Even worse, by dying intestate, you make it possible for swindlers to lay claim to your estate, and you virtually guarantee that your entire private life will be made public.

The most common excuse for not having a will or living trust is laziness. Well, Smart Women aren't lazy! After you finish reading this chapter, call your family lawyer and set up an appointment to draft a will or a living trust. Your lawyer can advise you on which would make the most sense for your situation.

WHAT ARE A LIVING TRUST AND ESTATE FREEZE?

Before we go any further, I probably should explain a little about living trusts, which are often executed in conjunction with the formation of a holding company. A living trust is basically a legal document that does two things. First, it allows you to transfer the ownership of any of your assets (your house, your car, your investment accounts, whatever you like) to a trust while you are still alive. Second, it designates who should be given those assets after you die. Those designated individuals ultimately receive the growth accumulated by your assets. In the meantime, by naming yourself the trustee of your trust, you control your assets—which means that, as long as you live, the transfer of ownership will have no practical impact on your ability to enjoy and manage your property.

The main advantage a living trust has over a simple will is that if you create a living trust properly and fund it correctly, your assets won't have to go through probate—that is, the courts won't review your instructions regarding the distribution of your assets. This can be very important. Among other things, by avoiding probate, you can save thousands of dollars in legal fees.

However, the cost of executing an estate freeze, which includes a living trust and a holding company, can be high. Also, estate freezes are difficult and costly to reverse once they're in place. Still, they're

sometimes advisable, especially in complicated family structures in-
volving large amounts of assets

In the meantime, because estate planning is so important and so
complicated, I strongly recommend that you hire an estate-planning
expert who specializes in drafting wills and trusts.

WHAT TO DO IF YOU ALREADY HAVE A WILL
OR LIVING TRUST

If you already have a will or a living trust, that's great. If it was
written more than five years ago, however, don't assume it's still
good. In all likelihood some things in your life have changed, and
your will or trust probably needs updating. I have sat with clients reviewing wills that still talked about who would take care of the
kids—even though the "kids" were now in their 50s. (People always
laugh when I tell that story, but the situation is more common than
you would believe.)

Once you've written or updated your will or living trust, make
sure your loved ones know where you've stored it. And *don't* keep it
in a safety deposit box. If your heirs don't have the keys to your box,
they may need to obtain a court order to get it opened—and that
could take weeks (sometimes even months). If you store important
documents in a safe or strongbox in your home or office, make sure
someone (like your lawyer or your children) knows where it is and
how to find the combination. You might think this is obvious, but
even professionals sometimes forget. Not too long ago, my own father, who's been a financial advisor for over 30 years, casually happened to mention that he and my mother kept their wills and other
important papers in a "hidden safe" in their house. It was the first I'd
ever heard of it.

The point is, if you are hiding any valuables, make sure your heirs
know where they're hidden. If you don't, they may well stay hidden
after you pass away.

And don't be penny-wise and pound foolish and try to draft a will
or trust by yourself—not even with one of those "family lawyer"
software programs that have become so popular. Just one mistake on
a self-created will can make the entire document invalid—in which
case your estate will end up in the courts, at a cost to your family of
thousands of dollars and endless heartache. Spend the money (and
time) to have your will drafted properly by a professional. The bill
may run from $400 to $1,000, but I promise you, it will be worth it.

Finally, if you have older parents and you don't know if they have a will or living trust in place, you really should have a talk with them about getting things organized. The conversation may be uncomfortable, but it will almost certainly spare you and your family much heartache later on.

> ## SAFEGUARD NO. 3
> ### IF YOU HAVE DEPENDENTS, YOU SHOULD HAVE LIFE INSURANCE.

If you have dependents—children or other relatives who depend on you financially—you must protect them by buying life insurance. Most people hate to talk about life insurance, but if someone depends on you and your income, then you need to have some sort of protection plan in place in case something happens to you. And that's all life insurance is—a protection plan.

LIKE IT OR NOT, MEN DIE

One of the sadder aspects of my job as a financial advisor is how often I hear horror stories about women who thought their husbands had life insurance coverage—only to find out after it was too late that they didn't. Remember, no one really knows when he or she is going to go. That's why you have to have insurance . . . to protect against the unexpected.

As I noted in Step One, men are the worst when it comes to dealing with this reality. So if you are married, put this book down right now and go find out if you and your husband have life insurance. Then find the insurance policy and read it. (By the way, when you pull out the policy, if the pages are yellowed and stick to the plastic folder they came in, chances are you have a really old policy that definitely needs to be reviewed.)

When you start reading your policy, the first two things you really want to know are who is covered and how much money will be paid out if the insured individual dies.

IF YOU ARE MARRIED WITH CHILDREN, DON'T INSURE JUST YOUR HUSBAND

Many family men naively assume that, if their wife is a stay-at-home mom, she doesn't need to be covered. This is a huge mistake. After all, if you are a stay-at-home mom and something happens to you, who's going to take care of the kids? Your husband will have to hire a nanny or stay at home himself (and thus have to stop or cut back working). Either way, that will require more money.

IF YOU ARE A SINGLE MOM, YOU'D BETTER OVERINSURE!

If you are a single mom raising kids on your own, it's even more essential that you have life insurance to protect your children's future. Indeed, as a single mother, getting adequate life insurance could be the most important thing you ever do for your children.

Life insurance is not the place to cut corners. Stop for a moment and think about it. If you were to pass away, who would take care of your kids? Would it be your parents? A relative such as a sister or brother? Or would your kids end up with your ex-husband? Whatever the case, you want them to be safe and secure, and this means, among other things, protecting them financially—that is, leaving them with enough money to live comfortably and ultimately with sufficient savings to pay for university or college.

So make sure you have enough life insurance not simply to provide for your children's needs over the next years if something were to happen to you, but to cover their expenses straight through four years of post-secondary education.

That's bound to be a lot of money, of course, but if you don't provide it, who will? Don't make the terrible mistake I personally have seen too many single moms make and assume that your parents will be able to handle the financial burden of taking care of your children. Over the last few years I have had to sit in too many meetings with clients who are now struggling because of the obligations they inherited when a grown child of theirs died, leaving them to take care of their orphaned grandchildren.

SO HOW MUCH IS ENOUGH?

To come up with a ballpark number, you should ask yourself the following questions:

1. Who will be hurt financially if I should die? In other words, who relies on my income? (By the way, if you could be hurt financially by a death in the family—your husband's, for example—then you definitely want to make sure you are protected yourself.)
2. What does it cost those who depend on me to live for a year? (This figure should include everything—mortgage, taxes, university or college costs, etc.)
3. Are there any major debts, such as a home or business loan, that would need to be paid immediately if I or my significant other were to pass away? (You'd be surprised how often smart people overlook these sorts of financial obligations. If you own a business, what costs would your family or children incur if you died? Do you own a second home? If you do, make sure the mortgage payments are covered. What about funeral expenses and probate costs? These can amount to thousands of dollars.)

MOST PEOPLE ARE UNDERINSURED

As a starting point to determine the minimum amount of life insurance you need, take your gross annual income (that is, your total earnings before taxes) and multiply it by six. I say "minimum" because depending on the level of your debts and expenses, you might want a death benefit as high as 20 times your annual income.

Whether you insure yourself on the low or high end of that range depends on your situation. Some people like to have just enough insurance to cover their dependents' major expenses for a few years. Others want to make sure that, if something happened to them, their family's independence would be assured indefinitely. As with the amount of your security savings, this is a decision you must make for yourself personally. I recommend that you cover your family's living expenses for at least 10 years—more if your dependents happen to be very young.

NOT EVERYONE NEEDS LIFE INSURANCE

Life insurance is meant to protect dependents who can't otherwise take care of themselves and would be at risk if you weren't around. It's not meant to leave your significant other in the lap of luxury. Therefore, if you don't have kids (or some other relative who depends on you), there is no reason for you to make financial sacrifices to buy life insurance. I'd rather see you put the money away for retirement.

Indeed, if you are single and childless (and have no other dependents), then the only possible reason you should buy life insurance is because you want to cover an outstanding mortgage, leave an estate for a charity, or you are using it as a retirement vehicle. As far as your Security Basket is concerned, the point of life insurance is to protect your dependents; if you don't have any, you don't need any.

SO WHAT KIND OF LIFE INSURANCE SHOULD I BUY?

If you are confused about life insurance, don't worry—you are not alone. Today there are more than 500 differently named types of policies. It's no wonder the public is confused. For the sake of your Security Basket, I am going to try to keep the insurance game simple.

First and foremost, there are really only two types of life insurance: term insurance and permanent insurance.

TERM INSURANCE

Term insurance is really very simple. You pay an insurance company a premium, and in return the insurance company promises to pay your beneficiary a death benefit if you die. Specifically, term insurance provides you with a set amount of protection for a set period.

The chief advantages of this type of insurance are that it is very cheap and generally it is very easy to get. The disadvantage of term insurance is that it does not allow you to build any cash value. What this means is that you never accumulate any equity in the policy, no matter how long you pay premiums to the insurance company. All term insurance provides is a death benefit. You can literally pay premiums into a term policy for 30 years, but if you then decide you don't want it any more, you walk away with nothing.

Term insurance comes in two basic "flavours"—annual renewable term and level term.

Annual Renewable Term. With annual renewable term insurance, your death benefit remains the same while your premiums get larger each year. More than likely, this is the type of policy you have if you work for a company and signed up for life insurance through the benefits department. The biggest advantage of an annual renewable term policy is that it is really inexpensive when you are young. Indeed, it is by far the cheapest way to buy insurance when you are just starting out. The problem is that, as you get older (and the likelihood of death increases), the premiums can become prohibitively expensive.

Level Term. Under a level term policy, both the death benefit and the premium remain the same for a period that you select when you first sign up. The period can range anywhere from five to 30 years. While this type of term insurance is initially more expensive than annual renewable term, it actually can turn out to be cheaper over the long run. If you choose this type of term insurance, I recommend you take it for a minimum of 15 to 20 years. If you are in your 30s or younger, a 20-year policy would at least protect your family in the years in which they are likely to have the greatest need for your income.

WHO SHOULD BUY TERM INSURANCE?

Unless you are looking for an investment vehicle, I would recommend that everyone with dependents to protect should buy term life insurance—ideally, a level term policy. Depending on your particular situation, you probably would do well to look into getting as long term a policy as possible, at least 20 years. If better rates become available, you can always go shopping for a new policy. (If you do this, make sure you don't cancel your old policy before you've been approved for your new one.)

The great news about term insurance these days is that it has never been more affordable. In fact, if you have a life insurance policy that is more than five years old, you probably should get it updated. Typically, you should be able to buy a new policy that provides two to three times the death benefit for the same price you're paying now, or the same size death benefit at just half or a third of your current premium cost.

Why hasn't your insurance company told you about this? Come on. Do you really think your insurance company is going to phone you up and say, "Hey, guess what? We've cut our prices 50 percent, and we'd like to send you some of your money back." Of course it won't—which is why you should be constantly reviewing your financial situation.

FIVE-STAR TIP: *As attractive as it may seem, don't get term life insurance through your employer unless the policy the company is offering is guaranteed renewable and portable. This means that if you leave your job, you can take the policy with you. If your policy isn't portable, you could find yourself without a job and without insurance—a bad combination.*

PERMANENT INSURANCE

Permanent insurance is known in the industry as "cash-value" insurance. Basically, it combines term insurance with a forced savings plan that can help you build a nice nest egg. The catch is that permanent insurance can cost up to eight times as much as term.

There are three main types of permanent insurance: whole life, universal life, and variable universal life.

Whole Life. With whole life insurance, the premiums remain level as you grow older (just as with level term), but a portion of what you pay in is funnelled into a basket of tax-deferred savings, where it can accumulate and earn dividends. At first, the portion is quite small, but as time goes on, it increases. As your policy's cash value builds, you can borrow against it or cash out by cancelling your coverage. The problem with whole life is that the dividends your savings earn are generally not that high; indeed, they may not even keep up with inflation. The returns on whole life insurance are comparable to what you'd get by keeping your money in a chequing account, often running as low as 1 to 5 percent a year. As a result, it can take literally decades to build any substantial cash value in a whole life policy. In my opinion, this makes it a very poor vehicle for a retirement nest egg.

Universal Life. Universal life insurance is a lot like whole life, except that it is supposed to offer much better returns, and it's a lot more flexible. Specifically, you can change the size of the death benefit—and thus the size of your premium payment—any time you want. This is a great feature if your income tends to go up and down; in years when you don't earn so much, you can reduce your premium by reducing the size of your death benefit.

The downside to universal life is that the projected rates of return that the insurance company quotes when it's trying to sell you on the policy are just that—projections. Nothing is guaranteed. Universal life works when the insurance company invests well, but it can be a disaster when the company doesn't. Many people who bought universal life policies back when rates were in the high teens have been shocked in recent years by annual returns of just 5 or 6 percent—and they still have to make premium payments.

Variable Universal Life Insurance. If you are looking for life insurance that also can double as an excellent retirement vehicle, I'd recommend variable universal life insurance. With variable universal life you get a cash-value policy that allows you to control how the savings portion of your premium dollars is invested. A good variable life policy may offer over a dozen different high-quality mutual funds for you to select from. Your choices may include stock funds (both domestic and global), bond funds, money market funds, and sometimes even fixed-rate securities. The advantages over a whole life or universal policy are plain. If you make good investment decisions, you can make significantly more money over the long term than you would with a whole life or a regular universal policy.

WHY HASN'T MY INSURANCE AGENT TOLD ME ABOUT VARIABLE LIFE?

If your insurance agent never told you about variable life insurance, chances are it's because he or she does not have the regulatory credentials that allow him or her to sell a policy that involves stocks or other securities. This is not the sort of financial advisor or insurance agent a Smart Woman wants to have. In the twenty-first century, you want someone who can offer you all types of policies and is up-to-date on the newest policies available.

FIVE-STAR TIP: If you buy a variable policy, you must be prepared to accept a certain amount of risk and volatility. Because you are investing in securities that may go down as well as up, there is a chance you may lose a portion of your cash value and be forced to make additional premium payments. If you are extremely conservative and like guarantees, don't consider a variable policy because you won't be happy with the volatility. Remember, permanent insurance works only if you are committed to it—and if you can afford to make premium payments over a long period. On average, it takes about 10 to 15 years for a permanent policy to really work as an investment vehicle. If you are not sure you can commit to fund a policy for this long, don't buy variable coverage. Start with a level term policy instead. It will cost less and protect your family just as adequately. You always can get permanent insurance later.

WHERE SHOULD I START?

If you are going to buy life insurance, you should meet with a life insurance professional—not a salesperson. Make a point of asking friends and getting recommendations. A good insurance professional can really add value, provided he or she is ethical and experienced.

Some people prefer not to buy through an agent or broker. Certainly, that can be more expensive than purchasing coverage directly from the company. If you're one of these people, do your research on the Internet. It's never been easier to buy life insurance on the Internet, and it's never been cheaper. Among the many web-based sources of information on life insurance are:

www.quality-ins.com
www.cheaplifeinsurance.ca
www.insurance-canada.ca
termlife.win.net
www.life-insurance-canada.com

SAFEGUARD NO. 4
YOU NEED TO PROTECT YOUR INCOME WITH
DISABILITY INSURANCE.

Because Canadians are covered by a government-operated universal health care program, they don't have to worry as much as Americans about the devastating expenses involved with medical- and health-related problems. That doesn't mean Canadians shouldn't pay attention to their insurance coverage. If they want to make sure they recuperate from an injury or illness in a comfortable private room, for example, they should invest in additional health-care coverage that includes hospitalization upgrades.

But health insurance addresses only part of the health-related risk that we all face in our day-to-day lives. We also have to consider how we'd cope if we became disabled.

I used to think disability insurance was a waste of money. I was wrong. Although far more people have life insurance than disability insurance, the chances of your becoming sick or hurt are much greater than the chances of your dying prematurely. Without disability insurance you are playing Russian roulette with your income.

U.S. researchers have compiled some daunting statistics about the chances of sustaining a disability during a person's lifetime. While Canadian figures may differ somewhat, the fact remains that we face a far higher chance of suffering a disability in our lifetime than we do of dying prematurely. Consider the following statistics. In one year:

- 1 out of every 88 homes will catch fire.
- 1 out of every 70 cars will be involved in a serious accident.

But . . .

> *The chances of becoming disabled are 9 to 11 times higher than a house fire or a serious automobile accident.*

What this means to you and me is that the greatest threat to our ability to finish rich may be the risk we all face of serious injury or illness! And the younger you are, the greater your risk. Indeed, it has been reported that between the ages of 35 and 65, the chances of suffering a disability serious enough to prevent you from working temporarily is 1 in 2.

Other than your health, your income is probably your most important asset. Lose it and you could be losing your primary means of financial security. That's why we all need disability insurance.

HOW MUCH DISABILITY INSURANCE DO I NEED?

Disability insurance is not designed to make you rich. Rather, it is a protection plan for your current earning power. Ideally, therefore, an adequate disability policy is one that would pay you the equivalent of your current take-home pay.

Most disability plans offer a benefit equal to about 60 percent of your gross (or before-tax) income. That may not sound like much, but if you've paid for the disability policy yourself, any income you receive from it will be tax-free, so 60 percent of the gross probably will be enough to maintain your standard of living. (After all, 60 percent of the gross is about what most of us actually take home after taxes.)

If your employer pays for your disability insurance, any benefits you receive from it will be taxed. This means that if the policy pays only 60 percent of your gross income, you're going to come up short. Indeed, once you've paid the taxes on your disability benefit, you're likely to find yourself with only a fraction of your normal take-home pay. To guard against this, you should consider purchasing what is known as a "gap policy" to make up the difference.

DON'T ASSUME YOU HAVE DISABILITY INSURANCE

Many people mistakenly assume they automatically get disability coverage from their employer. Don't assume anything. If you work for a company, first thing tomorrow check your benefits statement or phone your benefits department to find out whether you have disability insurance. If you don't, find out if you can get it through work and start the application process immediately. If you are a stay-at-home mom whose husband works, check to see if he is covered. If you are self-employed and don't currently have disability insurance, make getting it a top priority.

You should apply for disability insurance now while you are healthy. For some reason, people always seem to put this off, waiting until something is wrong with them before they start trying to get coverage. By then, of course, it is too late. And don't think you can fool the insurance company by fibbing on your policy application. Saying you're healthy when you know you're not or that you don't smoke when in fact you do is not only immoral, it's also pointless. Insurance companies will do just about anything they can to avoid having to pay out benefits—including hiring an investigator to thoroughly scrutinize your past medical history.

QUESTIONS TO ASK BEFORE YOU SIGN UP

1. **Is the disability plan portable and guaranteed renewable?** If you purchase your policy through your employer, you must make sure that you can take the policy with you if you leave the company. You also want a policy that is guaranteed renewable; there is no bigger ripoff than an insurance company that makes you "qualify" each and every year. This is how a bad insurance company gets out of having to pay you when you file a claim!

2. **Under what circumstances will the policy pay off?** Specifically, you want to know whether the policy will cover you in the event you can no longer do the work you currently do or whether it pays off only if you are rendered unable to do work of any kind. In the insurance industry, this is known as "-owner-occupation" and "any-occupation" coverage. Make sure you buy an owner-occupation policy. Why? Well, take me, for

example. I happen to make my living talking on the phone to clients. Now, if I lost my voice and couldn't talk, I would, for all intents and purposes, be out of a job. But unless I had owner-occupation coverage, the insurance company could say to me, "So what if you can't talk on the phone? There are plenty of other jobs you could do—like digging ditches. So we are not going to pay you any disability benefits." With owner-occupation coverage, they can't do that to me. This sort of coverage is more expensive, but it is much, much safer.

3. **How long does it take for the coverage to kick in?** Most disability policies start paying benefits within three to six months after you've been declared disabled. The easiest way to reduce the cost of a disability policy is to lengthen that waiting period. The more cash you have in your Security Basket, the longer you can stretch it out.

4. **How long will the policy cover me?** Ideally, your disability policy should pay you benefits until you turn 65 at least. However, many disability insurers require claimants to apply for Canada Pension Plan Disability benefits after a certain period. These benefits currently amount to a maximum of $900 a month. Whether or not you apply, the insurer will notify you and then deduct the benefit for which you qualify from your monthly insurance payment.

5. **Is my coverage limited to physical disability, or are mental and emotional disorders also covered?** A major cause of disability these days is stress. Not all disability policies cover it, however. If you are in a high-stress occupation, make sure yours does.

FIVE-STAR TIP: *As with all good and important things, there is a catch to disability insurance. It is expensive (plans often cost between 1 to 3 percent of your annual income), which is why most people don't have it, especially if they have to pay for it themselves. (In Canada, for example, 60 percent of self-employed people have no disability coverage.) The reason it costs so much is that insurance companies know there is a good chance they will have to pay off on the policies they write. (This alone should convince you that you need disability insurance.) In any case, I recommend that you contact your company's benefits department first and see if you can get it through them. Group policies tend to be less expensive and easier to get. If your employer won't cover you—or if you are self-employed—check with a broker or visit the insurance websites to see what is available.*

Once again, like life insurance, disability insurance is very complicated, and you may want to consider hiring a disability specialist to assist you.

The following sites provide information about disability insurance
and comparisons of rates charged by providers of this type of insurance.

Insurance Canada
www.insurance-canada.ca
Administered and overseen by the publishers of
Insurance Canada magazine

Cheap Life Insurance
www.cheaplifeinsurance.ca
Toll-free: (877) 830-7000
Despite the tacky name, this website provides good background
information and enables you to compare rates from different
providers. You will be contacted by phone, however, after you
submit your information.

Human Resources Development Canada
www.hrdc-drhc.gc.ca
Provides information you need to apply for Canada Pension Plan
Disability benefits.

SAFEGUARD NO. 5
IF YOU ARE IN YOUR 60s, IT'S TIME TO CONSIDER
LONG-TERM CARE COVERAGE.

Once upon a time, individual families provided their own support
systems to take care of sick or aged parents. Today, families are often
spread out all over the country and as a result there is often no support system. With average life expectancies climbing, more elderly
people thus find themselves in need of either home care or a long-
term care facility. Indeed, studies indicate that no fewer than one out
of every three Canadians over the age of 65 will eventually need this
sort of help.

The cost of such care can be staggering—as much as $30,000 to
$60,000 a year for residence in a long-term care facility. Provincial
health plans provide extensive services for the elderly and infirm. In

Ontario, for example, 380,000 people used the services provided by government-sponsored community-care access centres. Provincial initiatives focus increasingly on providing long-term care in the home rather than in an institution. Nevertheless, long-term care (LTC) coverage can enhance your comfort and peace of mind. (A good source of information on the resources available for long-term care can be found at Health Canada's website, *www.hc-sc.gc.ca*.)

DON'T JUMP THE GUN

As valuable as it can be, LTC coverage isn't necessarily something you need to buy right away (especially if you are under the age of 60). Most people start thinking about LTC coverage in their 50s and purchase it in their 60s. If you wait until you're in your 70s or 80s, it can become prohibitively expensive. Unless you're in terrible shape, you can still get a pretty good deal in your early 60s.

When you're looking for LTC coverage, the first thing you need to understand is what it will not do. Long-term care insurance will not pay for acute care that you get in a hospital (say, in the immediate aftermath of a heart attack or a broken hip). This is typically the province of health insurance. What LTC insurance will cover is the kind of care you get in a nursing home, a residential-care facility, a convalescent facility, an extended facility, a community hospice or adult-care centre, or in some cases your own home.

When you're shopping for LTC coverage, I recommend that you consider a comprehensive policy. The reason is that right now you are probably healthy and as a result can't really predict what type of coverage you (or you and your spouse) will need in the future. A comprehensive policy will typically give you the most options. It will cost more, but should you eventually need the care, I'm confident it will more than justify the extra expense.

HOW TO KEEP YOUR LTC PREMIUMS DOWN

The cost of LTC coverage depends on a number of variables. These include your age, the level of care you want, the amount of coverage ($100 a day, $200 a day, and so on), the length of waiting time before your policy kicks in, your state of health and age, and how long you want your policy to last should you need to use it.

Not counting short stays of less than three months, statistics show that most people spend an average of about three years in a nursing-care facility. Nonetheless, I recommend paying the extra 10 to 15 percent it costs to get lifetime coverage. If the extra cost is too much for you, you can reduce the premium price by requesting a higher deductible on your policy. What this means is that your policy will take longer to go into effect. Most LTC policies start paying off within 30 to 60 days after you enter a nursing facility or put in a claim for home care. By stretching that out a bit, you can bring down your premium costs quite nicely.

Delaying the start of coverage may sound scary, but it's actually quite sensible, since you will probably be able to afford the first few months on your own. It's later on that you will need the most help. By taking a higher deductible and getting lifetime coverage you are covering the worst-case possibility, which is why you are buying this type of coverage in the first place. (By the way, the cost of this type of insurance can be tax deductible, so check with your accountant if you decide to purchase it.)

QUESTIONS TO ASK BEFORE YOU SIGN UP

1. **What exactly does the policy cover?** Remember, there are different types of coverage available. Make sure you know exactly what type of coverage you are being shown before you sign up.
2. **How much will the policy pay out in daily benefits? Will it be adjusted for inflation? At what point do your benefits kick in, and how long will they last?** As I noted above, you can keep your premiums down by requesting a higher deductible. Also, it's worth paying a little more to get yourself lifetime coverage.
3. **Does the policy contain a premium waiver, or will you still have to pay the premiums after you start receiving benefits?** With a waiver, you won't have to worry about continuing to pay premiums while you are in the nursing-care facility.
4. **Is there a grace period for late payments?** Make sure there is. You would hate to find yourself in a situation where you accidentally missed a payment and then discovered that you'd lost your coverage.
5. **Are there any diseases or injuries that are not covered?** The answer should be no.

BE CAREFUL WHOM YOU BUY FROM

Long-term care insurance is still a relatively new product, and even the experts have found it difficult to gauge the financial impact of our rapidly aging population. As a result, there has been enormous upheaval in the LTC industry in recent years, although this has occurred more often in the U.S. than in Canada.

> FIVE-STAR TIP: *Given all the companies that have withdrawn from the LTC business in recent years, I have serious doubts about whether LTC insurance is a product you can count on. All things being equal, I think a woman in her 40s or 50s is better off investing her money than using it to purchase an LTC policy. Bottom line, this is truly a "buyer beware" product, so be careful and use only an established carrier.*

You have now completed your Security Basket. In the process, you have done an amazing amount—far more than 95 percent of the population ever does—to protect both your future and that of your family.

BASKET TWO:
YOUR RETIREMENT BASKET

In Step Four we talked about the importance of paying yourself first—of putting aside a portion of your income (ideally, 12 percent of your income before taxes), and how you should have it transferred out of your paycheque automatically, before you even see it. Well, where this money actually goes is into your Retirement Basket.

Remember: Even though we discussed the Security Basket first, that doesn't mean you should put off funding your Retirement Basket until after you've funded your Security Basket. *You should be doing both at the same time!*

The point of paying yourself first is to put money away now so you can have a great retirement later. As you will see, accomplishing this is not only easy, it also can be a lot of fun. Why? Because nearly every dollar you put into this basket goes in tax-free! If that's not fun, I don't know what is. What's more, because your retirement money is not taxed as long as it stays in the basket, you are in essence getting "free money" from the government to invest. When was the last time that happened to you?

You may be wondering how this works. It's simple. When you put money into your Retirement Basket, you actually are putting it into a pretax retirement plan.

What Exactly Is a Retirement Savings Plan?

A pretax retirement plan is a retirement plan into which you and/or your employer are allowed to deposit a portion of your earnings before the government takes its usual bite out of them. What's great about this is that normally that bite amounts to at least 28 cents out of every dollar you earn.

Funnelling your hard-earned dollars into a pretax retirement account spares the money from this kind of shrinkage. When you put your earnings into a retirement savings plan, all 100 cents of each dollar goes to work for you. And as long as the money stays in the account, it can continue to work for you without any interference from the tax man.

The Wonderful World of Retirement Plans

There are basically two kinds of pretax retirement plans: the kind your company provides for you (known as an employer-sponsored plan or Registered Pension Plan) and the kind you provide for yourself (known as an individual plan or Registered Retirement Savings Plan).

Over the next few pages, I'm going to describe how these work. Regardless of your status—that is, whether you are self-employed or on a company payroll—I suggest you read about both types of accounts. After all, self-employed people do wind up working for companies sometimes. And in this era of corporate restructuring, company people all too often suddenly find themselves self-employed. What's more, even if you are lucky enough to have a secure job with a company that offers a good retirement plan, opening an individual retirement plan of your own still might make sense for you. So please don't skip over a section just because you don't think it applies to your situation right now.

How Employer-Sponsored Retirement Plans Work

According to Statistics Canada, more than 5 million Canadians belonged to registered pension plans in 1998. Of these, the majority, almost 4,373,000 people, belonged to defined-benefit plans. That means they know the precise formula that will be used to determine their retirement benefit, but they do not know precisely how much they and their employers will have to contribute to achieve that benefit.

Fewer than 10 percent, about 636,000, Canadians belonged to defined-contribution plans, also called money-purchase plans. With this type of plan, employees know precisely how much money they and their employers contribute every month, but they don't know exactly how much they will ultimately receive. The benefits they receive depend on the amount of money they contribute and the returns generated by money in the plan.

Recent legislation and tax and accounting rules have made defined-benefit plans more complicated to administer. Although most people currently belong to defined-benefit plans, the majority of employers that start employee pension plans now choose a defined-contribution plan, because it's simpler to administer.

Up to a specified amount, employee contributions to Registered Pension Plans (RPPs) are tax-free. The most important detail that you need to know about your pension plan is the maximum amount that you can contribute every year to your plan.

TAX-FREE RETIREMENT SAVING

There are three types of defined-benefit plan, which I'll discuss in more detail in the next section. Regardless of the type of plan, however, the combined contributions of the employer and employee are tax-deductible up to a specified amount.

Federal legislation that governs pension contributions is aimed at providing a fair and equal opportunity for all working Canadians, as they save for their retirement, to enjoy the same tax advantages. That means that an employee who belongs to a defined-benefit plan should not be able to make a larger tax-free contribution to her pension than a person who belongs to a defined-contribution plan or a self-employed individual administering her own pension.

As a rule of thumb, individuals in Canada can contribute up to 18 percent of their income to a maximum of $13,500 tax-free to their pension plans.

If you belong to a defined-benefit plan, there is a fairly complicated formula for determining how much you can contribute tax-free. More important, you will receive a statement every year based on this calculation that tells you how much *more* you can contribute, tax-free, to your own Registered Retirement Savings Plan. This amount is called your pension adjustment (PA).

DEFINED-BENEFIT PLANS

As I mentioned, there are three types of defined-benefit pension plans:

- Flat-Benefit Plans
- Career-Average Plans
- Final-Average Plans

About 18 percent of Canadians belong to a flat-benefit plan. The rest belong to either a career-average or a final-average plan.

Flat-Benefit Plans. These plans are most common among unionized employees who receive wages at a uniform level. In such a plan, you receive a specified number of dollars for each year of service. If the specified amount per year is $20, for example, and you retire after 30 years of service, you would receive $600 a month ($20 x 30).

These plans are simple to administer. Usually all contributions are made by the employer. And you receive the benefit in addition to Old Age Security and Canada Pension Plan/Quebec Pension Plan benefits. However, the benefits are calculated according to the value of the dollar today. Unless regular increases are negotiated, inflation can erode their value.

Career-Average Plans. Employees usually contribute a fixed percentage of their salary to this type of plan. The benefit is then calculated as a percentage, usually around 2 percent, of their career earnings.

If you worked for 20 years, for example, with average monthly earnings of $2,000, and you were eligible to receive 2 percent of your earnings for each year of service in the plan, you would calculate your monthly pension benefit like this: 2% x $2,000 x 20 = $800.

These plans can be readily integrated with OAS and CPP/QPP benefits to the maximum advantage of the employee. Many companies also regularly change the year on which the pension formula is calculated. If the company moves the year to 2001, for example, your service prior to 2001 will be calculated on your 2001 earnings rather than your actual salary during those preceding years.

Final-Average Plans. Instead of basing the benefit calculation on all your years of service, final-average plans base the calculation on a specified period, usually the average of the best five consecutive years of earnings in the last 10 years of employment or the average of the best three consecutive years of earnings in the last five years of employment. Employees often contribute a percentage of their salary to these plans, while employer contributions vary according to such factors as investment yield, mortality, and employee turnover.

These plans protect employees somewhat against inflation, and they're easily integrated with OAS and CPP/QPP benefits. But if your earnings drop as you near retirement, you may end up with a lower pension benefit.

DEFINED-CONTRIBUTION PLANS OR MONEY-PURCHASE PLANS

With a defined-contribution plan, your employer contributes a certain percentage of your income, usually equivalent to your contribution. You have some choice over the way in which the funds are invested. It's a fairly important choice, because the performance of the underlying investments determines how much money you receive at retirement.

A defined-contribution plan shifts the risk of poor investment performance from the employer to the employee. If investments don't do well within a defined-benefit plan, the employer is going to have to contribute more in order to ensure you get the promised benefits. In a defined-contribution plan, if the investments don't do well, you are going to have to tighten your belt—the employer is off the hook.

ELIGIBILITY AND MAXIMUM ALLOWABLE PENSION

Pension legislation varies from province to province, but in most cases, employees have to work for the same employer for at least two years before they become eligible for an employer-sponsored pension plan.

Under the rules governing Registered Pension Plans, an employee can receive a maximum of 2 percent of her best three-year-average earnings, times the number of years of service, not to exceed $1,722 for each year of service.

VESTING AND PORTABILITY

Vesting is a term used to describe an employee's eligibility for the portion of her pension savings contributed by her employer. Until that portion is vested, you are not eligible for any pension earned by your employer's contribution.

In Alberta, British Columbia, and New Brunswick, vesting occurs after five years of service. In other provinces, except Newfoundland, it occurs after two years. In Newfoundland, an employee must be 45 years old with 10 years of service before her employer's contributions become vested.

Most jurisdictions stipulate that you can transfer your vested pension benefits to another financial vehicle if you move to another company or quit working before you reach retirement age. Usually, your vested pension funds are transferred into a locked-in retirement account (LIRA).

DEFERRED PROFIT-SHARING PLANS (DPSP)

Some companies set up a trust, registered with the Canada Customs and Revenue Agency, for some or all of their employees, into which the employer deposits cash contributions out of business profits. These contributions vest with the eligible employee after two years. The employee's share of the contribution is deposited tax-free, and it grows tax-free until the employee withdraws the money.

On behalf of each member of the DPSP, the employer cannot contribute more than 18 percent of the employee's salary or $6,750, whichever is less. If the employee leaves the company after DPSP payments have vested, the money must be paid to the employee as a lump sum or in periodic payments over 10 years or less. Alternatively, if the employee wants to continue sheltering the funds from taxes in a DPSP, the money must be transferred directly into another employer's pension plan or into the employee's RRSP.

If Your Company Doesn't Have a Retirement Plan

In my view, companies that don't offer retirement plans are doing their employees a disservice. I happen to believe that employers have a moral obligation to provide programs that allow workers to secure their own financial futures by contributing to tax-advantaged savings plans.

Some employers—especially the owners of small businesses—complain that they simply can't afford to offer such programs. In recent years, however, the cost of setting up and administering retirement plans has dropped to the point where even small businesses should be able to manage it. Indeed, when you figure everything in, it's probably less expensive for an employer to set up a retirement plan than to replace a fed-up worker who has quit to join a competitor who cares about his or her people's futures!

As an employee, you should make sure your boss knows how unhappy you are about not having a retirement plan. You might add that, if she expects you to make a long-term commitment to her company, she'd better do something about putting this sort of benefit in place.

That being said, it's still entirely possible to love your job even though your company does not now and never will provide you with a retirement plan. If that describes you, don't worry. You don't have to quit. But you do have to do something.

It's quite simple, really. If your employer won't provide a retirement plan for you, you must provide one for yourself. In other words . . .

You should open a Registered Retirement Savings Plan.

Registered Retirement Savings Plans

A working Canadian can contribute the lesser of 18 percent of her earned income or $13,500 per year to an RRSP. The contribution can be deducted from your income for tax purposes, and it grows within the RRSP tax-free.

Think of an RRSP as a briefcase. A briefcase keeps its contents protected from outside elements. In the case of an RRSP, the briefcase protects your money from the sticky-fingered tentacles of the government.

You pay no taxes on money held in an RRSP. And when you first put the money into an RRSP, you can deduct it from your total annual income when you're calculating your income tax for the year.

That means you pay less tax. And your money grows tax-free.

Outside an RRSP, for example, your money may earn $100, and you'd pay, say, $25 in tax, leaving you with $75. Inside an RRSP, your money may earn $100, and you'd pay no tax. So you still have $100 left to reinvest.

Even if you're employed by a company with a pension plan, you can still shelter a portion of your income within an RRSP.

You can figure out how much you can contribute to your RRSP by checking last year's tax assessment from the CCRA. If you can't find your assessment, you can call the CCRA hot line in your area, listed in the blue pages of your phone book. (Have your social insurance number handy.)

If you haven't used all of your allowable RRSP contribution room, you can carry it forward indefinitely. But the sooner you invest as much as you can within your RRSP, the sooner it can begin to grow tax-free, and the longer it can grow before you retire.

EARNED INCOME

The CCRA defines earned income as:

- Employment income
- Self-employment income after expenses and losses
- Rental income after expenses and losses
- Alimony
- Royalties

The following are not considered earned income:

- Investment income
- Pension income
- RRSP or RRIF income

FIVE-STAR TIP: *You get a tax deduction equivalent to your contribution to an RRSP. After that, all the interest, dividends, and capital gains compound themselves tax-free, as long they remain in the RRSP.*

THE TWO KINDS OF RRSPS

There are basically two kinds of RRSPs:

Managed RRSPs. In a managed RRSP, the plan holder invests in any of a variety of segregated pooled funds or mutual funds. These funds are held in trust under the plan and administered by the fund company, trust company, life insurance company, chartered bank, credit union, or investment dealer. Some people rely on a financial institution to invest the money in their RRSP in such instruments as Guaranteed Investment Certificates (GICs) and savings accounts. Managed funds are by far the more popular choice in Canada.

Self-directed RRSPs. People who set up a self-directed RRSP select their own investments to put in it. A financial institution or investment dealer must administer the RRSP, in return for an annual fee of about $125 a year.

A self-directed RRSP gives you much greater flexibility in selecting the types of investments you want to hold, and you can move your money around within your RRSP as you see fit. You can also maximize the foreign content within your RRSP. (Currently it's restricted to 30 percent of the book value of your plan.)

In many cases, people select the investments within their self-directed plan with the help of a financial advisor. Qualified investments range from stocks and bonds, cash held on deposit in a bank, GICs and mutual fund units, to call options, Bankers Acceptances, and mortgages.

WHAT IF I OWN MY OWN BUSINESS?

First, let me say congratulations! I say this because I admire entrepreneurs and because, as a business owner, you are eligible for the best retirement accounts around. Second, let me urge you to avoid a mistake that too many business owners make—deciding that setting up a retirement plan is too much of a bother.

Remember, you are in business to build a financially secure future for yourself and your family—and how can you do that unless you pay yourself first? As a business owner, the best way to pay yourself first is by setting up an RRSP.

If you are among the fortunate few small-business owners who earn more than $100,000 a year, you should consider setting up an

Individual Pension Plan (IPP). These are more complex than an RRSP, but they permit higher tax-deductible contributions, so you can save more for retirement.

THE IMPORTANCE OF "MAXING OUT" YOUR RETIREMENT PLAN

Whatever your maximum allowable RRSP contribution happens to be, that's the amount you should be putting in. This is called "maxing out" your retirement plan, and it is by far the single most important thing you can do to create a secure financial future. There is nothing I know of that is better at transforming otherwise ordinary Canadians into financially secure individuals than the simple act of each month putting as much of their paycheque as they are allowed directly into an RRSP.

It's reported that only about 40 percent of Canadians who are eligible to invest within an RRSP even bother to do so, and of those, only 25 percent contribute the maximum eligible amount. Why? In a word, ignorance. I am convinced that if people knew what they were missing out on—how they were cheating themselves out of a secure and comfortable future—hardly anyone would fail to take full advantage of their RRSP.

Here's a simple example that made a tremendous impact on me.

TWO WOMEN, SAME PLAN, BUT A $280,000 DIFFERENCE!

Last year, I held what is known in the investment industry as a Pension Plan Rollover seminar for a local company. This is a seminar where you teach workers who are about to change employers or retire how to "roll over" the money they've saved in their company's Registered Pension Plan into an RRSP.

After this particular class, two women came into my office. One was named Betty; the other, Lynn. Both had worked for the company for more than 35 years. Indeed, they were best friends who had started work at this company the very same week.

I met with Lynn first, and after I reviewed her retirement plan, which included her company's pension plan and her own RRSP, I was able to tell her that she was in great shape to retire. Her total retirement savings amounted to $530,000—enough to produce plenty of income for her to live comfortably for the rest of her life. Not surprisingly, Lynn left my office with a big smile on her face.

Betty, by contrast, wore a worried expression when she came in. "You know," she told me, "even though Lynn and I started at the same time and have made close to the same amount of money, I'm not in nearly as good as shape as she is financially."

"Oh, really," I said. "And why is that?"

Betty then showed me the documentation for her company pension plan and her own RRSP. Her total accumulated savings amounted to a little less than $250,000. Not bad, but not nearly as good as her friend's $530,000. "David," she said with a sigh, "I can remember it like it was yesterday. Sitting down at lunch 35 years ago, Lynn and I discussed how much of our income we were going to put into our pension plan and RRSPs. Lynn told me she was going to max hers out and put away the full 18 percent. She figured it might hurt the first few months, but after that she wouldn't really notice it. I said, 'Eighteen percent? No way! That's just too much.' I figured I'd start with maybe 4 percent and, when I got a raise, I'd increase my contributions."

Betty shook her head ruefully. "You know what? So many raises came and went, but I never got around to increasing the size of my RRSP contribution. There always seemed to be some new expense that came first—a new car, a special vacation, college costs. Now Lynn gets to retire and I have go find another job. I'll probably need to work for another 15 years. Pretty stupid, huh?"

My heart went out to Betty. But there wasn't much I could do. Don't make the same mistake she did. Maximize your retirement contribution now.

WHAT DO I DO WITH MY CONTRIBUTIONS?

Okay, so you've decided what type of RRSP makes the most sense for you, and you've figured out how much you are going to contribute to it this year. Now comes the really big decision.

As I noted earlier, deciding where and how to invest your retirement money probably is the most important financial decision you ever will make.

Some of you may find that baffling. I can hear you asking, "Haven't I just made that decision? I'm investing my money in an RRSP."

No, you are not. An RRSP is not an investment. It is, rather, just a holding tank for your retirement money.

People are often confused about this. They will tell you that they've gone to the bank and "bought an RRSP." Sorry, but you can't "buy" an RRSP. That's like saying you bought a chequing account.

What you do with an RRSP is this: You open it, and then you put money into it, and then you inform the bank (or brokerage or plan administrator) *how you want the funds invested*.

I once explained this to a class of mine, only to have a woman named Brenda stand up and tell me that I didn't know what I was talking about. "I've been buying RRSPs at my bank for years," Brenda insisted.

When I asked her how she had invested her RRSP funds, she shook her head angrily. "You're not listening to me, young man," she snapped. "I said I *bought* an RRSP, I don't take risks with my money with foolish investments."

"Brenda," I said, "I'll bet you 10 bucks that your RRSP money is invested in a GIC that's paying you less than 5 percent a year."

"You're on," she replied.

As it turned out, I was wrong. When she brought her RRSP statements to my office, I discovered that she was *not* invested in a GIC. Rather, she was invested in nothing! It's true. When we called Brenda's bank to find out what exactly her RRSP funds had been doing for the last 10 years, the officer who answered the phone told us the money was sitting in a savings account.

"Great," I said. "And what rate of return is the savings account paying her?"

The bank officer stammered a bit. "Well," he said finally, "it's not actually paying her anything. It's just a place where we hold money until the client tells us how they want it invested."

Can you believe it? Brenda had her RRSP money sitting in a holding account earning nothing for 10 years! In other words, when you figure in inflation, her next egg had shrunk, not grown.

If you think that's dumb, you are right. The only thing dumber is that there are literally thousands of Canadians walking around right now thinking they "own" RRSPs, when in fact they have no idea how their retirement money is invested or what it is earning. Equally bad is the fact that thousands of Canadians really don't know what their retirement money is invested in.

Please, please don't be one of these people. Pull out all your RRSP and/or company money-purchase plan statements right now and review them.

Make sure your retirement money is working as hard for you as you worked for it!

Don't let it sit in some miscellaneous bank account that pays you just 1 percent a year—or even worse, maybe nothing at all!

To help you make the most of your retirement money, here is a list of rules I've compiled over the years.

RULE NO. 1
WITH RETIREMENT FUNDS, INVEST FOR GROWTH!

This may strike you as painfully obvious, but it's so important that I think it's worth emphasizing. All too often, women come into my office and show me retirement plans that are invested in GICs or other fixed-rate securities. Now, with their guaranteed returns, GICs are perfectly appropriate if your goal is what the professionals call "short-term capital preservation"—that is, you've got a bunch of money that you're going to need to use sometime soon, and you want to make sure nothing happens to it in the meantime.

Unless you are planning to retire in the next year or two, however, your goal with your retirement account is not short-term capital preservation. It's long-term growth. So don't make this mistake. Review your retirement plan options carefully and make sure your choices include at least some growth-oriented investments.

If you are at all unsure about what the best available investment options may be for you, seek professional guidance. Speak with your company's benefits director or call your personal financial advisor and ask him or her to go over your retirement-plan options with you. The Bach Group does this sort of thing for our clients all the time . . . at no cost. If your financial advisor isn't willing to review your RRSP investment options, you probably should look for a new advisor.

WHY INVEST FOR GROWTH?

Many people make the crucial mistake of thinking that, when it comes to their retirement money, the thing to do is play it safe. They couldn't be more wrong. Remember back in Step One, on page 31, when we showed that, because of inflation, the cost of living has been climbing steadily at an average of slightly more than 3 percent a year? Playing it safe will not allow you to beat that rate and, if your retirement account doesn't grow faster than inflation, you are not going to have very much to live on 20 or 30 or 40 years from now.

To secure your future, in other words, what you've got to do with your retirement money is go for growth. Yes, seeking growth requires you to invest in stocks, and they are generally more volatile and riskier over the short term than some other types of investments. But over the long term—and that's what we're concerned with here, the long term—they can be significantly more rewarding.

According to data compiled by Canadian MoneySaver, stock gains in the next decade are likely to average about 7.5 percent a year after inflation. Fixed-income securities like Treasury bonds will yield less than 5 percent.

The obvious lesson here is that you should invest a significant portion of your retirement money in stocks or mutual funds that invest in stocks. How big a portion? Well, that really depends on your age, your personal goals, and your willingness to accept a certain amount of volatility.

THE VALUE OF A HYPOTHETICAL
$100,000 INVESTMENT AFTER 25 YEARS

$267,000	$429,000	$685,000	$1,083,000	$1,700,000
4%	6%	8%	10%	12%

Rate of Return

ASSET ALLOCATION: CREATING THE PERFECT BALANCE

Figuring out the right mix of growth investments vs. fixed investments is what is known in the investment industry as determining your asset allocation. Asset allocation is a fancy way of saying, "You need to put your eggs in different baskets." This may not sound like a big deal, but it is. In fact, it is a huge deal. *Studies indicate that more than 91 percent of all investment returns are attributable to proper asset allocation, as opposed to clever stock selection or good market timing.*

The first step in determining the asset allocation of your retirement plan is to decide how much of your money you want to put into growth vehicles (basically, stocks and stock-based mutual funds) and how much you want to put into safer but slower-growing fixed-income securities (basically, bonds or bond funds).

I use the following rule of thumb to help determine how much money a particular individual should invest in stocks vs. bonds:

Take your age and subtract it from 110. The number you get is the percentage of your assets that you should put in stocks or stock-based mutual funds. The rest of your assets should go into something less volatile, such as bonds or fixed-rate securities.

For example, let's say you are 40 years old. Following the rule, you subtract 40 from 110, which leaves you with 70. That means you should consider putting about 70 percent of your retirement fund into stock-related investments, with the remaining 30 percent going into bonds.

Obviously, the older you are, the smaller your stock investment will be. (According to the rule, a 50-year-old should have 60 percent of her assets in stocks, while a 30-year-old should have 80 percent.) This makes sense, since the closer you are to retirement age, the less risk you want to incur.

While this process may sound simplistic, it is widely used and based on a theory created by an acclaimed scholar named Dr. Harry Markowitz, who was awarded a Nobel Prize in economics for his work on modern portfolio theory.

Once you have determined the ratio of stocks vs. bonds that is right for you, you will need to figure out more specifically what kinds of investments you should make in each category. This is something you should consider discussing in detail with a trusted and knowledgeable advisor. (Later in this chapter, I'll give you some tips on how to find a terrific financial advisor.)

IT'S TIME TO DO YOUR OWN RESEARCH

You should also do your own research. Today with the Internet, gathering information about fund performance is a snap. There are countless websites that offer financial information. I have personally visited more than 500 of them. To make it easier for you to find a good financial website, I've listed some of my favourites below where you can review everything from stocks to bonds to mutual funds and learn a lot about overall financial planning:

www.morningstar.ca Morningstar is the company that really started it all in terms of ranking mutual funds, and its website is probably the best one of its type around. The Morningstar site not only allows you to review your portfolio and find top funds quickly and easily, it also provides general descriptions of the funds, along with an in-depth analysis that is nothing short of incredible. One of the things I like best about this site is a page called Fund Quickrank, which allows you to screen funds quickly based on their performance, their Morningstar ratings, or their volatility. To find Fund Quickrank, simply go to the Morningstar home page and look on the left side of the page, under "Funds." There you'll see a link to Fund Quickrank. Click over to the page and it will take you through the process in three easy steps. You can also screen for stocks on this site.

www.canadianmoneysaver.ca This website provides practical investment advice researched, used, and described by more than 60 financial practitioners, including financial planners, tax experts, portfolio managers, lawyers, and successful investors from across Canada. For less than $25 a year, you can subscribe to the entire range of services, which include expert advice, an investment library, and money tips.

www.globeinvestor.com Administered by *The Globe and Mail,* this site delivers a wealth of financial and investment information. One useful feature allows you to build your own portfolio of mutual funds and stocks and follow their performance from month to month and year to year.

http://ca.finance.yahoo.com Yahoo Finance is probably the most popular financial site on the web, and for good reason. This is a true full-service financial portal, offering stock analysis, portfolio tracking, message boards, research, and on-line bill paying. To get detailed information on mutual funds, click on the link labelled "Mutual Funds." It will take you to a list of all the different types of fund categories.

From there, you can quickly run a search. Once you've found a fund that interests you, a click on the "Profile" link next to the fund's symbol will summon up a quick analysis courtesy of Morningstar.

www.financenter.com This site offers the best collection of financial tools anywhere on the Internet. There are calculators for just about everything you could imagine—from how long it will take you to pay down your credit card debt to how much will it cost you to retire. Wondering if you should lease a car vs. buy one? Want to figure out how much of a house you can afford? One of Financenter's calculators will tell you. When you need to crunch numbers, this is the place to go.

www.quicken.com Quicken gets it. It's that simple. This company makes the best retirement and expense-tracking software in the world, and its website is equally phenomenal. It's both easy to use and well integrated—not only with Quicken's personal-finance software, but with just about everyone else's as well.

RULE NO.2
CONSIDER BORROWING THE MONEY YOU NEED TO MAKE YOUR MAXIMUM RRSP CONTRIBUTION.

People who don't have enough cash on hand to maximize their RRSP contributions should consider borrowing the money.

When we borrow money to invest outside an RRSP, the interest on the loan is tax deductible. Interest on money borrowed for RRSPs, however, is not deductible. But it can still be worth borrowing, as long as you can pay back the loan within a year. The longer it takes to pay back the money, the less benefit you'll receive.

Most financial institutions will lend you the money at the prime interest rate, providing you purchase your RRSP through that institution. At a rate of 7.5 percent, for example, a $5,000 loan for an RRSP would cost $375 in interest over one year. If it earns a 5 percent return, your borrowed $5,000 will generate $250. So your real cost of borrowing is only $125. If you're in the top tax bracket, you will receive a refund of $2,500. Even if you're in a lower tax bracket, you'll still save more than $1,300 in tax. And your money grows tax-free within your RRSP. So the cost of the loan is worth it.

> ### RULE NO. 3
> TRY TO AVOID WITHDRAWING MONEY FROM YOUR RRSP.

If you cash in all or part of your RRSP, then the amount you withdraw will be added to your income for that year and will be taxed as ordinary income.

Meanwhile, the financial institution that administers your RRSP will withhold a percentage of the money you withdraw and send it to the CCRA. This withheld money is simply a prepaid tax. The size of the withholding tax depends on the amount you withdraw.

- up to $5,000, you pay 10 percent withholding tax;
- $5,001 to $15,000, you pay 20 percent;
- over $15,000, you pay 30 percent.

For this reason, you're better off withdrawing $5,000 or less at a time. This allows you to keep more cash until you file your next tax return, although Ottawa will demand that you pay the tax when it comes due, whether you have the money or not. The best option is not to withdraw the money at all.

The point is, none of us knows what the future holds. Ideally, your RRSP should be the last place you turn to for money. If you can, leave your retirement money alone until you are ready to retire.

> ### RULE NO. 4
> CONSOLIDATE YOUR ACCOUNTS.

Many people remember Grandma's advice about not putting all your eggs in one basket, but they often misunderstand it. Not putting your eggs in one basket means diversifying your risk—putting your money into different kinds of assets, such as stocks, bonds, mutual funds, and other investment vehicles. It doesn't mean opening an RRSP at a different bank or brokerage firm each year.

Every day I meet people who have four, five, or six—sometimes more than a dozen—different RRSPs. The record in my office currently is held by a client named Ben. Ben always had been what we call a GIC shopper. Every year he would literally spend days going from bank to bank to find the best rate on GICs for his new RRSP. The trouble was, he was so focused on "buying" his next RRSP that he never thought about the pitiful rates his old RRSPs were earning. (Those "terrific" rates he got lasted only for a year; when his "premium" GICs matured, the bank would roll them over into new certificates that didn't pay nearly as much.) When I met with Ben he had over $160,000 in GICs at 18 different banks—earning an average of less than 5 percent a year! I showed him how much better off he would be consolidating all his GICs into one RRSP and then managing his money for a combination of growth and income.

The fact is, there is simply no way you can do a good job managing your retirement accounts if they are spread all over the place. If that's what you've done, consider consolidating them into one self-directed RRSP. Not only can you completely diversify your investments within a single RRSP but also you'll find it much easier to keep track of everything.

RULE NO. 5
CHOOSE THE BENEFICIARY OF YOUR RRSPs WISELY, AND
NAME THE BENEFICIARY IN YOUR WILL.

If you die with an RRSP, your estate has to pay tax on the accumulated value of the assets within the plan, unless you specifically designate your husband or your dependent children as the beneficiaries of your RRSP.

The tax liability on even a modest RRSP can be substantial, and your survivors may not have the financial means to pay it. This makes it all the more important to make sure you specify that your husband or children should inherit your RRSP.

If your RRSP passes to your husband or a spousal trust, the proceeds of the inherited plan can be transferred into your husband's RRSP, tax-free. If your dependent children or grandchildren inherit your RRSP, they can avoid paying tax if they use the proceeds to purchase an annuity effective until they reach the age of 18. If the youngster is financially dependent because of a physical or mental infirmity, the inherited proceeds can be transferred to an RRSP.

In all cases, you should specify your intentions regarding your RRSP in your will. This gives the executor the authority to transfer your RRSP as you specify, in the event of your death.

Unless you live in Quebec, you can also name the beneficiary of your RRSP directly in your RRSP. If you take this route, you should still insert a clause into the RRSP that gives your executor the authority to transfer your RRSP to your spouse's RRSP if you die.

However, I recommend that you specify your RRSP beneficiary in your will. If you have to change the name of the beneficiary at a later date (after a divorce, for example), it requires much less paperwork to do it in your will.

While we're on the subject of beneficiaries, if your husband has been married before, you might want to make sure his ex still isn't listed as the beneficiary on any of his RRSPs. I've seen this happen more than a half dozen times in the last five years—and not just on RRSPs, but on insurance policies too!

In addition, you also should make sure you have a "contingent beneficiary" listed on your RRSP—that is, a second choice in case your primary beneficiary dies before (or at the same time as) you do. For example, let's say you are married with children, and you and your husband are killed together in a car accident. If you had listed your kids as contingent beneficiaries on your RRSP, they would automatically get control over your retirement money. (They could then take the proceeds and pay tax on them or buy an annuity, as I mentioned earlier.) If, on the other hand, you hadn't listed a contingent beneficiary, the courts might be forced to have your accounts distributed, which would mean subjecting them to tax.

RULE NO. 6
MAXIMIZE THE FOREIGN CONTENT IN YOUR RRSP.

RRSP legislation allows you to hold up to 30 percent of the assets in your RRSP in the form of foreign stocks, bonds, mutual funds, and other instruments. You should try to take full advantage of this capacity. Here's why:

All the money that's invested in Canada adds up to only 3 percent of all the money in the world. That means 97 percent of the action goes on somewhere else. If you want to participate in the opportunities available in the global investment marketplace, you have to look beyond Canada for promising investments.

Diversification is another reason to maximize your foreign content. Just as you don't want to put all your money into a single stock, why should you invest all of your money in a single country? Markets perform differently in different countries, at different times. Between 1995 and 1999, for example, the best-performing equity market in the world was in Finland, with an average return of almost 60 percent a year. Over the same period, Canada generated a return of about 21 percent, the ninth best performer in the developed world.

Currency rates are another reason to invest outside Canada. In 1991, the Canadian dollar was worth US89¢. Three years later, it was worth US72¢. It's now worth about US65¢. If you held a U.S. investment over that period, and all it did was break even, you would have made money, because your U.S. dollars would be worth more than they were when you made the investment.

RULE NO. 7
DON'T SHORTCHANGE YOURSELF.

Whatever else you do in your financial life, please take retirement planning seriously. I know I sound like I'm preaching here, but as I said before, there is really nothing you can do that will have more impact on your future financial security than maximizing your contributions to an RRSP and then making sure that money works really hard for you.

The fact is, if you are not currently maxing out your retirement contributions—to a company-sponsored plan, an RRSP or both—you are living beyond your means. This is not meant to be harsh; it is meant to be a wake-up call. Contributing to a retirement plan is not a luxury; it is a necessity! Please give yourself the opportunity to retire as early as you would like, with enough money to have all the fun you deserve.

BASKET THREE:

YOUR DREAM BASKET

Pretend for a moment that you had a magic lamp with a genie inside. As we all know, genies are obliged to grant their masters (or mistresses) three wishes. So what would yours be? If you could have—or be—anything you wanted, what would you wish for?

That may seem like a childish question, but it's not. What it's really asking is something quite important—namely, what dreams of yours currently are going unfulfilled? Do you long to see the world? Quit your job? Start your own business? Devote yourself to some charitable organization?

It is one of the sadder facts of life that most people stop dreaming as they get older. The number-one reason, I'm sorry to say, is money. For the most part, it takes money to make our dreams come true, and most of us simply don't have enough. Lacking the necessary resources, we find ourselves frustrated; eventually, we stop bothering to dream at all.

That's the bad news. The good news is, it doesn't have to be that way. You *can* make your dreams come true . . . and you won't need a magic lamp—or its modern-day equivalent, a winning lottery ticket—to do it. Nor will you be restricted to just three wishes.

To make your dreams a reality, you have to do only two things: identify what your dreams are and create a plan to finance them. That may sound pretty obvious, but you know what? Most people never do it.

Smart Women, however, aren't like most people. So let's get started . . .

Recapture Your Wide-Eyed Optimism

You know why so many people play the lottery? It's because, for the price of just a dollar or two, they get the opportunity to dream. Unfortunately, that's generally all a person gets. The reality is that you have a better chance of being hit by lightning than actually winning a lottery.

Even though most of us know that, we play anyway. That's how powerful our need to dream is. Dreams energize us. They add passion to our lives. It's hard to be depressed when you are excited about your future, and that's what dreams do: They make us believe that tomorrow is going to be better than today.

Think back for a moment and recall, if you can, what it was like when you were a kid. Can you remember a time in your life when you believed you could be anything and have anything you wanted? Do you remember what it felt like not to have to worry about bills and work and family responsibilities? Try to imagine that for a moment. Pretend you are a little girl who feels she can have or be anything she wants. What would it be? Who would you become?

Try to pursue these questions more deeply than you did in Step Three, when you were coming up with goals for yourself. We are not talking here about earning 10 percent more income or losing 10 pounds. We are talking about *dreams*. Do you want to climb the Himalayas? Study painting in Paris? Open a women's shelter?

Remember, you are trying to be young and imaginative like you were when you were a kid, not stressed out and conventional like you are now. (Just kidding!) Seriously, though, what do you want to see happen in your life? What's missing? Where do you want to go? Perhaps your dream is to own your own home. Or to take off from work for a whole month and not call the office once! Maybe you would like to write a book.

Whatever your dreams happen to be, I want you to write them down. On the following Dream Sheet, list your five top dreams. If you don't have the time to do this right now, then set up a time later to meet with yourself and create your dream list. That's right—make an appointment with yourself to reserve somewhere between 30 and 60 minutes in which you will write down the dreams that excite you. And don't make excuses. Your dreams are worth half an hour of your time.

DREAMS

Designing and Implementing the Fun Factor!

THERE ARE TWO PARTS TO THIS EXERCISE:

- Ten blanks for writing down your most important dreams
- A form in which you specify your five most important dreams over your lifetime

STEPS:

- On this page, below, fill in the 10 blanks with as many dreams as possible that you want to accomplish during your lifetime.
- On the next page, specify:
    1. Five Most Important Dreams
    2. Make Specific, Measurable, and Provable (i.e., How much will it cost?)
    3. Immediate Action in the Next 48 Hours
    4. With Whom Will You Share Your Dreams?
    5. What Values Does It Help You Accomplish?
    6. What Challenges Will You Face?
    7. Strategies to Overcome Anticipated Challenges

1.   6.

2.   7.

3.   8.

4.   9.

5.   10.

FIVE MOST IMPORTANT DREAMS	MAKE SPECIFIC, MEASURABLE, AND PROVABLE	IMMEDIATE ACTION IN THE NEXT 48 HOURS	WITH WHOM WILL YOU SHARE YOUR DREAMS?	WHAT VALUES DOES IT HELP YOU ACCOMPLISH?	WHAT CHALLENGES WILL YOU FACE?	STRATEGIES TO OVERCOME ANTICIPATED CHALLENGES
1						
2						
3						
4						
5						

Making Your Dreams a Real Part of Your Life

Once you have written down your top five dreams, the next step is to spend a little time thinking about what it would take to make them a reality. How much money will be required? How long will it take you to save that much?

The more defined your dreams are, the easier it will be to estimate what it will cost to realize them. You definitely should spend a little time on this for, as I explained back in Step Three, the key to getting what you want in life is to be specific about it. Once you have a good idea of what it will take, you can determine how much you need to put away each month. By putting money away each month, you will feel your dream come closer to reality, and as it does, you will find yourself getting more and more excited about your future.

WHAT IF I DON'T HAVE ANY SPECIFIC DREAMS RIGHT NOW?

I usually suggest to my clients that they should fund a Dream Basket whether they are able to come up with a list of dreams or not. After all, just because you don't have a specific dream right now doesn't mean you never will. And wouldn't it be nice to have some money already put aside when something comes along (as it inevitably will) that falls into a "dream" category?

Sometimes dreams are not what we expect. I once suggested to a young woman named Lisa that she start funding a Dream Basket even though she didn't have any specific dream in mind. Six months later, Lisa's dog Dexter got really sick. Without an operation that cost $1,500, Dexter would die. Lisa immediately turned to her Dream Basket for the money, and today Dexter is wagging his tail and doing whatever else happy dogs do. As Lisa explained to me later, "I had no idea what my dream was at the time I started putting money aside, but when Dexter got sick, I knew that my dream was to help him live. If I hadn't funded my Dream Basket, I would have lost Dexter. My Dream Basket kept him alive!"

How to Fund Your Dream Basket

Your Dream Basket is the place where you put aside the money you will need to make your dreams (other than security or retirement) come true. You should fund it the same way you fund your retirement basket—that is, with a fixed percentage of your income that you automatically contribute every month. As I said earlier, making the process automatic is the best way I know to ensure that you actually stick to your savings plan. Set up a systematic investment plan, in which a set amount of money either is deducted directly from your paycheque or is transferred from your chequing account the day after you are paid.

The size of your regular contribution should be determined by the likely cost of your dreams. As a rule of thumb, it probably should be at least 5 percent of your after-tax income (which is to say, a lot less than the 18 percent of pretax income that you should be putting into your retirement basket). While 5 percent of your after-tax income isn't a huge amount, it is certainly big enough to create a very powerful long-term savings vehicle. Needless to say, if your dreams happen to be of the particularly expensive variety, you will want to put away a larger percentage of your income. The key here is to realize that it's up to you; the more money you put away, the faster your dreams will become a reality.

The form in which you keep this money will depend on how long you expect it will be before you're ready to make your dream a reality. Some dreams require just a year or two of planning and saving; others may take half a lifetime. Over the next few pages, I will discuss a variety of different investment vehicles and explain which are right for what time frame.

In order to keep things simple (and there's certainly no point in making them more complicated than they need to be), you should think of your dreams in terms of how long it will likely take you to realize them. Specifically, you should categorize them as being either short-term, mid-term, or long-term dreams. Short-term dreams are those that can be accomplished within a year or two. (An example might be getting yourself in a position to be able to take a luxury vacation.) Mid-term dreams take a bit longer to fulfill—say, between two and five years. (A typical mid-term dream might be having the funds to put a down payment on a house). Long-term dreams require even more time than that. Some (such as being able to quit your job so you can move to Tahiti and live on the beach) may take decades.

Obviously, you don't fund a short-term dream with a long-term investment strategy. Here are my recommendations for the best ways to construct your Dream Basket.

FOR SHORT-TERM DREAMS
(LESS THAN TWO YEARS)

If you're saving to finance a short-term dream, you need to keep your funds as safe and liquid as possible. As far as I'm concerned, that means investing in cash or cash equivalents. In this case I consider three kinds of cash investments to be appropriate: money market funds, guaranteed investment certificates, and Treasury bills.

Money Market Funds. A money market fund is a mutual fund that invests in short-term securities (typically, federal and provincial Treasury bills and senior corporate notes). Generally, buying into a money market fund requires a minimum investment of $500, and as of this writing interest rates of around 2 percent a year are not uncommon.

Deposit Accounts. Under severe competition for your money, financial institutions have come up with high-interest savings accounts. Such an account may be called a premium account, investor account, or cash performance account. Whatever the bank or trust company calls it, the bottom line remains the same: They all provide investors with a higher interest rate on their money than a conventional savings account. Unfortunately, many institutions require a hefty deposit of at least $25,000 to get a piece of the action.

Term Deposits. A term deposit involves a contract between you and the financial institution. It's usually a short-term contract, for 30 days to one year, although term deposits can extend over five years. Under the contract, you lend your money to the financial institution for a specified period. In return, the financial institution pays you a fixed rate of interest until the contract expires. In general, the longer the term, the higher the interest rate. Sometimes the interest rate on a term deposit is less than the rate on a premium savings account offered by banks. Also, you can cancel a term deposit prior to maturity, but only if you pay a penalty. There is often a substantial spread between the highest and the lowest rates offered for the same term. So shop around for the best rate of return.

Guaranteed Investment Certificates. GICs are securities that promise to pay you a given rate of return over a given period on a deposit that can range from $500 to $100,000. They're sold by trust companies and banks. GIC maturities can be as short as six months or as long as 10 years; as of this writing, rates for one-year GICs are running at about 4 percent. Unlike money market funds, GICs are federally insured by the Canadian Deposit Insurance Corporation (CDIC) up to $60,000. That's their big advantage. Their disadvantage is that if you need to get your cash out before your GIC matures, you will likely have to forfeit your interest.

FIVE-STAR TIP: *Any money that you have in a savings account, chequing account, guaranteed investment certificate (GIC), or term deposit is guaranteed up to $60,000 per institution, not per branch. If you have over $60,000 sitting in a bank, you can get around the guaranteed limit by keeping up to $60,000 in your name, up to $60,000 in your husband's name, up to $60,000 in a joint account, and up to $60,000 in an RRSP, all within the same institution and all guaranteed.*

Treasury Bills. Issued by the federal government, Treasury bills (T-bills) are fixed-income securities that can be purchased through a bank or brokerage firm. They are issued in increments of $10,000 and mature in a year or less. The main difference between a Treasury bill and a GIC is that technically T-bills do not pay interest. Rather, they are issued at a discount and then can be redeemed at full price (known as par value) when they mature. For example, if the one-year T-bill rate happens to be 5 percent, you would pay $9,500 for a certificate that a year later you could redeem for $10,000.

There are a number of reasons people like Treasury bills. For one thing, they are backed by the federal government, which makes them just about the safest investment you can buy. T-bills generally can be sold on a moment's notice simply by making a phone call, and you usually can collect your money within three days.

FOR MID-TERM DREAMS
(TWO TO FOUR YEARS)

Given the slightly longer time frame, liquidity should be less of an issue for mid-term dreams than for short-term ones. The same goes for safety. You've got a little more time to play with, so you can afford to take a bit more risk—which means you can expect a bit more reward. Not that you should take any big chances, mind you; the idea, after all, is to protect your money, not gamble with it.

With that in mind, I generally recommend mid-term dream money be invested in bonds. Although bonds are slightly less liquid and slightly more risky than cash equivalents, they are still relatively safe, and they pay better interest.

Essentially, a bond is an IOU; when you buy one, you literally are lending money to the issuer (usually a company or a government agency). The bond specifies when you will be paid back (the maturity date) and how much interest you will be paid in the interim (usually in two instalments a year).

Bonds typically are issued in increments of $1,000, $5,000, or $10,000. Maturities can be as quick as one year and as long as 30 years. The shorter the period, the less risk for the bond buyer—and the lower the interest rate.

You can invest in literally hundreds of different kinds of bonds, from super-safe government savings bonds to high-yield "junk." For our purposes, I suggest you restrict your choices to one of the following categories.

Canada Savings Bonds (CSBs). CSBs are one of the most popular savings instruments in the country. Each fall, CSBs are sold through financial institutions like banks and trust companies to Canadian residents in denominations of $100, $300, $500, $1000, $5000, and $10,000. Currently the limit on the total value of CSBs that you can purchase in one year is $100,000. They are available, within a certain purchase limit, to Canadian residents through cash purchases and payroll deduction programs. Purchasers can choose bonds that pay regular or compound interest. Interest rates for CSBs are set each year when they're issued, and are guaranteed for only one year. Each year, the CSB yield may stay the same or go up or down, depending upon the current economic climate. CSBs currently pay an annual compound rate of just 2.7 percent, and you have to hold them for three years to get even this return. After the first three months, interest is payable on a CSB up to the end of the month prior to the date when you redeem it. (Provincial governments also sell savings bonds with similar conditions and returns.)

Corporate and Municipal Bonds. While CSBs are backed by the wealth and majesty of the Canadian government, a corporate or municipal bond is only as solid as the particular company or municipality that issued it. That's not to say there aren't some very safe corporate and municipal bonds. There are. But there are also some very risky ones. Before you buy any bond, you need to check out the grade it has received from one of the major rating firms, such as Dominion Bond Rating Service, Standard & Poor's or Moody's. Your broker can give you the rating for any bond that interests you (see the chart below). At The Bach Group, we almost never buy for our clients corporate or municipal bonds that are less than A-rated. Of course, the higher the rating, the lower the interest rate. (To sell their bonds, healthier companies don't need to offer as much interest as riskier companies do.) But that's okay. The extra interest you can earn from a lower-rated bond is generally not worth the extra risk. As of this writing, rates range from 5 to 10 percent, depending on the company's creditworthiness and the bond's maturity.

KNOWING THE RATING BEFORE YOU BUY IT!

Two recognized agencies that assign credit ratings to corporate issues are Moody's and Standard & Poor's. Their investment grade rating levels, which reflect the credit quality of an issue, appear below.

RATING/QUALITY	MOODY'S	S&P
Highest grade— smallest degree of investment risk.	Aaa	AAA
High grade— slightly more risk than highest grade.	Aa1	AA+
	Aa2	AA
	Aa3	AA-
Upper medium grade— interest and principal regarded as safe, but not risk-free.	A1	A+
	A2	A
	A3	A-
Medium grade— adequate security, but susceptible to changing economic conditions.	Baa1	BBB+
	Baa2	BBB
	Baa3	BBB-

INTEREST RATES MAKE BOND PRICES FLUCTUATE

Most investment-grade bonds are fairly liquid, meaning you don't necessarily have to wait until they mature to get your money back. While you probably won't be able to get the company that issued your bond to pay you back early, you always can sell the bond to another investor. There is, of course, no guarantee that it will fetch the same price you originally paid for it. Bond prices at any given time depend on the general level of interest rates. If rates have risen since your bond was first issued, you'll probably have to sell at a bit of a discount. On the other hand, if rates have fallen, your bond will likely fetch a bit of a premium.

Of course, none of this matters if you hold your bond until it matures. Assuming that the company that issued the bond is still solvent, you will be repaid in full regardless of where interest rates are or what the market is doing.

THE SIMPLEST WAY TO INVEST IN BONDS

One of simplest ways for a nonexpert to invest in bonds is through a bond fund. The advantages of this approach are numerous. Not only are bond-fund portfolios managed by full-time professionals, they are also diversified, with a typical fund owning hundreds of different bonds. What's more, while you generally can't buy an individual bond for less than $1,000, you can buy into a bond fund with an initial investment of as little as $500. And, unlike individual bonds, which usually pay interest only twice a year, you can arrange to get a payout from a bond fund every month if you like. As a result, I typically recommend bond funds to people with less than $50,000 to invest in bonds.

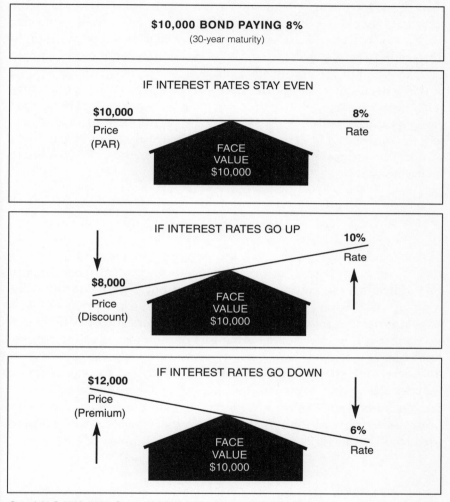

$10,000 BOND PAYING 8%
(30-year maturity)

IF INTEREST RATES STAY EVEN

$10,000   8%
Price   Rate
(PAR)   FACE
                   VALUE
                  $10,000

IF INTEREST RATES GO UP
                                       10%
                                       Rate
$8,000
Price   FACE
(Discount)   VALUE
                  $10,000

IF INTEREST RATES GO DOWN
$12,000
Price
(Premium)
                                        6%
                   FACE   Rate
                   VALUE
                  $10,000

FOR LONG-TERM DREAMS
(FOUR TO 10 YEARS)

Nothing has created more wealth for individuals in this country than the stock market. While no investment is a sure thing, over the long haul stocks are hard to beat. As I noted earlier, since the late 1920s, stocks have generated an average annual return of close to 11 percent. Beginning in the early 1980s, stock prices rose nearly 15 percent a year until the end of the century.

It's statistics like these that make the case for putting your long-term dream money into the stock market. Yes, stocks are riskier than cash equivalents or bonds, but if you can wait out the inevitable market downturns—and if you're saving for a long-term dream, you should be able to—for the long-run stocks are the best investment game in town.

WHAT IS A STOCK?

When you buy a stock, you are purchasing a piece of a publicly traded company. (How big a piece depends on how many shares you buy.) There are two ways to make money from stock ownership. The most obvious way is to buy a stock at a relatively low price and then have it appreciate in value. In addition, some companies pay dividends on their stock, in effect distributing part of their profits to their shareholders.

There are basically three ways to invest in stocks. You can purchase individual stocks directly, you can invest through a mutual fund or, if you've got at least $100,000 to invest, you can use a managed money portfolio. For greater simplicity for you, the investor, I am going to focus the Dream Basket investments on mutual funds.

3,000 MUTUAL FUNDS AND COUNTING . . .

To say that we have seen an explosion in mutual fund investment over the past decade is to understate the situation wildly. Since 1990, the open-end mutual fund industry in Canada has seen its asset base grow from less than $50 billion to more than $433 billion. There are an additional 1,200 funds categorized under such relatively obscure terms as closed-end, hedge, tax-advantaged, managed, and so on.

I often joke in my classes that a new mutual fund is born just about every seven hours. Actually, that's not so far from the truth. Currently more than 3,000 mutual funds are available to Canadian investors. Although these funds were created originally as part of an effort to simplify the investment process, their enormous proliferation has left most of us more confused than ever. Over the next few pages, I'll try to clear up some of the confusion.

WHY BUY A MUTUAL FUND?

The reason you want to consider investing in a mutual fund is that as an investor, your goal is going to be to put away money each month regardless of what the outside world is doing. Remember the pay-yourself-first concept we discussed in Step Four? Now I want to suggest that you also should fund your Dream Basket automatically. Whether you make $3,000 or $30,000 a month, my goal for you is to put money away automatically each month that represents a specific percentage of your income. You can do this very easily with what is known as a systematic investment plan, an automated process by which your chequing account is debited (typically once a month) to fund an investment (typically a mutual fund).

Now, whatever the dollar amount that you select to invest monthly turns out to be, it needs to go into an investment. Let's say that after taking the Seven-Day Financial Challenge of tracking your money (you are doing this, right?), you find $200 that you can save each month. If you automatically put this money into your Dream Basket and your dream is five years out, then you want the money to be invested for growth. If it goes into a mutual fund that invests in stocks, your money will be put to work for you immediately, and a professional money manager will be working full time investing your $200 in a pool of money to make it grow. This mutual fund manager has at his or her disposal the best research and support that money can buy and access to information that you and I do not have unless we want to spend hundreds of hours a month becoming investment savvy. Now, how realistic is it that you are going to start focusing even 10 hours a month on the stock market looking for investments? Pretty unlikely, right? But even if you did want to do this and you felt you could pick stocks yourself, are you going to want to do it each and every month? Even if you have $3,000 a month to invest, do you want to invest it in just one stock each month, and then have to worry if you picked the right stock? Chances are you'll want to do other things with your life. That's why mutual fund investing has become so popular in the last 10 years.

Entire books have been devoted to the question of how to pick a mutual fund, so I am not going to pretend that I can tell you all you need to know about mutual fund investing in just a few pages. The truth is that you probably should consider hiring a financial professional to assist you in the critical process of selecting and building a mutual fund portfolio. In the meantime, however, I can suggest a few basic steps you can take.

WHERE SHOULD I START?

As far as I'm concerned, the first place you should put your long-term Dream Basket money is in an index fund. Index funds are simple, inexpensive, easy to set up, and they work. What more could you ask?

Index funds are stock mutual funds that mimic a specific index. In recent years, the most popular of these have been S&P/TSX Composite Index (formerly TSE 300) funds. These funds invest in the stocks that make up the Toronto Stock Exchange index. Next to the S&P/TSX 60 (which consists of 60 "blue chip" stocks), the Composite Index is one of the most commonly quoted stock market indicators. That's because the performance of the S&P/TSX Composite Index pretty much matches the performance of the market as a whole.

The main reason index investing has become so popular is that it costs less than investing in other kinds of funds. What's more, index funds offer real tax advantages. Because index fund managers move in or out of particular stocks only when those stocks are added to or dropped from the index they're mimicking (something that happens relatively infrequently), there is barely any trading that results in taxable capital gains. In addition, while index funds may have lagged behind some actively managed funds in the go-go years of the late 1990s, historically they have tended to do better than most other funds. (Over the last 20 years or so, index funds have outperformed roughly 75 percent of the actively managed funds.)

You can find a list of popular index funds at *www.bylo.org*, the website operated by Bylo Selhi. Most of these low-cost funds have management expense ratios of less than 1 percent. Remember, they all represent investments in the stock market—meaning there is risk involved. So read their prospectuses before you invest any money.

A NEW CLASS OF INDEX FUNDS

In the last few years, a new class of index funds has become increasingly popular. Known as Exchange Traded Funds (or ETFs), they are basically index mutual funds that trade like stocks on the Toronto Stock Exchange, meaning you can buy and sell them during market hours just like you can buy and sell common stock. What makes these funds so exciting to investors is that they are incredibly liquid, incredibly tax efficient, and extremely low cost. The average ETF has an expense ratio of about 0.55 percent—which happens to be less than half the cost of an index fund and about one-sixth the cost of an actively managed fund. And most of these funds sell for less than $50 a share. How's that for ease of investing and diversification with very little money?

As of this writing, the most popular ETFs are Barclays iUnits, followed by ETFs sold by TD Bank and one sold by State Street. You can also buy ETFs based on U.S. and other foreign exchanges.

ETFs can be purchased through virtually any brokerage firm or on-line trading company. As time goes on, I expect to see more and more investors and financial advisors (myself included) building portfolios with a combination of ETFs and actively managed funds. For more details on this exciting new investment vehicle, go to *www.bylo.org* or contact the Toronto Stock Exchange at *www.tsx.ca*.

FIVE-STAR TIP: *Exchange Traded Funds are exploding in popularity. By mid-2002, there were 16 Canadian ETFs and more than 90 U.S. and foreign ETFs available on the market. More and more investors are using ETFs to lower their taxes and their costs. In my view, the ideal long-term portfolio should include ETFs, balanced with actively managed mutual funds. If you have a financial advisor, ask him or her about ETFs. If you are handling your investments yourself, make sure to visit the websites I listed earlier to keep up with the latest developments.*

MOVING BEYOND THE "GETTING STARTED" PHASE

When you are just getting started, index funds are a great way to get your feet wet. Over time, however, you should consider building a diversified portfolio of mutual funds. To me, a diversified portfolio is one that contains shares in somewhere between four and 10 different funds.

One of the biggest mistakes that investors make these days is investing in too many different mutual funds. At The Bach Group, we sometimes see portfolios in which people have accumulated shares in 20 or more funds. That's simply too many funds. This usually happens when someone subscribes to an investment newsletter or magazine. Every time the magazine recommends a new fund, she invests in it. The result is what we call portfolio redundancy (meaning, you have too many investments that serve basically the same purpose). The problem with this is that it usually dilutes your returns.

BUILD YOUR PORTFOLIO AROUND "CORE" FUNDS

I'm a huge believer in building a portfolio that consists of what I call "core-type" mutual funds. The key to successful investing is to keep the process relatively simple and straightforward. With this in mind, here are the five types of funds I believe you should consider when building a mutual fund portfolio. They are listed in the order of what I consider most conservative to most aggressive.

Large Capitalization Value Funds. A large-cap value fund invests in companies with large market capitalizations—that is, companies whose outstanding stock has a total market value equal to 1 percent or more of the total market capitalization of the S&P/TSX Composite Index. Companies of this magnitude tend to be more secure and established than most, and about 50 of them pay quarterly dividends to shareholders. The "value" part of the name reflects the basic strategy these kinds of funds pursue. Generally speaking, the manager of a value fund looks for high-yielding large-cap stocks that sell at low price-earnings multiples. (That's a fancy way of saying that these funds like to invest in solid companies whose stock is selling at bargain prices.) By investing in these types of stocks, you can often get consistent returns with relatively low volatility. Although I'm a big fan of value investing, I have to admit that the years between 1995 and 2001 were very hard on this approach. Indeed, many people considered the strategy to be old-fashioned, arguing that value stocks couldn't compete with the high-tech, "new economy" stocks. But since 2001, value stocks have come back with a vengeance, and value-style fund managers have, for the most part, been vindicated. As far as I'm concerned, every portfolio should contain some value stocks.

Large Capitalization Growth Funds. This type of fund invests in what are commonly referred to as "growth stocks." Typically, growth stocks do not pay dividends because growth companies prefer to invest their profits in research, development, and expansion. In the last few years, large-cap growth stocks have outperformed practically every other category of investing, producing great returns for the funds that invest in them. Of course, there is no guarantee that this trend will continue.

Because of the small size of the Canadian market and the limited number of large companies relative to stock markets in the U.S., many large-cap funds in Canada follow a style that combines growth and value, sometimes called Growth at Reasonable Prices (GARP). These funds are usually listed as large-cap equity funds.

Small Capitalization Funds. Typically, small-cap funds invest in companies with market caps that range from about $250 million to $1 billion. This reflects an ultra-aggressive approach, in which the fund managers are basically swinging for the fences each time they come to bat. As a result, they tend to strike out a lot. To switch metaphors, small-cap investing is a lot like betting on the hare instead of the tortoise. The younger you are—which is to say, the more time you have to recover from a potential disaster—the more you can afford to invest in this way. But be careful. I don't recommend putting more than 25 percent of your assets into this type of fund.

International or Global Funds. As the name implies, these funds invest in stocks from foreign countries. While an international stock fund invests solely in foreign stocks, a global fund will usually have only about 60 percent of its assets invested abroad; the remaining 40 percent will be in domestic stocks. Remember, Canada represents only 3 percent of the total world economy, and if you invest only in domestic stocks, you're missing out on a lot of opportunities. Experts often recommend that investors keep up to 30 percent of their portfolio in international or global mutual funds.

WITH 3,000 FUNDS TO CHOOSE FROM, HOW DO I KNOW WHICH ONE IS RIGHT FOR ME?

Let's face it, even mutual fund investing has become pretty complicated in recent years. There are so many different funds (upwards of 3,000 at last count). So many ads screaming about performance. So many books, magazines, websites, television shows—all of them with their own suggestions on how to pick a mutual fund. It's enough to make a Smart Woman confused to the point of not taking action.

To help you get started on your Dream Basket, you should check the mutual fund companies that allow you to invest as little as $50 or $100 a month. (You can find this information at *www.globefund.com*) There are very few companies in the former category in Canada, and many of them operate closed-end funds. There are more than 150 funds in Canada that require a minimum monthly investment of $100. If you belong to a union or professional association, you might have access to a family of mutual funds sponsored by the organization that requires a minimum investment of $50.

A lot of people say you should invest only in no-load funds. I don't believe that. What matters most when it comes to mutual funds isn't load vs. no load, but which particular fund best suits your needs and how long you should hold onto it. There are times when it's definitely worth paying a small commission in order to get the professional advice that comes with a load fund. In any case, given that many financial advisors now work on a fee basis (something I'll explain on page 175), you can often get the commission on a load fund waived.

MUTUAL FUNDS THAT ALLOW YOU TO INVEST WITH AS LITTLE AS $100 A MONTH!

There are more than 150 funds in Canada that allow you to invest as little as $100 a month. The list includes some well-known mutual fund companies such as Dynamic, which provide systematic investment plans. Under a systematic investment plan, you arrange to have a specified amount of money (say, $100) automatically transferred from your chequing account each month and invested in a mutual fund (or funds) of your choosing. Because it all happens automatically, you don't have to remember to write any cheques or make any deadlines. In other words, it couldn't be easier. No discipline is required (except to make sure you have enough money in your chequing account to cover the monthly debit). Indeed, you'll probably stop thinking about it after the first few months—and the next thing you know, your Dream Basket will be full of money!

AVERAGE FUND PERFORMANCE
For the Period:
12/31/84–5/31/01

Portfolio Investments	Period's Average Annual Return
Dow Jones 30 Industrial Average w/ divs.	14.33%
S & P 500 Composite Index w/ divs.	13.07%
Mid-Cap Funds Average	17.40%
Small Company Growth Funds Average	13.18%
Growth Mutual Fund Index	12.79%
Growth & Inc. Fund Index	13.40%
International Mutual Fund Index	13.96%
Global Fund Average	12.55%
Balanced Mutual Fund Index	12.37%
High-Yield Bond Fund Index	10.62%
General Municipal Fund Index	8.64%
Money Market Fund Average	5.62%

Source: 2001 Lipper Analytical Services, Inc.

Needless to say, you should never invest in any mutual fund without first reading its prospectus. And don't invest in any fund until any and all questions you may have about the risks involved have been fully answered by your advisor or the fund company itself.

For a complete list of funds and their minimum investment requirements, check the Globefund website at *www.globefund.com*.

FOR REALLY LONG-TERM DREAMS
(10 YEARS OR MORE)

There are long-term dreams and then there are really long-term dreams. Say your dream is to build a second home in Whistler, but you know it won't be possible until your kids are out of college, which is at least 10 years away. Where should you put your Dream Basket money in the meantime?

BUYING INDIVIDUAL STOCKS

Even though I strongly prefer systematic investing in mutual funds, it is possible now to do the same thing with individual stocks. The disadvantage of this route is that you must decide which stocks to invest in, and you don't get the same immediate diversification and professional money management as mutual funds provide. Nonetheless, some people insist on including some individual stocks in their portfolios. If you're one of them, here's how to go about doing it.

"DRIP" INVESTING

A great way to invest systematically in individual stocks is to start what is known as a Dividend Reinvestment Program (or DRIP). Essentially, DRIP plans allow investors to purchase stocks directly from the companies that issue them. Once an account is set up, investors can continue to buy more stock systematically and have any stock dividends they earn reinvested automatically, often with no commission costs.

What makes DRIP programs so great in my opinion is that an investor who wants to build his or her Dream Basket can get started buying stocks with an investment as little as $10 a month. MDS Inc., for example, allows shareholders to invest as little as $50 every six months. (Check its website at *www.mdsintl.com*.) You can check a website for a list of companies that provide DRIP programs (*www.stingy-investor.com*) There are about 70 companies listed, but companies from time to time discontinue their DRIP arrangements, so you should check directly with the issuer, as well.

HOW DO I SET UP A DRIP PROGRAM?

Setting up a DRIP program is relatively easy. You first need to become a shareholder (that means owning at least one share of stock). This can be done through a full-service brokerage firm or a discount brokerage firm or through the trust company that administers the dividend-issuer's shares. You can buy a share in TransCanada PipeLines Ltd., for example, through Computershare Trust Company of Canada (formerly Montreal Trust). For detailed information on DRIPs, I highly recommend going to *www.stingyinvestor.com*. This is a great site that lists all the companies that currently offer DRIP programs.

There's Nothing Wrong with Asking for Help

We've covered an awful lot of ground in this chapter. Between all the recommendations I've made about how to fill your three baskets, I'm sure your head must be spinning. But remember—financial planning really isn't that complicated. For the most part, smart investing (which is the only kind of investing Smart Women do) is simply a matter of knowing what steps to take and in what order.

The fact is, becoming financially secure and being able to fund your dreams is a lot like opening a safe. Unless you know what numbers to turn to and how, you'll never get inside. With the right combination, however, the world's strongest safe can be opened with very little effort. You now know the combination to your financial safe. Use the tools I have given you, in the right order, and your financial dreams will become a reality.

While I believe that every Smart Woman is capable of managing her finances on her own, if that is her goal, I still strongly suggest that before you start making investments, you consider getting some professional guidance. Now, hiring a professional to help you does not mean you are weak or lazy or lacking in confidence. It's like hiring a coach—and there's nothing wrong with hiring a coach. The most accomplished people in the world hire and work with coaches on a daily basis. Take Barbra Streisand. She is one of the greatest singers in the world, yet she still has a voice coach. Same with Tiger Woods. Perhaps the greatest golfer on the planet, he's got a golf coach. Throughout his playing career, Michael Jordan worked with basketball coaches as a matter of routine. Meryl Streep, the brilliant Oscar-winning actress, uses drama and dialect coaches.

Why do these people, all of whom are at the top of their respective games, still rely on coaches? Because they want to keep improving—and because a coach can give you something that is very difficult (if not impossible) to give yourself: accurate and objective feedback on how you're doing.

Rich People Hire Financial Advisors

Wealthy investors almost always employ financial advisors. This is not just my opinion; it is a fact. According to a recent study by Dalbar, a financial-services ratings firm in the U.S., nine out of 10 investors with portfolios worth more than $100,000 prefer working with a financial advisor. This is something to think about if you are not yet as rich as you want to be.

So consider hiring a financial coach. Not only will he or she make the job of managing your finances much easier, but if you hire a good one (which is the only kind you should consider), you probably will end up achieving better results than if you tried to do it on your own.

How do you find a good financial advisor? The interesting thing is that, while this may be one of the most important professionals you ever hire to help you in your lifetime, most investment books don't discuss how you should specifically go about hiring one. Having grown up in the financial world my entire life, there are a couple of things I know for a fact. One is that if I were to leave the investment business, I would not continue to manage my own money. I'd hire someone to help me, because every year the laws and conditions governing the financial arena change, and if I were not managing money full-time, I'd soon lose my edge and ability to manage my money well. As a result, I'd be forced to go out and do what you may need to do right now, which is to start interviewing prospective financial advisors.

Since the first edition of this book was published, I've heard from literally thousands of readers asking me to recommend a financial advisor for them. To help you do your own research, I've created the 13 Golden Rules for Hiring a Financial Pro.

Based on my experience as a financial advisor, these are the rules I would use if I were going to go out and interview someone to help me manage my money. If you really apply these rules, I am confident you will be able to find a financial professional who can help you make smart decisions about your money. Most importantly, you'll be able to hire the best advisor possible and get the best attention possible.

Therefore, I've added a new rule to help you find a financial advisor in your own area. Rule number 13 now provides you with some of the best referral sources. My recommendation is that you consider hiring a local financial advisor, someone you can meet with face to face. Use these rules and the referral sources I listed. There are literally thousands of great advisors out there and all you need to do is find one. And if by any chance you meet with someone that you're not totally comfortable with, simply keep looking. Remember, this is your money and ultimately, even if you hire a financial coach, you are still in charge!

The 13 Golden Rules for Hiring a Financial Pro

RULE NO. 1

GO WHERE THE MONEY IS.

Rich people do not manage their own money. As a rule, they work with top-notch financial professionals. So why reinvent the wheel? Go to someone you know who is wealthy and ask her who she works with. She doesn't have to be a close friend. Maybe it's the owner of the company you work for. Maybe it's someone you have read about in the local paper. Ask her if she is happy with the financial guidance she receives and why. Ask her how she pays for this financial guidance and if she would refer you to her advisor. Then call the financial professional and ask if you can set up a meeting to discuss the possibility of hiring him or her to help you make smart decisions with your money.

You might think, "Well, a top-notch financial advisor won't work with me. I don't have millions of dollars." You might be wrong. Here's how the real world works. Let's say I have a client named Margaret with a $5 million portfolio. Let's also say that Margaret happens to be the president of the company you work for and that you've asked her to recommend a financial advisor. So Margaret calls me up and asks if I would be willing to meet with an employee of hers (namely, you) who wants some advice. Well, what type of service do you think you're going to get? Million-dollar service, that's what! Why? Because regardless of how much or how little money you have, I'm going to want to keep the million-dollar client who referred you happy.

So go out and find someone who is wealthy and ask if he or she would be willing to refer you to a financial advisor. I guarantee you will start out an "A" client, even if you don't have a lot of money to invest.

RULE NO. 2
GO TO YOUR FIRST MEETING PREPARED.

A real professional will insist that you come to your first meeting prepared. That means he or she will ask you to bring copies of your investment statements, net worth, current expense breakdowns, and your most recent tax returns—in short, the kind of information called for in the worksheets in Appendices 1 and 2. There are thousands of people in this country who call themselves financial advisors, financial planners, or financial counsellors. They are not all equally excellent. A professional who doesn't ask you to bring this sort of information is not the kind of professional you want to hire.

If you are not willing to take the time to get organized prior to your first meeting with a financial advisor, or if you are reluctant to show your personal financial documents to a professional, then you probably are not ready to work with one. That's not intended to be harsh; it's intended to be realistic. Some people are very uncomfortable showing their financial documents to anyone and have a deep-rooted problem with trust. A person like this will not be happy hiring a financial professional regardless of how good the advisor may be.

RULE NO. 3
DURING YOUR FIRST MEETING, YOU SHOULD DO MOST OF
THE TALKING.

Your first meeting with a financial advisor is like a financial checkup. The goal is for the advisor to determine your financial health and to discover (or help you discover) what your financial goals and values are. A good financial professional will conduct the meeting in such a way that you end up doing most of the talking. If the advisor spends a lot of time telling you how great he is, how much money he makes for his clients, and how powerful his firm is, thank him politely for his time and continue with your search. This is not the type of financial advisor you want.

> ### RULE NO. 4
> A GOOD FINANCIAL ADVISOR SHOULD BE ABLE TO EXPLAIN HIS OR HER INVESTMENT PHILOSOPHY.

Ask the financial advisor about his or her investment philosophy. He or she should be able to explain it quickly and in simple terms. A real professional should have this part of the process down to a science and be able to explain it both easily and comfortably.

What you don't want is someone who says "Oh, you like stocks— I specialize in stocks! Oh, you like mutual funds—I'm a mutual fund specialist! Oh, you like gold—I think gold sounds great!" What you are getting with this kind of financial advisor is a salesperson, not a financial pro. A financial pro has a set philosophy, a long-term plan or strategy, that shapes all his or her dealings. What you should look for is someone whose philosophy coincides with yours, not someone who is willing to do whatever you want.

> ### RULE NO. 5
> FIND OUT WHAT THE FINANCIAL ADVISOR CHARGES.

Some financial advisors are paid by commission (that is, they take a small percentage of every transaction they make on your behalf). Some are paid a flat annual fee on assets managed. Some are paid on an hourly basis. Some are paid a combination of commissions and fees. Don't be reluctant to ask the advisors you are considering to explain how they are compensated and what their services will cost you. Get them to list and explain all the associated fees they charge, including hidden costs such as internal mutual fund fees. (I call these "hidden" because many financial advisors—and even some no-load mutual fund companies—often don't explain them in detail. A good advisor will.)

> # RULE NO. 6
> ## BE PREPARED TO PAY FOR THE ADVICE YOU GET.

Professional financial advisors do not give you free advice. You'd think this would be obvious, but in this Internet world where we've gotten so used to everything being given away (or at least offered at steep discounts), many people actually think they can go into a financial professional's office and get the benefit of his or her experience and knowledge for nothing. Sorry, but it doesn't work that way.

So how do you pay for your advice? The financial services industry has been going through massive changes in recent years, but there are two basic fee structures used by most professional financial advisors.

COMMISSION-BASED ADVICE

A commission-based advisor earns a fee each time he or she buys or sells an investment for you. For the past hundred years or so, this is how the majority of stockbrokers have worked, and it's very popular among financial advisors.

The good thing about commission-based advice is that if your advisor is an ethical person who doesn't trade the account much, it can turn out to be very inexpensive. Say you invest in 10 stocks or a half-dozen mutual funds and hold them all for years. Chances are you're not going to have to pay very many commissions. Unfortunately, some commission-based advisors will yield to the temptation to keep moving your money—that is, to create transactions that might not be really necessary in order to generate fees. This practice is called "churning," and it's illegal.

If you ever suspect that your account is being churned, stop approving all those trades and get a second opinion. I'm constantly stunned when I meet with prospective clients whose accounts have been churned. One lady I met a few years ago handed me a brokerage statement that contained eight solid pages of trade confirmations. Her account totalled just $50,000 in assets—and yet it had generated $10,000 in brokerage commissions. It was sickening. The broker must have been calling her virtually every day to get her to okay this ridiculous level of trading.

When I asked her how this had happened, she said she thought this was how it worked. "I didn't know any better," she told me.

Make no mistake about it—an ethical advisor will never trade your account like this. The annual commissions on your account should not come to more than 2 to 3 percent of the account's total value. In other words, that poor woman's $50,000 account should have generated maybe $1,500 in commissions for the year . . . max! In fact, the industry standard for a commission-based account is less than 1 percent.

Don't get me wrong. There are a lot of fantastic advisors out there who charge commissions. (Indeed, in some cases, we still do this at our group.) But if you hire a commission-based advisor, make sure it's someone you trust, and keep an eye on the level of trading.

FEE-BASED ADVICE

With fee-based advice, you pay an annual fee for all the services your financial advisor provides, including all your trades, meetings, proposals, performance reports, etc. Generally speaking, the fee is a set proportion—normally between 1 and 2.5 percent—of the amount of money the advisor is managing for you. So if you have $100,000 to invest, the advisor will charge you $1,000 to $2,500 a year.

Just a few years ago, fee-based advisors were relatively rare. Now virtually every major brokerage firm in the country is embracing this kind of payment structure. And because of the competition, the price of fee-based advice is quickly coming down. It's now possible to get a professional advisor to manage a professionally structured portfolio of mutual funds for just 1 percent annually.

Most of my new clients are fee-based. As far as I'm concerned, this structure has a lot of advantages. For one thing, there is now no possible conflict of interest. Since the advisor's pay depends on the value of your assets, it's in the advisor's interest to see your assets grow. Moreover, fee-based advisors get paid only if their clients are serviced well and kept happy. If they invest their clients' money and then forget about them, the clients will leave and the fees will stop coming. For this reason, fee-based advisors tend to be more service-oriented. To fee-based advisors, new clients represent more than a one-time sale; their businesses are based on long-term relationships. (By the way, if you hire a fee-based advisor, make sure you tell your accountant, because under some circumstances the fees you pay may be tax-deductible.)

> ## RULE NO. 7
> ### MAKE YOURSELF AN IMPORTANT CLIENT . . . BY SAYING "THANK YOU."

It is not enough simply to hire a good financial advisor. You want whomever you hire to pay attention to you—ideally, to consider you one of his or her most important clients. Most people think that, in order to be important to a financial advisor, you need to have lots of money. Nothing could be further from the truth. I have clients with assets that range from $25,000 to $100 million, and I can assure you that some of the smaller ones are just as important to me as the biggest ones.

The fact is, it's not just money that determines how much your financial advisor cares about you. It's how you treat your financial advisor that matters. As an example, I have a client, Francine, who opened an account with me with just $1,000. I put Francine's money into a stock that tripled in value, so all of a sudden she had $3,000. I also bought this stock for more than a half-dozen other clients. Most of them made significantly more money than Francine, because they had more invested. Unlike any of them, however, after the stock took off, Francine showed up at my office one day with four bottles of wine as a gift for me and each of my assistants. Now, I don't know what the wine cost Francine. I don't even remember whether it was red or white. What I do remember is that this small gesture of hers was talked about in our office for weeks. We couldn't believe how special it was. I'm still talking (and now writing) about it three years later.

So when your financial advisor makes you some money, take a moment to say "thank you." Sure, it's his or her job to make you money. But that's no reason not to show your appreciation. No matter how small your portfolio, a small gesture like a simple thank-you note or a bottle of wine can transform you to an "A" client.

Another great way to say "thank you" to your advisor—and become as a result an "A" client—is to refer the advisor some new business (that is, to recommend that a friend hire your advisor). Not only will this show your advisor how much you appreciate what he or she has done for you, it may turn out to be just what your friend needs to get her financial life together.

And it's not just financial advisors who should get this sort of consideration. When Francine gave me that little gift, it made me realize that I had never once expressed my appreciation to any of the professionals on whom I depend: my lawyer, my accountant, my doctor, my haircutter, the mechanic who looked after my car—the list goes on and on. So three years ago I started sending them all thank-you notes and in some cases a gift basket at Christmas. The first time I did this, my doctor called me personally to say "thank you." Guess what? Even though my doctor is routinely booked up three months in advance, I never have to wait for an appointment anymore. I just seem to get right in. My car mechanic framed my thank-you letter and posted it on the wall of his waiting room. My accountant seemed to find more deductions the next year.

I'm not kidding. Because of my small gifts and notes, my relationship with all these professionals is now different. They remember me because I made a small gesture to say "thank you." Try it. Our parents were right: Saying "thank you" goes a long way.

RULE NO. 8
CHECK OUT A PROSPECTIVE ADVISOR'S BACKGROUND.

As I said earlier, there are more than 30,000 people in this country who call themselves financial advisors, financial planners, financial managers, investment advisors, or investment managers. They may be certified by one of several organizations, including the Financial Planners Standards Council, the Canadian Association of Financial Planners, the Institute of Canadian Bankers, and the Investment Funds Institute of Canada.

How can you tell if the one you are talking to is someone you can trust? The newspapers always seemed to be filled with stories about dishonest financial managers who swindle their clients out of their life savings. Recently in the Bay Area there was a case of a man who called himself a financial planner and allegedly fled the country with over $10 million of his clients' money. He was even said to have conned his own employees. The worst thing about this tale is that it was totally avoidable. This man had a record of negligent financial behaviour, as a result of which he had been fired by a major brokerage firm. This fact was documented by the National Association of Securities Dealers (NASD).

In Canada, regulation of the securities industry is carried out by provincial securities commissions and self-regulatory organizations, which include the Investment Dealers Association of Canada (*www.ida.ca*). Each province has government bodies—securities commissions or administrators—that oversee a provincial securities act, which outlines what participants in the market can do.

Securities commissions delegate some aspects of securities regulation to the Investment Dealers Association of Canada, the Mutual Fund Dealers Association of Canada, Market Regulation Services Inc., and the Montreal Exchange.

The Investment Dealers Association is responsible for the regulation of its member firms (Member Regulation) and monitors the bond and money markets. To find out if a firm is a member of the Investment Dealers Association, you can check the IDA's website.

The provincial securities commissions and administrators have formed a national group to work toward making securities regulations consistent and harmonized across Canada. This group is called the Canadian Securities Administrators (*www.csa-acvm.ca*). Among the objectives of the CSA is the protection of investors from fraudulent, manipulative, or misleading practices.

Provincial securities commissions keep a file on every financial professional in the province licensed to sell securities. Most reputable firms will not hire a financial advisor who has any sort of black mark on his or her record.

Financial planners in Canada are regulated by the Financial Planners Standards Council. If you are considering hiring a financial planner, you can go to the FPSC's website (*www.cfp-ca.org*) and type in the planner's name to see if he or she is a member in good standing.

Before you hire a financial advisor, check out his or her file with the organization that regulates his or her activities. (In Ontario, for example, you can reach the Ontario Securities Commission at (877) 785-1555 or visit its website at *www.osc.gov.on.ca*.) Also take a look at the firm where the advisor works. If you hire someone from a large firm, you are buying built-in safety. Large firms have what are known as compliance departments, which see to it that all employees of the firm observe the highest ethical and legal standards when it comes to investing and money management. At the investment firm where I worked, every single piece of mail that comes in or goes out is photocopied and reviewed. Every single transaction we make is monitored. If an advisor seems to be trading a client's account too actively, the firm checks with the client to confirm that he or she is aware of what's going on.

Of course, hiring a financial advisor who works for a large firm does not guarantee performance results. But it does provide you with one very important protection against the damage an unethical advisor can do—namely, deep pockets. If a broker somehow slips under the compliance department's radar and you get burned by unethical or illegal investment practices that should have been caught, there's a much better chance that firm will compensate you for the damage done. The same cannot always be said of a small independent financial planner.

> ## RULE NO. 9
> NEVER, EVER, HIRE AN INVESTMENT ADVISOR WHO BRAGS ABOUT PERFORMANCE.

In recent years, with the stock market's unprecedented run-up, many investment portfolios and mutual funds have had little trouble producing double-digit returns. As a result, currently it is quite easy for a financial advisor or mutual fund company to come up with a recommended portfolio that's generated earnings of better than 20 percent a year over the last five or 10 years.

Looking back at the last five years means very little going forward. I call it "rearview mirror" investing, and it does not make for good solid financial forecasts. A good financial advisor will talk to you about historical returns going back not five years or even 10 years, but at least 20 to 30 years. That's important because by looking at the returns generated by different investments and asset classes since the 1960s and 1970s, you will see that, over the long term, investing in the stock market is more likely to produce annual returns of about 11 percent, not 20 percent.

The key to creating an intelligent financial plan is to use realistic projections—which is to say those that are based on more than just the last five to 10 years. Often a prospective client will ask me why some other advisor is promising her returns of, say, 18 percent a year, while I'm willing to project only 8 to 12 percent over the next five years. My answer is that I am being honest and the other guy is not; he's basing his projections on the last five years, while I base mine on the last 50. No one knows what the future holds. All we know is what history has shown us. The more history we use—that is, the farther back we go—the safer our projections are bound to be.

Once your potential advisor gives you a proposal on how to invest your money, ask the advisor what the breakdown is between stocks, bonds, and cash. Then compare what you're told to the chart on page 181. If you are meeting with someone who tells you he can earn 18 percent a year for you when the graph shows that, historically, the asset breakdown he is suggesting has achieved just 10 percent, you know you are dealing with a less than ethical person. Find someone else.

> ### RULE NO. 10
> A GOOD FINANCIAL ADVISOR EXPLAINS THE RISKS
> ASSOCIATED WITH INVESTING.

It's easy to forget about risk when the stock market is running the way it did in the 1990s, but that doesn't mean you should. A good advisor will spend time explaining and educating you about the risks associated with investing. At The Bach Group, before we implement an investment plan, we show our clients exactly how often in the past the market has dropped, how long it has stayed down, and, based on the history of the last 45 years, what we believe the risks associated with our proposal to be.

This is incredibly important because many people today do not fully understand—nor are they being prepared for—the risks inherent in any stock market investment. If you meet with an advisor who does not discuss the notion of risk with you and ask you specific questions to get a feeling for your comfort level, thank her for her time and continue on with your search.

ASSET ALLOCATION - RISK & REWARD

Annual average returns

April 1992 – March 2002

Portfolio Mix		Average annual return	Return per unit of risk
US equity Intl equity Cdn equity Bonds	100% 0% 0% 0%	15.90%	1.22
US equity Intl equity Cdn equity Bonds	60% 10% 20% 10%	13.86%	1.17
US equity Intl equity Cdn equity Bonds	30% 30% 30% 10%	11.99%	1.02
US equity Intl equity Cdn equity Bonds	15% 15% 70% 0%	11.53%	0.82
US equity Intl equity Cdn equity Bonds	10% 0% 90% 0%	11.48%	0.75
US equity Intl equity Cdn equity Bonds	0% 0% 90% 10%	10.71%	0.71
US equity Intl equity Cdn equity Bonds	0% 10% 90% 0%	10.70%	0.69
US equity Intl equity Cdn equity Bonds	10% 10% 10% 70%	10.11%	1.58
US equity Intl equity Cdn equity Bonds	0% 0% 20% 80%	9.44%	1.43
US equity Intl equity Cdn equity Bonds	0% 10% 10% 80%	9.255	1.60
US equity Intl equity Cdn equity Bonds	0% 0% 0% 100%	9.06%	1.63
US equity Intl equity Cdn equity Bonds	0% 100% 0% 0%	9.01%	0.62

> ## RULE NO. 11
> GO WITH YOUR GUT INSTINCT.

When you interview a financial advisor, ask yourself if you feel comfortable with this person. Is this the kind of person you want to open up to and work with for years to come? Do you feel deep down inside that this is someone you can trust? The answer should be a "gut level" yes. If it is not, continue your search. You have not yet found your trusted advisor.

> ## RULE NO. 12
> KEEP IN REGULAR CONTACT WITH YOUR
> FINANCIAL ADVISOR.

If you haven't heard from your financial advisor by phone or by letter in the last 12 months (statements don't count), then you may have fallen into what we call the client abyss. Get out quick. Either go in immediately and reacquaint yourself with the professional with whom you are working, or start interviewing for a new advisor. As a rule, your advisor should contact you at least twice a year, and you should sit down together to review your financial situation at least once every 12 months.

> ## RULE NO. 13
> IF YOU CAN'T GET A REFERRAL, DO YOUR OWN RESEARCH.

There is a lot of great free information out there about financial advisors, and you should definitely take advantage of it. Then use the power of the Internet to do your own research. Here are some places to start.

Finding a Financial Advisor

The Financial Planners Standards Council
(800) 305-9886
www.cfp-ca.org
This site provides a wealth of good information on financial
planning and allows you to check if a Certified Financial Planner
has been disciplined by the FPSC. There are more than 13,000
CFPs in Canada. However, not all financial planners in Canada
hold a Certified Financial Planners' designation.

Canadian Association of Financial Planners
(800) 346-2237
www.cafp.org
The CAFP represents over 3,300 financial planners in Canada.
Among other things, you can use its website to search for a planner with a Registered Financial Planner's designation. It's currently of only limited value, but promises to get better as more
financial planners offer their services on a fee-for-service basis.

Checking Out an Advisor's Background

Investment Dealers Association
The IDA operates five offices across the country. In Toronto, for
example, you can reach the IDA at (416) 364-6133. On matters
of enforcement, contact the IDA by fax at (416) 364-2998.

Provincial securities commissions
You can find these commissions listed individually on a number of
websites, including the Bank of Canada's (*www.bankofcanada.ca*).

In Conclusion

These 13 rules are meant to make your search for a lifelong financial guide easier. Don't let anything I have said scare you off from searching for one. There are many, many good and ethical professionals out there who can help you with your financial decisions.

Remember, it's now time for you to move on your decision. If you have decided that you do want professional help, make hiring an advisor a priority. Your ultimate goal should be to hire an individual or a team that you can see yourself working with for a long time—perhaps even the rest of your life. Therefore, the hiring process is something you should take very seriously. Ask people within your community, talk to friends and wealthy people you know and respect, and find out whom they are working with. Spend time, interview more than one professional, ask for references, and then follow up and call those references.

I promise you—it will be worth the effort.

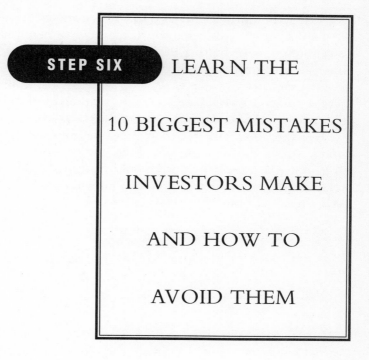

STEP SIX

LEARN THE 10 BIGGEST MISTAKES INVESTORS MAKE AND HOW TO AVOID THEM

When I was five, my friend Marvin and I thought it would be fun to see what was behind those electric sockets our mothers were always warning us not to touch. I think I was the one who found the screwdriver, but it was definitely Marvin who stuck it in the socket.

Wham!

Before either of us had a chance to react, Marvin went flying backward across the room and all the power in the house went out. "Wow," I said, gaping at my friend, who was now lying in a heap against the opposite wall. "Was that fun?"

Poor little Marvin looked at me with a dazed expression, then burst into tears.

I can't remember what lame story we eventually concocted to cover up what we'd done, but I do recall clearly that the experience taught me two important things. The first was never to stick a screwdriver in a light socket. The second was that while it's important to learn from your own mistakes, it's probably a better idea (and certainly a much safer one) to learn from other people's.

I bring this up because both these lessons are important to remember when you're trying to decide how to invest all that money you should now be putting in your three baskets. The fact is, when it comes to investing, many of us act like five-year-olds sticking screwdrivers into electric sockets. That is, we experiment ignorantly—and invariably wind up making some horrendous mistake that sends us reeling across the room in financial shock.

Over the course of this chapter, we're going to focus on what I consider to be the 10 most "shocking" mistakes that investors generally make. My hope is that as a result of studying other people's mistakes, you'll be able to avoid the painful and expensive experience of having to learn from your own.

MISTAKE NO. 1
BECOMING AN INVESTOR BEFORE YOU ARE ORGANIZED AND HAVE SPECIFIC GOALS IN MIND

Back in Step Three, we talked about the importance of knowing exactly where you are today financially and what eventual destination you've got in mind before you go charging down the road to riches. Well, I hope you don't mind if I repeat myself a bit here. The fact is, going off half-cocked—that is, without having a clear idea of how you stand and where you want to go—may well be the most common (and most avoidable) mistake investors make.

There's no getting around it. Before you invest any of your money, you must invest some of your time. The rule is simple: *In order to become a successful investor, you first have to get your values and goals written down on paper and your finances organized.* You absolutely must do a family financial inventory and balance sheet and determine precisely your current net worth. You also must get a good handle on what you earn and what you spend. This is not a guessing game or a time for estimates. Remember, until you know where you stand financially, you should not invest in *anything.* As I noted earlier, use the FisnishRich Inventory Planner in Appendix 2 to get a solid grip on where you stand today financially.

I can already hear you protesting: "Worksheets? Financial inventories? This stuff takes time. What if I miss out on a great investment opportunity while I'm busy getting my finances organized?"

Believe me, I know that doing the foundation work is not nearly as exciting as investing in a hot stock. No one goes to a cocktail party and brags about the fact that she spent the weekend cleaning her financial house. Rather, people like to talk about the hot new investment they just bought—and now with all those personal-finance magazines, television shows, investor newsletters, and Internet chat rooms, it's very easy to be tempted into investing without first getting your money in order and your investment goals down on paper.

Resist the temptation. You can't invest successfully without knowing where you are starting from and what your investment goals are. Only after you have figured out these things will you be able to evaluate intelligently the opportunities around you and figure out whether (and how) they might make sense for you.

MISTAKE NO. 2
NOT TAKING CREDIT CARD DEBT SERIOUSLY

Credit card debt can be incredibly destructive. If you're single, it can keep you from achieving your goals and make you miserable. If you're part of a couple, it can destroy your relationship. I don't care how much two people may love each other; if one of them is constantly spending the couple into debt, I can promise you that eventually the relationship will fall apart. If both parties are running up debts, it will simply end that much sooner.

Why do I say this? First of all, carrying credit card debt is stressful. Knowing that you owe a company money and that you're being charged as much as 20 percent interest on the outstanding balance will make even the most laid-back person anxious. Second, the anxiety never goes away; it's there—all day, every day—until the debt is paid off. And not only does it hang over you like a cloud, it hits you smack dab in the face every month when the bill shows up.

Don't wait to find out about your credit record!

Nothing is worse than finding out that you have credit problems just when you're about to make a major purchase—say, when you're ready to buy your first home.

This happened to one of my closest friends, a woman named Renee, who makes a good living as a computer executive. When she and her new husband, Alan, started to look for a house in San Francisco a few years ago, she called a mortgage broker to get preapproved for a loan. This, she figured, was a no-brainer. She'd already asked Alan if his credit was clean, and he'd said of course it was.

So imagine her surprise a few days later when the broker called her back and asked if she was sitting down.

"What's wrong?" Renee asked the broker.

"Well," he said, "Alan has some credit problems. In fact, his credit rating is so bad that there's no way the two of you can qualify for a loan together."

Renee was stunned. "How can that be? My credit is perfect, isn't it?"

"Sure," the broker said, "but his isn't."

The problem was those nice companies that give away the free T-shirts and make it so easy to get a credit card when you're a student. With their encouragement, Alan had opened a couple of those accounts when he was in college, charged a few items, and then had forgotten about them.

Unfortunately, those nice credit card companies don't forget. Instead, they had placed nasty little "no payment" flags on his record. And even though the amounts in question were relatively small (less than $200 on two accounts), that was enough to ruin his credit rating—and along with it, any chance he and Renee had of getting a mortgage together.

Fortunately for them, Renee's credit rating was strong enough to qualify them for a home loan on her own, and so they were still able to buy a house. Anyway, the point here is not to single out Alan, but to demonstrate how easy it is to be blindsided by a bad credit report. Even when you think you have your act together, you may not. The moral . . .

Find out your credit rating now!

Don't wait to be surprised. This week go and get yourself a copy of your credit reports. It's actually quite simple. There are two main credit-reporting companies in Canada—Equifax and TransUnion—and on request they will each provide you with a free copy of your personal credit report. For a charge of $15 to $22, you can also order a copy of your credit report on-line.

Here's how to contact the companies:

Equifax Canada Inc.
Box 190
Station Jean-Talon
Montreal, Quebec
H1S 2Z2
(800) 465-7166
www.equifax.ca

TransUnion Canada
Consumer Relations Centre
Box 338
LCD 1 Hamilton, Ontario
L8L 7W2
(866) 525-0262
Residents of Quebec: (877) 713-3393
www.tuc.ca

If you discover any inaccuracies or mistakes in any of your credit reports, get them fixed immediately. The procedures for doing so are relatively simple, and the individual companies will tell you exactly what's required. Basically, if you tell a credit-reporting company that your file contains inaccurate information, the company must look into your claim (usually within 30 days) and present all the relevant evidence you submit to whomever provided it with the information you're disputing. If this does not resolve the dispute, you may add a brief statement to your credit file, a summary of which will be included in all future reports.

If you discover that you've got some legitimate black marks on your credit reports (for example, some old unpaid bills that you've forgotten about), do whatever you can to correct the situation. In general, that means pay off those old debts and don't let any new bills go past due.

Beware of companies that say they can "fix" a bad credit report or give you a new "clean" one overnight. There is nothing that will "fix" a bad credit report except the passage of time and a consistent record of responsible bill paying, and you contacting the credit-report companies and working with them to get your credit record clean.

There are some reputable non-profit groups that can advise you on how to clear up a bad credit report or straighten out an inaccurate one. One of the best is Credit Counselling Canada, reachable at one of dozens of local offices across Canada (check your phone book) or on-line at *www.creditcounsellingcanada.ca*.

You can't live rich if you're in a rat race

If you currently find yourself deeper in debt than you would like to be, you are not alone. Why do we borrow so much money? Basically, it's because we get hooked into thinking about the price of things not in terms of their total cost but in terms of how much the monthly instalments will be. This is a marketing gimmick that you find almost nowhere else but in North America. From car payments to mortgage payments to credit card payments, virtually every kind of price tag in Canada is denominated in monthly payments.

Unfortunately, if you want to live happily ever after, you can't be living paycheque to paycheque or credit card payment to credit card payment. You can't live rich if you're stuck on the rat race of life working yourself silly to just pay off debt.

If credit card debt is a problem, here's what you must do.

1) **Cut up the cards.** As I mentioned in the "Latté Factor" chapter, you (and your partner, if you have one) need to have a credit card "haircut." It's not complicated. Just take a $2 pair of scissors and cut up every piece of plastic cash you have. From then on, do all your spending in cash. I dare you to waste $75 on a "must-have" sweater or $100 on a "killer" pair of shoes when you have to pay for them with "real" money. Even better, I'd really be surprised if you could easily go into an appliance store and buy a $1,000 television with 50 twenty-dollar bills. Counting out 50 twenties will make you realize just how much that new television really costs.

2) **If you're married, stop fighting with each other.** The two of you are on the same team. Debt is a "we" problem, not a "you" problem. This is true in a moral sense for partners in any committed relationship, but for married couples it has a legal dimension as well. When you are married, you are jointly responsible for all your debts, regardless of who incurred them. Say your husband runs up $50,000 in credit card debts, divorces you, and then files for bankruptcy. Guess who the creditors will come after? You, if you've got any assets. I've seen this happen more than once. What this means is that, if either of you has a credit card problem, you need to get help together. Remember, your enemy is debt, not each other; you need to rally against it together.

3) **Get help.** Contact a reputable, non-profit credit-counselling organization such as Credit Counselling Canada. (As I noted above, stay away from outfits that promise to "fix" your credit problems—usually for a healthy fee.) Generally speaking, these groups can help you consolidate your debt, renegotiate interest rates, and get creditors to stop harassing you. Most importantly, they can help you identify just how you got into debt in the first place and help you get out much more quickly.

4) **Stop the barrage of credit card applications to your home.** If you have a good credit record, you can easily find yourselves

receiving three or more applications a week for new credit cards. I swear, Michelle and I sometimes get them daily. Do what many of our Canadian friends recently did. Contact the Canadian Marketing Association at (416) 391-2362 or *www.the-cma.org* and add your name to its Do–Not–Contact service.

MISTAKE NO. 3
HAVING A 25-YEAR MORTGAGE

In my opinion, without question the biggest mistake house buyers make in Canada today is assuming a 25-year amortization on their mortgage. On a 25-year mortgage of $150,000 at 8 percent, you end up paying almost $200,000 in interest.

What's the alternative? Well, if you paid off your mortgage in 15 years, your total interest payments would come to just under $110,000. That's still a lot, but it is nearly $90,000 less than it would have been with a 25-year mortgage. How difficult is it to pay off a home in 15 years instead of 25 years? Not very.

To begin with, you don't have to run out and get a new mortgage. All you need to do is the following.

First, call your mortgage holder and ask him or her how much you would need to add to your principal payment each month in order to pay off your mortgage in 15, 18, or 20 years. Also ask how much you would save in reduced interest costs. Once you see the savings in black and white, you will be motivated to start making extra principal payments. Trust me on this. This one phone conversation could end up saving you literally hundreds of thousands of dollars. So make the call.

Once you have decided how much more quickly you would like to pay off your mortgage, you need to decide whether you want to reach your goal by making a small extra payment each month or by forking over a larger lump sum at the end of the year. I recommend you do it monthly; the smaller bites make it more likely you will stick to your plan. If you can manage it, consider making an extra 10 percent payment each month and then adding an extra month's payment at the end of the year. This would almost guarantee that your 25-year mortgage will be paid off in close to 18 years (maybe even less, depending on whether your loan is fixed or adjustable). That's 12 years' worth of mortgage payments that you could now devote to something else—such as your retirement fund, or maybe even a vacation home.

If you need another reason to consider speeding up your mortgage payments, think about this: The faster you pay off your home, the sooner you can retire.

Now, there are some experts who disagree with this philosophy. Indeed, one school of thought suggests that rather than trying to pay off a 25-year mortgage more quickly, you should take a 25-year mortgage, then extend it and strive to never pay it off. Well, that sure sounds like a lot of fun. What woman wouldn't look forward to making mortgage payments for the rest of her life?

Even crazier, some financial planners say that you should cash out whatever equity you happen to have in your home and invest the proceeds in the stock market or in an insurance policy. In my opinion, this advice is totally out of touch with reality. The reality is that you need a place to live in which you can feel safe and happy. You can't live in a mutual fund or in an insurance policy. I don't care how great the return is, you can't park your car in it. And, despite what these experts would have you believe, there are going to be years when the stock market goes down and that "perfect" mutual fund actually appreciates less than your home.

Let's get back to basics. Most people dream of owning their own home. Most people also dream about being able to retire early so they can enjoy their lives and spend time with their loved ones. If you buy a home and pay it off early, you can accomplish both of these dreams. So pay off your mortgage sooner rather than later, and don't ever let some slick salesman tell you that having money in your home is like having cash "in them thar" walls or under your mattress. Cash in a home is your ultimate equity and your ultimate security. In my opinion, the sooner you own your home free and clear, the better.

If you're at all confused by this, call your bank or mortgage company and tell them you want to pay off your mortgage earlier than the schedule calls for. Ask them exactly how much extra a month you would have to send them to pay off your mortgage in 15, 18, and 20 years. Make sure to ask if there are any penalties for paying off your mortgage earlier (chances are the answer is no). Then ask them to send this information to you in writing. Most likely, they'll be happy to help you and, in any case, it shouldn't take them very long to do the calculations.

You can also get a pretty good idea on your own by using the mortgage calculators at the following website: *www.freemortgageanalyzer.com.*

One thing to keep in mind: When you make these extra mortgage payments, pay close attention to your monthly statements. Banks often don't credit mortgage accounts properly. I've had it happen twice with my own mortgage. In one case, we had been making extra payments for eight months—without a penny of it ever being credited against our principle. When we finally noticed, the bank said it thought the extra payments were meant to cover future interest we might owe. Can you believe that? It took us three months to sort things out. The moral: Even if you're not making extra payments, watch your bank like a hawk!

What about paying off your mortgage right away?

If you're fortunate enough to enjoy some huge windfall—say, a lump-sum inheritance or a big bonus at work—you may be tempted to take the money and pay off your mortgage in one fell swoop. But before you do anything like that, first get some professional financial advice. While I believe in paying off your mortgage more quickly than the bank would like, it doesn't always make sense to pay it off all at once. There are a lot of variables involved—such as how long you intend to stay in your house, how much money you have, and when you were planning on retiring—and the right course of action isn't always obvious.

```
╭──────────────────────────────────────────────╮
│                 MISTAKE NO. 4                  │
│             WAITING TO BUY A HOUSE             │
╰──────────────────────────────────────────────╯
```

I've received countless e-mails from single women—especially those in their 20s and 30s—wondering if they should they buy a house or condo. Many ask if it makes sense to hold off on buying real estate until they meet Mr. Right and get married.

The answer is unequivocally no! Don't wait. Do it now.

Why the hurry? It's simple. When you own your own home, you are building equity for yourself. When you rent, you are building someone else's equity. (In other words, by renting, you make someone else rich; by owning, you make yourself rich.)

More fundamentally, you should never put off taking a financial action (like buying a house) because of something that might happen later (like getting married). When it comes to your finances, you should always live in the now. If you are single and want your own home, why wait for some man to come along? Go for it.

The number-one reason people put off buying a home is because they think they can't afford it. More often than not, they're wrong. It's a common misconception that in order to buy a house you need to have tens of thousands of dollars in the bank for a down payment. Not true. These days, many banks will lend you 95 percent of the purchase price—which is to say, you won't need to make a very large down payment.

Second, many people don't realize how much of a house they could get for the equivalent of their current rental payment. To put it really simply, for every $1,000 you pay in monthly rent, you can afford about $125,000 in a mortgage. Say your rent is currently $2,000 a month. For that kind of money, you could get a $250,000 mortgage. In most of the country, $250,000 can buy you a lot of house.

And here's something else to think about. You aren't really in the game of building wealth until you get in the real estate game. Moreover, until you own your own home, you're at the mercy of others. I found this out the hard way. Thirty days before my wedding to Michelle, I was evicted from my apartment in San Francisco. (I was renting, and the owner decided to move his kid into my unit.)

It was horrible. Not only did it make me feel helpless, but because I had to scramble to find a new place for us to live, I ended up having to pay twice as much for an apartment half the size.

About a year later, Michelle and I purchased a condo. It was 1998, and real estate prices were sky high. Friends told us we were crazy to buy. Since then, however, the market price of our condo has increased. We have a wonderful home that we own, and we've built real equity. My single biggest regret is that I didn't buy sooner.

The National Association of Realtors operates a website called Homestore, where you can find listings for houses, condominiums, cottages, farms, and other properties located throughout the country. You can find it at: *www.realestate.ca*.

MISTAKE NO. 5

PUTTING OFF SAVING FOR RETIREMENT

At the beginning of this book, I noted that almost 45 percent of Canadian women age 65 or older live below the poverty line. And they live to an average age of 81 years. As I pointed out, that means that only half the women in Canada over the age of 65 are in any position to lead a life of financial comfort.

This situation is not only totally unacceptable, it's also totally unnecessary. The difference between a comfortable future and destitution is literally a matter of no more than a few dollars a month. The problem is, by failing to plan, most of us in effect plan to fail.

The problem is not complicated. The longer you wait to get started, the more you need to save. The following chart illustrates this quite dramatically. It shows the savings records of two women, Susan and Kim. Susan began saving for retirement at age 19. For eight years she put $2,000 a year into an investment account; then, at age 26, she stopped, never putting in another dime. Kim, on the other hand, waited until she turned 27 to begin putting money away for retirement. Starting then, and continuing right up through the age of 65, Kim put $2,000 into an investment account every year. Who came out ahead? The following chart shows the answer, and I'll bet you'll find it surprising.

As we discussed in Step Five, the best way to get started saving for retirement is to arrange to have it done without your having to think about it—that is, to have your monthly contribution either deducted directly from your paycheque or automatically transferred from your chequing account each month. The benefits of this approach are enormous. First (and most important), you can't spend what you don't see in your chequing account. Second, it spares you having to debate with yourself whether you *really* need to make a contribution this month. Third, contributing once or twice a month is a lot easier than writing a big cheque at the end of the year. The fact is, most people who wait until the end of the year to fund their retirement plans end up either not doing it or putting too little away.

Remember, the sooner you start saving for retirement, the sooner you will be able to finish rich and go play!

THE TIME VALUE OF MONEY
Invest Now Rather Than Later

SUSAN Investing at age 19 (10% Annual Return)			SEE THE DIFFERENCE	KIM Investing at age 27 (10% Annual Return)		
AGE	INVESTMENT	TOTAL VALUE		AGE	INVESTMENT	TOTAL VALUE
19	$2,000	2,200		19	0	0
20	2,000	4,620		20	0	0
21	2,000	7,282		21	0	0
22	2,000	10,210		22	0	0
23	2,000	13,431		23	0	0
24	2,000	16,974		24	0	0
25	2,000	20,871		25	0	0
26	2,000	25,158		26	0	0
27	0	27,674		27	$2,000	2,200
28	0	30,442		28	2,000	4,620
29	0	33,486		29	2,000	7,282
30	0	36,834		30	2,000	10,210
31	0	40,518		31	2,000	13,431
32	0	44,570		32	2,000	16,974
33	0	48,027		33	2,000	20,871
34	0	53,929		34	2,000	25,158
35	0	59,322		35	2,000	29,874
36	0	65,256		36	2,000	35,072
37	0	71,780		37	2,000	40,768
38	0	78,958		38	2,000	47,045
39	0	86,854		39	2,000	53,949
40	0	95,540		40	2,000	61,544
41	0	105,094		41	2,000	69,899
42	0	115,603		42	2,000	79,089
43	0	127,163		43	2,000	89,198
44	0	139,880		44	2,000	100,318
45	0	153,868		45	2,000	112,550
46	0	169,255		46	2,000	126,005
47	0	188,180		47	2,000	140,805
48	0	204,798		48	2,000	157,086
49	0	226,278		49	2,000	174,094
50	0	247,806		50	2,000	194,694
51	0	272,586		51	2,000	216,363
52	0	299,845		52	2,000	240,199
53	0	329,830		53	2,000	266,419
54	0	362,813		54	2,000	295,261
55	0	399,094		55	2,000	326,988
56	0	439,003		56	2,000	361,886
57	0	482,904		57	2,000	400,275
58	0	531,194		58	2,000	442,503
59	0	584,314		59	2,000	488,953
60	0	642,745		60	2,000	540,048
61	0	707,020		61	2,000	596,253
62	0	777,722		62	2,000	658,078
63	0	855,494		63	2,000	726,086
64	0	941,043		64	2,000	800,895
65	0	1,035,148		65	2,000	883,185

EARNINGS BEYOND INVESTMENT $1,019,148

EARNINGS BEYOND INVESTMENT $805,185

SUSAN EARNS	$1,019,148
KIM EARNS	$805,185
SUSAN EARNS MORE	$213,963

Susan invested one-fifth the dollars but has 25% more to show
START INVESTING EARLY!

MISTAKE NO. 6
SPECULATING WITH YOUR INVESTMENT MONEY

Show me a gambler and I will show you a future loser. The reason Las Vegas is America's fastest-growing city is that the odds favour the house. People who gamble eventually lose.

The same holds true when it comes to investing. In the investment world, of course, we don't call it gambling. We use the word "speculation," but it really means the same thing. A speculator, like a gambler, is someone who is looking for a fast buck. And just like at a casino, every once in a while someone does get lucky. But over the long haul, nothing will more effectively prevent you from ever becoming financially secure than speculating with your investment money. This should be obvious, but it's not; otherwise, millions of Americans wouldn't be speculating in the market every day.

Here are the most common ways to speculate—avoid them!

Investing in Options. One of the easiest ways to speculate in the stock market—and in the process probably lose everything you've invested—is to buy what are called *options*. Options allow you to speculate on the future price of a given stock. Essentially, you're placing a bet that the price of a certain stock will reach a certain point by a certain date. The problem is, if you bet wrong and the stock doesn't reach that price by that particular date, your option could expire worthless—and the money you paid for it is down the drain. (An amazing thing about options is that they are one of the only investments where you are actually told in advance what day your investment could be worthless. It's called option expiration day.)

Unless you are willing to put in the considerable time required to master the complexities—or if you happen to work with a professional who has a *proven* track record in options trading—I recommend you avoid them altogether.

Investing in Companies That Don't Make a Profit. It may sound obvious, but the second easy way to lose money in the stock market is to invest in companies that don't make a profit. When you buy a stock, you are making an investment in a business. Some businesses are well run and make money year after year; some are poorly run (or just new) and lose money. Now, all things being equal, doesn't it make more sense to invest in a company that consistently makes money rather than one that doesn't? Of course it does. Nonetheless, thousands of people buy stock every day in companies that have never shown a profit—or even produced a proven product. Most recently, we've seen this phenomenon in Internet-related stocks. In the late 1990s, it seemed all you needed to do was put the words "Internet" or "cyber-something" in your prospectus, and the investing public would go bananas. As a result, some companies that had been in business for only a year or two were worth billions of dollars on paper—even though they consistently lost money. Eventually, of course, most of these "hot stocks" cooled off, and the investors who were sucked in by all the excitement ended up losing their shirts (think Amazon.com).

Some people argue that investing only in proven companies with solid earnings records is a great way to miss the next Microsoft. That's ridiculous. You don't have to get in on the absolute ground floor of a promising new company to do well with it. You can easily wait to buy into it until after it has compiled four or five years of steady profits. Take Microsoft itself. Let's say you decided to be really cautious and wait for it to report profits for 10 years in a row before you were willing to invest. Could you have made any money on the stock? Absolutely. Between 1995 (10 full years after the company reported its first profits) and 2001, the price of Microsoft stock more than quadrupled.

So why take chances? Leave the high-tech start-ups and other risky businesses to the venture capitalists. As long as you are investing to secure your future, you should stick to solid companies with proven track records.

FIVE-STAR TIP: *The above section was first written in 1998, before the technology boom really took off—and before it came crashing back to earth. For a long time after the first edition of this book was published early in 1999, I can't tell you how many people questioned my argument against investing in "dot.coms." Before the party ended, more than 500 such companies went public, feeding on our appetite for get-rich-quick schemes. Companies like Webvan, Pets.com, and Etoys spent hundreds of millions of dollars on ads aimed at "building a brand"— only to find that if you don't make money, you can't stay in business. By now, we all know that the dot.com craze became a dot.com bust. But don't think it's all behind us. Every decade has its own dot.com craze, and the mistake is always the same. Investors get caught up investing in what's hot, instead of in what's making money. Ultimately, they get their clocks cleaned. The rule is simple—no earnings, no investment.*

Actively Trading Your Account. One thing that makes women potentially better investors than men is that women generally are better at committing to the long term. When men buy stocks, they tend to get fidgety; they are constantly looking around, wondering if some better investment isn't waiting for them just around the corner. And while actively buying and selling investments may sound like a great way to stay on top of market developments, the fact is that there are only two winners when you trade frequently: the firm that executes your trades (because it earns a commission on every one of your transactions) and the CCRA (because it gets to collect a piece of your profits every time you sell an investment for more than you bought it). There's no getting around it; under current tax laws, you simply cannot win over the long term by actively buying and selling stock in the short term.

Let's say you buy a stock at $10 a share and less than a year later you sell it at $12. You might think you made a 20 percent return, but you really didn't. First off, it probably cost you 25 cents a share to buy the stock and 25 cents a share to sell it. Right there, your $2 profit is cut to $1.50. Second, if you sell a stock at a profit, you could end up paying almost 40 percent of your earnings in capital gains taxes. So there goes another 80 cents. Suddenly your 20 percent return has been reduced to 70 cents (7 percent). And that's assuming you actually did everything right and bought a stock that went up and then sold it at a profit.

The point is this: When it comes to investing in stocks, the key word is *investing*. You don't invest in a business by making a speculative stock purchase in the hope of a favourable short-term movement. You invest for the long term, with the goal of owning a particular company's stock for years. Trust me—this philosophy will make you significantly more money. At the very least, you'll end up paying far less in commissions and taxes.

Throwing Good Money After Bad. I can't tell you how often I've seen people persuaded to put more money into an investment that has just suffered a significant drop in price—the so-called logic being that, having fallen in price, the investment must now be a bargain. This is known in the investment world as buying on dips. Often financial advisors will suggest that if you liked a stock at $20 a share, it must be an even better buy at $10. But just because the price of a stock has dropped, that doesn't mean it's now "on sale." That's true only if the company is well run and its stock happens to be down simply because of some short-term market gyration, rather than business problems that could prevent it from making money in the future.

I learned this the hard way. I once owned a stock that hit $65 a share and then started falling like a rock. When it reached $3, I said the stupidest thing I've ever said to myself: "Gosh, $3 sure seems cheap. If management can turn things around, it will be back to $10 in no time." With that in mind, I bought a thousand more shares— and watched the price go straight down the tubes to zero. And this was a company with a board of directors whose membership read like a "Who's Who" of American business. (Think Nortel.)

The point of this expensive lesson was clear: When a stock price falls through the floor, and the company doesn't have a convincing explanation for the collapse (or a specific plan in place to correct the problem), don't add to your financial misery by doubling down. As investment guru Warren Buffett once put it: "The most important thing to do when you find yourself in a hole is to stop digging."

MISTAKE NO. 7
BUILDING A PORTFOLIO THAT'S NOT DIVERSIFIED

If the last few years (specifically, 1999–2001) taught us anything about the stock market, it's that without a properly diversified portfolio, you can get slaughtered financially!

Let this sink in for a moment. Greed makes people do really dumb things. Among other things, it had some irate clients calling me in 2000 wanting to know why all their money wasn't in technology stocks. These clients (almost all of them men) would call me and say, "David, why don't I own Yahoo? My friend bought it, and he's making a fortune."

Even worse, well-intentioned clients would call me and say they'd just heard some "expert" on the radio who insisted they had to own "the Nasdaq," whatever that was, so now they wanted to move all their money into it.

The worst part about all this was that most of these people were over 65! I actually lost a client, an 80-year-old woman, who was furious with me because I told her it was crazy to put half her assets into dot.com stocks. She told me I was an old fuddy-duddy.

There I was, 33 at the time, trying to protect an 80-year-old woman's nest egg, and I'm the fuddy-duddy.

Looking back, it would be funny if it wasn't so sad. The technology boom that supposedly made people instant millionaires in a matter of months (instead of the decades it's supposed to take) wound up going bust almost as fast as it went boom. And it was the "retail investors" (which is to say, you and me) who were the ones who got creamed—as usual. The winners were the institutional investors who bought shares of these risky companies at the initial offering price, sometimes as low as $10 a share, and then flipped them a few hours later for $90 a share. You and I didn't get that chance.

Still, some good did come out of it. It reminded us that there are no shortcuts. The only sure way to get rich is to do so slowly by building a well-diversified, rock-solid portfolio. As I noted earlier, you cannot time the market. Nor can you anticipate which sector of the market is going to be hot next week, next month, or next year.

Some people find this hard to accept. One of the worst things investors do is look at their portfolios at the end of a year and decide to sell stocks of theirs that didn't go up and buy ones that did.

In 1999, for example, value stocks and value mutual funds did horribly, either staying flat or going down. At the same time, growth stocks and growth funds went through the roof, shooting up as much as 40 percent that year. But if you had let hindsight be your guide and flipped out of value investments and into growth holdings at the end of 1999, you'd have gotten killed over the next 12 months as tech stocks tanked, in some cases falling more than 70 percent. And to make matters worse, while growth investments were collapsing, value stocks and funds were rising by more than 30 percent!

The chart on page 202 shows in simple terms exactly why you need to maintain a diversified portfolio. Trust me on this. You'll see lots of books in the stores written by "experts" who will tell you that one particular type of asset is fundamentally superior to all the others—and that, as a result, you should put all your money in it alone. In my opinion they are wrong. History has shown that no asset class will always outperform every other asset class. Because of human nature, strong asset classes inevitably become "overbought" (that is, overenthusiastic investors bid up prices too high). At that point, people panic and values plunge. So stay diversified.

A CASE FOR DIVERSIFICATION

In real estate, it's location, location, location. In asset allocation, it's diversification, diversification, diversification. A sound investment plan can include investing in assets in various asset classes. Large-company domestic stocks, small-company domestic stocks, real estate stocks, foreign stocks, and U.S. Treasury bonds have each been the top-performing asset class during calendar years. The table below illustrates the average annual total returns for these asset classes.

Year	Large-Company Stocks	Small-Company Stocks	Real Estate Stocks	Foreign Stocks	U.S. Treasury Bonds
1980	32.50	38.60	24.37	22.58	2.71
1981	-4.92	2.03	6.00	-2.28	6.25
1982	21.55	24.95	21.60	-1.86	32.62
1983	22.56	29.13	30.64	23.69	8.36
1984	6.27	-7.30	20.93	7.38	15.15
1985	31.73	31.05	19.10	56.16	22.10
1986	18.66	5.68	19.16	69.44	15.26
1987	5.25	-8.80	-3.64	24.63	2.76
1988	16.56	25.02	13.49	28.27	7.89
1989	31.63	16.26	8.84	10.54	14.53
1990	-3.11	-19.48	-15.35	-23.45	8.96
1991	30.40	46.04	35.70	12.13	16.00
1992	7.61	18.41	14.59	-12.17	7.40
1993	10.06	18.88	19.65	32.56	9.75
1994	1.31	-1.82	3.17	7.78	-2.92
1995	37.53	28.45	15.27	11.21	18.47
1996	22.95	16.50	35.27	6.05	3.63
1997	33.35	22.36	20.26	1.78	9.65
1998	28.60	-2.55	-17.50	20.00	8.69
1999	21.03	21.26	-4.62	26.96	-0.82
2000	-9.11	-3.59	26.37	-14.17	5.89

Source: AIM Distributors, Inc., and Lipper, Inc. All data as of 11/30/00.

```
┌─────────────────────────────────────────────────┐
│                  MISTAKE NO. 8                    │
│            PAYING TOO MUCH IN TAXES               │
└─────────────────────────────────────────────────┘
```

The biggest enemy of your financial future is taxes. Yet when I review the financial situation of new clients, you'd be amazed how often it turns out that their previous advisors never did any tax planning for them.

When you are building an investment portfolio, it is absolutely imperative that you take into consideration your potential tax liability. The reason I spent so much time in Step Four and Step Five talking about retirement plans is that the money in them grows tax-deferred, which helps you to grow your nest egg much faster. The difference in not paying taxes on your investments over a 10- to 30-year period can be huge! It can mean the difference between financial pain or financial pleasure. The following chart shows how much faster your money will grow if it is invested in tax-deferred vehicles. Over a typical 30-year period, you could literally be talking about millions of additional dollars in your pocket! (See chart on page 204.)

As you can see, your money grows significantly faster when the profits are not drained away by taxes. Always seek to minimize your taxes when investing; ideally you should seek investments that grow tax-deferred.

```
┌─────────────────────────────────────────────────┐
│                  MISTAKE NO. 9                    │
│        BUYING AN INVESTMENT THAT IS ILLIQUID      │
└─────────────────────────────────────────────────┘
```

An illiquid investment is one that you cannot sell immediately. To me, "immediately" means in less than five business days. If I can't sell it within five business days, I won't buy it. Why? Show me an investment you can't sell for a fixed period and I'll show you a potential problem.

Now, don't get me wrong. I'm not arguing against buying a home or an investment such as a government bond that takes 10 years to mature or a mutual fund with an annual sales fee. All of these things may have a perfectly proper place in your investment portfolio. What

NOTICE THE DIFFERENCE
TAX-DEFERRED INVESTING CAN MAKE

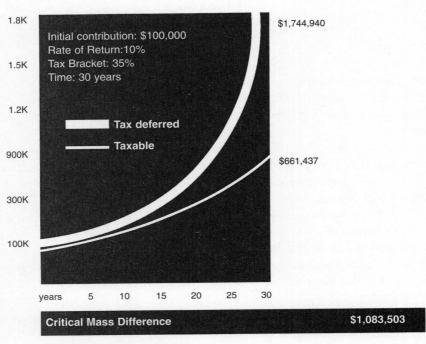

Initial contribution: $100,000
Rate of Return: 10%
Tax Bracket: 35%
Time: 30 years

$1,744,940

Tax deferred

Taxable

$661,437

years   5   10   15   20   25   30

Critical Mass Difference   **$1,083,503**

Tax deferral can grow more money.

Turning Growth into Income

From	Taxable	Tax Deferred
Accumulation	$661,437	$1,744,940
Rate of Return	at 10%	at 10%
Annual Earnings	$66,143	$174,494
Tax Bracket	at 35%	at 35%
Annual Income	**$42,993**	**$113,422**

Tax-deferred growth can lead to more income.

I'm warning you against buying is something that is not salable for a specific period, no matter what. An example of the kind of illiquid investment I hate is a *limited partnership*—the two most dreaded words in the Smart Woman's financial vocabulary. When I bring up limited partnerships in my classes, I often hear moans and groans from a few of the older students. That tells me they have some experience with the subject.

Limited partnerships generally are set up to pool investors' money to purchase certain types of investments, typically real estate. The problem is that most limited partnerships are not salable—that is, not liquid—usually for as long as 10 to 15 years. "Don't worry about it," the salesman typically tells a potential investor. "The money you're investing is for retirement and you won't need it for 20 years anyway." Sure, but what happens if an emergency arises and you've got to get your hands on your money early?

Now, I know some people will dispute this and insist that limited partnerships can make sense. Well, I'm sorry; I have seen too many account statements and heard too many firsthand stories from people who were burned by this kind of investment. As far as I'm concerned, limited partnerships are a bad idea for ordinary investors. They are not liquid, so don't buy them. Period. (If for some reason you come across a limited partnership that you feel you just have to be a part of, then my rule of thumb is *don't put more than 10 percent of your investable assets into it*. This way, if you lose your whole investment, your financial world won't be completely devastated.)

Limited partnerships are hardly the only illiquid investment out there, so don't let down your guard. For example, there are investment companies (offering everything from collectable coins to second mortgages) that claim to make a "secondary market" in the investment they are selling. That's all well and good, but in many cases they slip into the fine print a disclaimer saying that they are not obligated to buy out your investment if you want to sell. If that's the case, then what you're buying is not really a liquid investment.

One of the worst cases I know of in this regard concerns a former client of mine named Barbara. Back in 1991, a devastating fire wiped out over 2,800 homes in the hills above Berkeley, California. Barbara's home was one of them. Fortunately, she had adequate fire insurance. Her insurance company settled her claim for more than $500,000, and Barbara went about planning to rebuild her home.

Since construction wouldn't be ready to start for six months, Barbara put the money in a bank GIC (a great place, you will remember from our discussion of the Dream Basket, for short-term funds). A few weeks later a neighbour who was in a similar situation asked her what she'd done with her insurance money. When Barbara told him it was sitting in a GIC earning 5 percent, the neighbour rolled his eyes. His insurance money, he claimed, was earning 15 percent.

That got Barbara's attention. The neighbour explained that a friend of his who invested in secondary mortgages had let him in on a deal. Barbara was impressed and, to make a long story short, she wound up giving her neighbour's friend half her insurance money—$250,000 in all—to invest in secondary mortgages. The friend's pitch was simple. The money would be safe because it would be backed by real estate. In any case, Barbara didn't need to worry because short-term investments in secondary mortgages were very easy to buy and sell. She would be paid 180 days' worth of interest up front and then get her principal back at the end of the 180 days. It sounded too good to be true.

It was. Barbara got her interest payment up front, but when the 180 days were up, she found herself waiting in vain for her $250,000 principal to be returned. When she went to ask her neighbour's friend what was going on, she discovered he was nowhere to be found. In a panic, Barbara ran to the local courthouse to check the records on the property she supposedly had a second mortgage on. The property was in foreclosure—as a result of which, Barbara's investment was unsellable.

Had Barbara used the rule of not investing in illiquid investments, she never would have had this problem. The fact is, secondary mortgages are almost never easily liquid because they are backed by real estate that would have to be sold for you to get your money back.

Liquid means that the public (that is, anyone you choose to sell to) can buy you out easily and quickly—ideally, in less than five business days. Examples of liquid investments include stocks, bonds, mutual funds, money market funds, GICs, Treasury bills, and annuities. In fact, most investments are liquid. Just remember to ask the question: "If I absolutely had to, could I sell this and get my money within five business days?" If the answer is no, think hard before you put any money into the investment.

MISTAKE NO. 10
GIVING UP

I once asked my grandmother if she had ever made any major mistakes investing. She told me that the first stock she ever bought went straight down and she lost everything she had invested. As she explained it, she had gotten a "tip" and just jumped in. She actually invested only a couple of hundred dollars, but at the time that represented a full year's worth of savings. She told me she felt sick and embarrassed, and was afraid to tell my grandfather.

"Well, what did you do?" I asked her.

"What could I do?" she replied with a smile. "The money was gone." Still, she realized one important thing: The problem was not the stock market, the problem was her inexperience with investing. "So I set out to become smart about investing and do it right the next time," she told me.

And that's just what she did. She read books (like the one you're reading now) as well as financial magazines and newsletters, she took classes, and in general she made an effort to get smart about investing. Did she invest perfectly from then on? Of course not. She made plenty of mistakes at first, but she learned from them, and over the years she built a million-dollar portfolio.

People often make a financial mistake, get bad advice, and then give up on their dream of financial security. *Don't let this happen to you.* You now know more than most people about how to avoid the most common mistakes that can be made with your investment dollars. Are there more pitfalls out there? Absolutely. Might you stumble into one of them? Possibly. But don't let that keep you from getting where you want to go. As you continue on your journey and acquire more knowledge of and control over your finances, you will start to be able to spot bad money decisions a mile away. It will be as if they have a huge sign on them reading "kiss your money goodbye!"

Yes, you should be careful, but don't become overcautious. By learning to avoid the common pitfalls investors make, you can minimize your risk and put yourself on the road to financial security. But remember—the biggest mistake you can make is not to become an investor.

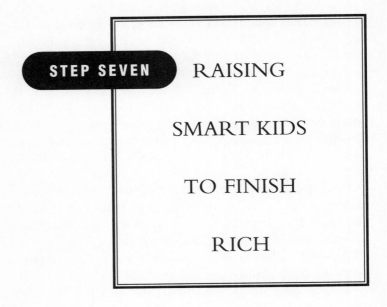

STEP SEVEN RAISING SMART KIDS TO FINISH RICH

Imagine for a moment how different your life would be if you had learned everything this book has just taught you about handling money when you were still a kid.

The fact is, you shouldn't have needed the material in this book. All this stuff should have been taught to you in school, along with math and reading and history. But for some reason, our educational system has decided that there is no room in the schools for lessons about money. Sure, there are some great creative teachers here and there who take it upon themselves to teach their students about handling their finances. But it's never been part of the mandatory curriculum.

To send a child off into the "real world" without teaching him or her how to be smart about money is to set that child up for failure. With this in mind, I ask that you read this chapter whether or not you have kids—even if you're single and are convinced you'll never have a family. Why? Because teaching smart kids to finish rich is not about just teaching your own kids, it's about teaching all kids.

Perhaps you have a friend who has a child. Maybe you've got a niece or nephew. You could become their mentor.

Perhaps your kids are grown. Maybe you're a grandmother. Remember, as I related in the introduction, my entire life was shaped by the fact that my grandmother Rose Bach started teaching me at the age of seven that even a kid could become an investor. It was Grandma Bach who told me, "David, if you saved your birthday money and your weekly allowance, you could start buying stocks—and one day you could become a millionaire!" Grandma knew how to get my attention.

Unfortunately, most parents and grandparents don't do what she did. They don't teach their kids about money. As a result, their kids grow up financially illiterate. You can do something about that—we all can, and we all should.

Our School System Is Failing Our Children

The majority of Canadian high school students have little understanding of basic economic principles.

Few of them know, for example, that the stock market brings people who want to buy stocks together with people who want to sell them. Few of them know that in times of inflation money does not hold its value.

Parents Are Failing Too!

The parents of these kids don't know much more than their kids, and they know it. In a survey sponsored by RBC Financial Group, more than half of wealthy investors said they have only a basic understanding of financial matters.

If we can use U.S. statistics as a guideline, even investors—the one group you would expect to know something about the subject—are woefully ignorant. Consider the following results of a 1997 study by the National Association of Securities Dealers.

- 78 percent could name a character on a television sitcom, but only 12 percent knew the difference between a "load fund" and a "no-load fund."
- 63 percent knew the difference between a halfback and a quarterback, but only 14 percent could tell the difference between a growth stock and an income stock.

The conclusion to be drawn from this is clear: We have a system that is set up for failure. Our schools don't teach kids anything about money, and the cycle of financial illiteracy goes on and on.

THE GOOD NEWS . . . EDUCATION ABOUT MONEY CAN HELP!

I find this situation frightening, and I hope you do too. I refer to it because I want you to understand at a gut level how bad the problem is.

But being concerned isn't enough. Unless we do something, the situation is not going to change. Ultimately, what we need is a mandatory national financial literacy program—something similar to Participaction, which Ottawa created back in the 1960s to teach kids about the importance of being physically fit.

That program and a similar program in the U.S. motivated millions of kids to get in shape. I know because I was one of those kids struggling on the pull-up bar in the third grade, unable to do a single chin-up. I remember being ashamed and humiliated by the experience of taking a national fitness test and failing. But it also motivated me.

It took me until the eighth grade, but I finally got my Fitness Badge. I felt proud that day, but more important, fitness became a way of life for me. To this day, I still work out four times a week.

If you agree with me that we need a national financial literacy program, you should make your voice heard. Let your representatives in Ottawa hear from you. (These days, it's easy to do on-line at www.parl.gc.ca.) Tell them you believe strongly that we need a mandatory national standard for financial education.

THE RIGHT TIME TO TEACH THE KIDS IS NOW

So when is the right time to begin teaching your kids about money? Here's a test to help you determine the answer. Put a one-dollar bill in your left hand and a $100 bill in your right hand. Then ask your child which one he or she wants.

Children who are smart enough to know that the $100 bill is the one to go for are smart enough to start learning about money. So far, the youngest child I've heard of who could pass this test was a three-year-old. Try it out. You may find you have a future Warren Buffett on your hands.

COACHING SMART KIDS TO FINISH RICH

The most important thing to understand when it comes to teaching children about money is that all kids are not created equal. Obviously, yours is smarter than most, but every child should be allowed to go at his or her own pace.

In any case, here are eight simple steps you can take to get your children started on the journey to living and finishing rich.

STEP NO. 1
EXPLAIN WHERE MONEY COMES FROM.

The first thing you need to explain to a young child about money is where it comes from. Many kids actually think money comes from a device that lives in a wall (what you and I would recognize as an ATM machine).

Perhaps the place to start is with the expression, "Money doesn't grow on trees." We've all heard that phrase, you can tell your child, but do you know where money does come from?

Take out a dollar bill and some change, and explain how the Canadian government manufactures currency. Then explain what it represents: how you earn it by working or investing, how you spend it to pay for the home you live in, the clothes you wear, and the food you eat.

The older your children are, the more detailed you can and should be. If your kids are over the age of 10, don't hesitate to tell them in excruciating detail exactly what happens to your paycheque—how much goes to taxes and Canada Pension Plan, to mortgage payments, to insurance, utilities, car payments, phone bills, and all the other necessities of life. Most children have no idea about their family finances. In fact, many parents find it easier to talk to their kids about sex than about money.

Be honest with your kids . . . and be positive.

If your family is having money troubles, don't try to hide it. Your kids are probably aware of your problems anyway. But whatever you do, be positive. Explain that money is a really good thing when it is used respectfully, how it can help you lead a better life and help others, but that it is not a measure of your worth as a human being.

Many parents give the wrong message about money to their kids. They either equate wealth with goodness or they say that people who have money are greedy. (Sometimes they deliver both these contradictory messages at the same time.) You want your kids to be attracted to money, not afraid of it. You want them to be comfortable with money.

> ## STEP NO. 2
> TEACH THEM THE MIRACLE OF COMPOUND INTEREST.

As I discussed earlier in this book, Albert Einstein once said that the most miraculous phenomenon he knew was the miracle of compound interest. Many adults are still in the dark about this. You're not, so don't keep it a secret. Show your kids the charts on pages 101 and 102. Explain to them what can happen to a dollar when you invest it, instead of spend it.

How a Dollar a Day Can Grow to be $1 Million

Here's what happens if you save a dollar a day and then put it to work for you.

$1	a day at 10%	=	$1 million in 56 years
$1	a day at 15%	=	$1 million in 40 years
$1	a day at 20%	=	$1 million in 32 years

Makes you wonder, doesn't it, why we don't place more value on a loonie. What if you really went crazy and saved $2 a day?

$2	a day at 10%	=	$1 million in 49 years
$2	a day at 15%	=	$1 million in 36 years
$2	a day at 20%	=	$1 million in 28 years

By the way, please don't start thinking like a skeptical adult and say, "Oh, but you can't find those kind of returns." You can. Go to *www.morningstar.ca* or *http://cafinance.yahoo.com* and do a search for mutual funds that have generated an average annual return of 10 percent or more over the last 10 years. You'll find there are plenty.

In any case, the point here is not about investment returns. It's about the power of compound interest. Kids get excited by it. So do teenagers. When you show them what compounding does, they won't react the way many adults do and look for reasons why it can't work. To the contrary, they will realize that the dollar they've been wasting on a candy bar every day could make them rich! They will want to save and become investors. Which is your goal.

FIVE-STAR TIP: *Here's a real nugget on compound interest that is sure to catch your kid's attention. (It comes from J. J. Pritchard's book on finances for children,* Quest for the Pillars of Wealth.*) If, when he arrived in the New World in 1492, Christopher Columbus had deposited one dollar into a savings account that paid 5 percent a year in simple interest, each year he would earn 5 cents on his dollar—which is to say that by 2002, his one dollar would have grown to $26.50. However, if he had taken that same dollar and placed it in a bank account that paid 5 percent a year in compound interest, it would now be worth more than $55 billion dollars! That's the power of compounding.*

> ## STEP NO. 3
> MAKE THEIR WEEKLY ALLOWANCE A TEACHING TOOL.

One of the best ways to teach children about money is to give them an allowance. However, this does not mean simply handing over a specified amount of money with no strings attached. In my view, your child's weekly allowance should be based on three principles:

- They should earn it
- They should value it
- They should use it to help others

Unfortunately, for many kids and their parents, allowances have become a rite of passage. The child hits a certain age and asks for an allowance. The parents then turn to their friends, take a survey on allowances, and settle on a dollar amount they feel comfortable with. They then proceed to dish out that amount every week to the child, who uses the money to buy candy, comic books, clothes, CDs, and other goodies that catch his or her fancy, fueling a vast army of consumers who as a group spend billions of dollars a year. Consider this . . .

Canadian Teenagers Spend Billions

There are 2.4 million tweens in Canada (between the ages of 9 and 14), according to a Creative Research International Inc. survey commissioned by YTV. This group spent approximately $1.5 billion in 2000. There are another 1.7 million people in Canada between the ages of 15 and 19, and they were responsible for spending an astonishing $12 billion in 2000. (To put it in context, that adds up to the annual gross domestic product of Jamaica.) Now, I know some of these kids had jobs, but an awful lot of them were using money that had been dished out to them by generous (and often guilt-ridden) parents.

I'm not saying we shouldn't give our kids money. But why not do it in a way that teaches them something about the nature of personal finance and money management? That's what the Rockefellers did, and they certainly knew something about money.

Handling the Allowance Question,
Rockefeller-Style

According to a snippet I read on the Internet from a book called *Kids and Cash* by Ken Davis and Tom Taylor, former vice president Nelson Rockefeller, who had earlier been the governor of New York (and the primary benefactor of New York City's famed Museum of Modern Art), once explained how his father, the legendary John D. Rockefeller, taught him about money. As Nelson Rockefeller told it, he and his five brothers were each given 25 cents a week. "If we wanted more money we had to work for it," he said. What's more, he added, "All of us had to keep a record of where our money went. We were required to give 10 percent to charity, save 10 percent, and then account for how we spent or saved the other 80 percent."

There is an amazingly powerful yet simple lesson from one of the wealthiest families in U.S. history. It comes down to this.

- To earn an allowance you have to work
- 10 percent of your allowance goes to charity
- 10 percent of your allowance goes to savings
- 80 percent of your allowance can be spent but you have to track each expenditure

If you think about it, that's pretty much what you've been learning in this book: Pay yourself first, watch your Latté Factor, and give back to others. Think how much easier it would have been to make these strategies a part of your life if you had been introduced to them when you were a child, like the Rockefeller kids were.

I recall seeing an episode of Oprah Winfrey's TV show that included a segment featuring parents talking about how they taught their kids about money. One couple said they required their children to put part of their allowance into a family investment account that the kids ran themselves. Each month, they held a family investment meeting at which they discussed investment strategies and how their holdings were doing. That's a brilliant idea.

The point is that when it comes to giving out an allowance, you can just dole out the dough—or you can turn the exercise into a teaching tool that will have a massive, positive impact on your children's financial literacy.

What If We've Already Been Giving Our Kids an Allowance with No Rules?

Be honest. Tell them that the rules have changed—that from now on, you intend to handle their allowance in a way that will teach them how to be future millionaires. They will get it. (And what are they going to do—go on strike?)

STEP NO. 4

TEACH THEM ABOUT RETIREMENT ACCOUNTS . . . NOW

The best time to open a retirement account is when you're a teenager! But how do you convince a teenager of that?

Actually, there is a way. Show your teenager the charts on page 217. The first one illustrates what would happen if a 14-year-old named Lucy were to open a retirement account and save $2,000 a year until she reaches 18—that is, depositing a total of $10,000. Even if Lucy never put in another dime after that, simply by letting the money grow in a tax-deferred retirement plan at 10 percent a year, she would wind up with more than $1 million in her account ($1,184,600, to be precise) by the time she was 65.

The other charts illustrate what happens if you don't start saving until you're older. One shows Susan, who starts at age 19; the other shows Kim, who waits until she's 27. Neither woman ever catches up to Lucy, even though both deposit significantly more money.

It's another demonstration of the miracle of compound interest, and it is extremely motivating!

How Can a Teenager Open a Retirement Account?

Very easily. Any teenager with a part-time job can eventually open a retirement account. All you've got to do is accompany your child to a bank or brokerage firm (or to the office of your financial advisor, if you've got one) to help with the paperwork. The key qualifications to open an RRSP is that your child must have earned income and that the RRSP deposit in any given year cannot exceed 18 percent of his or her income in that year.

If your teenagers have paying jobs, they can file annual tax returns even if their incomes are below taxable levels. By reporting their earned income, they will start to accumulate RRSP contribution room. Although they may not be able to take advantage of it right away, they can carry it forward indefinitely. And they can make a one-time overcontribution (currently the maximum is $2,000), which begins compounding tax-free as soon as they invest it.

THE TIME VALUE OF MONEY
Invest Now Rather Than Later

LUCY — Investing at Age 14 (10% Annual Return)				SUSAN — Investing at Age 19 (10% Annual Return)				KIM — Investing at Age 27 (10% Annual Return)		
AGE	INVESTMENT	TOTAL VALUE		AGE	INVESTMENT	TOTAL VALUE		AGE	INVESTMENT	TOTAL VALUE
14	$2,000	$2,200	S	19	$2,000	2,200	S	19	0	0
15	2,000	4,620	E	20	2,000	4,620	E	20	0	0
16	2,000	7,282	E	21	2,000	7,282	E	21	0	0
17	2,000	10,210		22	2,000	10,210		22	0	0
18	2,000	13,431	E	23	2,000	13,431	E	23	0	0
19	0	14,774		24	2,000	16,974		24	0	0
20	0	16,252		25	2,000	20,871		25	0	0
21	0	17,877		26	2,000	25,158		26	0	0
22	0	19,665	T	27	0	27,674	T	27	$2,000	2,200
23	0	21,631		28	0	30,442		28	2,000	4,620
24	0	23,794	H	29	0	33,486	H	29	2,000	7,282
25	0	26,174		30	0	36,834		30	2,000	10,210
26	0	28,791	E	31	0	40,518	E	31	2,000	13,431
27	0	31,670		32	0	44,570		32	2,000	16,974
28	0	34,837		33	0	48,027		33	2,000	20,871
29	0	38,321		34	0	53,929		34	2,000	25,158
30	0	42,153		35	0	59,322		35	2,000	29,874
31	0	46,368	D	36	0	65,256	D	36	2,000	35,072
32	0	51,005	I	37	0	71,780	I	37	2,000	40,768
33	0	56,106		38	0	78,958		38	2,000	47,045
34	0	61,716	F	39	0	86,854	F	39	2,000	53,949
35	0	67,888	F	40	0	95,540	F	40	2,000	61,544
36	0	74,676		41	0	105,094		41	2,000	69,899
37	0	82,144	E	42	0	115,603	E	42	2,000	79,089
38	0	90,359	R	43	0	127,163	R	43	2,000	89,198
39	0	99,394		44	0	139,880		44	2,000	100,318
40	0	109,334	E	45	0	153,868	E	45	2,000	112,550
41	0	120,267		46	0	169,255		46	2,000	126,005
42	0	132,294	N	47	0	188,180	N	47	2,000	140,805
43	0	145,523		48	0	204,798		48	2,000	157,086
44	0	160,076	C	49	0	226,278	C	49	2,000	174,094
45	0	176,083		50	0	247,806		50	2,000	194,694
46	0	193,692	E	51	0	272,586	E	51	2,000	216,363
47	0	213,061		52	0	299,845		52	2,000	240,199
48	0	234,367		53	0	329,830		53	2,000	266,419
49	0	257,803		54	0	362,813		54	2,000	295,261
50	0	283,358		55	0	399,094		55	2,000	326,988
51	0	311,942		56	0	439,003		56	2,000	361,886
52	0	343,136		57	0	482,904		57	2,000	400,275
53	0	377,450		58	0	531,194		58	2,000	442,503
54	0	415,195		59	0	584,314		59	2,000	488,953
55	0	456,715		60	0	642,745		60	2,000	540,048
56	0	502,386		61	0	707,020		61	2,000	596,253
57	0	552,625		62	0	777,722		62	2,000	658,078
58	0	607,887		63	0	855,494		63	2,000	726,086
59	0	668,676		64	0	941,043		64	2,000	800,895
60	0	735,543		65	0	1,035,148		65	2,000	883,185
61	0	809,098								
62	0	890,007								
63	0	979,008								
64	0	1,076,909								
65	0	1,184,600								

Total invested = $10,000.
Earnings beyond investment = $1,174,600.

Total invested = $16,000.
Earnings beyond investment = $1,019,148.

Total Investment = $78,000.
Earnings beyond investment = $805,185.

Lucy earns $1,174,600   Susan earns $1,019,148   Kim earns $ 805,185

Lucy invested $68,000 less than Kim and has $369,415 more!
START INVESTING EARLY!

As I see it, getting teenagers their own retirement plans is both a smart financial strategy and a phenomenal teaching tool. By doing it, you accomplish two things. You teach your children about saving at a young age and you get them in the habit of "paying themselves first."

> ## STEP NO. 5
> TEACH THEM TO THINK LIKE OWNERS INSTEAD
> OF SHOPPERS.

Earlier, I told you how Grandma Bach helped me make my first financial investment at age seven. Both my grandmother and my father changed my life by teaching me at a young age what it meant to buy stock in a publicly traded company.

The idea that there were things you could do with cash other than just spend it—that by investing you could turn a little money into a lot more—just blew me away. I remember asking my parents the first time we visited Disneyland, "Is this place for sale? Can we buy stock in this place?"

I couldn't believe it when they said yes. Don't get me wrong. I think mutual funds make great investments. But the experience doesn't match the feeling of owning a share of stock in a particular company. There is nothing quite like using the Bell phone system or logging on to Rogers High-Speed Internet and knowing that you own a piece of the company.

With this in mind, teach your kids how to buy stock. Take them down to a brokerage firm and help them open an account. You'll have to open the account in both of your names, but it will be a great lesson. Then teach them how to look up stocks in the newspaper and how to read the ticker on ROB TV and the other financial services. (If you don't know yourself, have someone at the brokerage show you. It's not really that complicated.)

Something else you can do is buy one share of stock in a company your child knows and likes, and then ask the broker to have the stock certificate "issued out." This means the certificate will be sent directly to you, rather than being kept on file at the brokerage. If it's a cool company like Disney, the stock certificate will be gorgeous—nice enough to frame and hang in your kid's room. When his or her friends come over, your child can explain what it is and how he or she is becoming an investor. Pretty soon, your friends may be wanting to teach their kids about stocks too.

There is a company called OneShare.com that will do all of this for you over the Internet. (You'll find them on the web at *www.one-share.com*) It's an American company, but it will buy shares for Canadians, too. The company will even have the stock certificate framed for you! If you want to do this as a gift, all you need is the child's name and social insurance number.

STEP NO. 6
TEACH THEM TO USE CREDIT CARDS RESPONSIBLY

According to the Association of Universities and Colleges of Canada, the average college undergraduate owes nearly $25,000 when he or she completes post-secondary education, making Canadian students the most indebted in the western world. Several thousand students a year file for personal bankruptcy. Moreover, many undergraduates have a credit card, or even more than one.

The Credit Card Companies Want Your Children

Credit card companies aren't stupid. They know that if they can get their cards into your children's hands, they will use them often, while making only the minimum monthly payments, thus staying in debt—and paying expensive finance charges—for years, if not decades.

For the companies, this is simply good business and they are not going to stop anytime soon. They are a fixture on college and university campuses around Canada, and they are good at marketing. Do you think it's an accident that the average Canadian owes an average of $10,000 in student loans and $3,000 in credit card debt?

You Must Teach Your Kids Now . . . Before the Credit Card Companies Get to Them

Sooner or later, your children are going to get a credit card, and they are going to use it. Just how they use the card will depend largely on how they were raised. If they've seen you constantly using credit cards, they will use credit cards constantly. If they've seen you run up bills you can't afford, they'll probably do the same.

Unless you start showing your kids the bills and explaining the stress that credit card debt can cause, they will not realize the real implications of their purchasing decisions. I speak from personal experience. I grew up watching my parents use credit cards all the time. The only lesson I really learned was that you were supposed to pay your cards on time—a very important lesson, as it turned out, but hardly the only one I needed to learn. As a result, when I got to college, I was woefully unprepared to handle all the credit cards that were offered to me.

When I signed up at my new dorm room in first year, I was greeted by representatives of three credit card companies. They were giving away "free" clock radios, bike locks, and dictionaries. All you had to do was sign up for a card.

When my friends saw all the stuff I'd gotten, they all rushed downstairs to sign up too. Three weeks later, our mailboxes were stuffed with shiny new credit cards. Now picture this: You're 18 and you and everyone you know has instant access to "free money," courtesy of some brand-new plastic. What do you suppose we did? That's right—we went to town and partied.

By my second year, I owed $5,000 in credit card debt. When I confessed my plight to my parents, my father told me something I will never forget. "David," he said, "welcome to adulthood."

He went on to explain that the cards had my name on them and that, if I didn't pay the bills on time, I'd ruin my credit record and be scarred financially for years.

It was a splash of harsh reality that caused me to grow up fast. It took me a year to get out of that credit card debt, but I did it. In the process, I learned a valuable lesson. Don't spend what you don't have. Today I use a debit card and an American Express card, and I never carry credit card debt.

If only my parents had drilled it into my head earlier not to use credit cards and always to pay off the card in full each month, it would have saved me so much trouble and anguish.

Here's what you should teach your kids specifically about credit cards.

Explain what happens if you run up a credit card balance and don't pay it off. Explain how brutal it is to have to keep paying 18 percent interest on purchases that have long since lost their shine. Share with your kids how if they don't pay their cards on time each and every month, they can literally damage their credit so badly that even years later they won't be able to get a mortgage to buy a house. All it takes is one little credit card with a $500 balance you forgot to pay off.

This is so important that before your kids leave for college, you absolutely have to have a "credit card talk." In addition to emphasizing the importance of paying off their balances, make them understand that multiple credit cards are a disaster waiting to happen. All they really need is one card for use in case of emergencies. In no event should they have more than two.

Good luck on your talk. I know it won't be easy, but it will be worth it. You could wind up saving a child from future bankruptcy.

FIVE-STAR TIP: *The biggest single mistake I see university and college kids make with credit cards is neglecting to give the credit card company their new address when they move. This is easy to do when you are moving once or twice a year. As a result, many kids wind up "forgetting" about their bills—and by the time the credit card company tracks them down, they have months' worth of late fees and charges, and their credit record is permanently scarred. If you're the parent of a college student, don't let your child make this mistake. If he or she lives in a university residence, tell them to arrange to have their bills sent to your home or get them a post office box at school, because mail at dorms and fraternity and sorority houses gets lost all the time.*

STEP NO. 7
TEACH THEM TO GO FOR THEIR DREAMS.

This last step has very little to do with money but a lot to do with life. I think one of the greatest gifts a parent or adult can give a child is the feeling that "this child is special." We need to literally douse our children with love—to keep reinforcing the feeling that they are special. You can't err by giving too much love or support. Nor do I believe that it's ever a mistake to tell children again and again that they are special and that if they try, they can accomplish anything they want. I think the biggest mistake we make with our kids is inadvertently teaching them not to try because they may fail. If anything, rather than discouraging failure, we should reward it.

A Child Who Fails Trying Something New Is a Child Who Will Learn Faster

What's great about children when they are really young is that they have no fear. They aren't afraid of not looking good. They don't worry about not knowing how to do something. They just storm right ahead and try.

Unfortunately, society quickly changes this. Society teaches children as they grow older that failure is to be avoided. Our grading system at school reinforces this idea. Don't fail, the schools say. You must be good at all things. You must get good grades in all your subjects or you won't move ahead in life.

This idea that you need to be good at everything is absurd. The truth is that to be incredibly successful in life you may need to be really good at only one thing. In fact, this describes some of the most successful and richest and happiest people around. They've become so good at one particular thing that society rewards them for it, and refers to them as "stars."

Become a Cheerleader for Your Child

You can be a cheerleader for your kids and still enforce discipline. I had very strict parents, but they also cheered me on. They urged me to try new things and always "go for it." They encouraged me to take risks.

I don't think this kind of approach can ever be a mistake. The idea that we need to raise realistic kids is crazy. What's reality? Look at our world. New realities are created every day.

One of the most disappointing things about our schools and the way we raise our kids is that we don't spend more time teaching kids to take more risks. Instead, we teach them to play it safe. Be good, get good grades, get a good job, and eventually you can have a good retirement. That's the lesson society endorses.

But what if that lesson is totally out of date? What if the idea that getting good grades and then going to a good university and then getting a good job represents an outmoded plan? In fact, most of our schools today are based on a model created over a hundred years ago for an industrial society in a world totally different from the one into which most of us were born. Back then, you went to work, punched a clock, did what you were told, and eventually were handed a gold watch (maybe). There was hierarchy and a well-defined system within which to work.

Not anymore. Today, ideas created out of thin air can become billion-dollar enterprises. The people who get ahead are the ones who know how to communicate, how to think outside the box and persuade others. Unfortunately, many of our schools are still preparing our kids for the old system. Sit still. Be quiet. Do what you are told and we will give you good grades. Get good grades, get a good job, and get lifelong security.

I'm not suggesting that kids shouldn't get good grades and go to university. Of course they should. But it seems to me that our schools are creating worker bees at a time when society is rewarding entrepreneurs.

We need to raise our children to think bigger and more creatively than we did. So ask yourself right now, "What am I teaching my kids about life's challenges?" Are you raising your children to go for their dreams or simply to avoid failure?

STEP NO. 8
USE THE INTERNET TO TEACH YOUR KIDS ABOUT MONEY.

The Internet is an amazing tool that you can use to teach your kids more about money—and it's free. I've spent a lot of time looking for great sites on this subject. These are some of my favourites.

www2.cibc.com/smartstart Canada's major banks have set up websites to teach kids about the basic principles of banking and finance. This one is administered by CIBC. It teaches kids of all ages how to think about money and how money works.

www.bankofcanada.ca The Bank of Canada's website includes a downloadable game called The Adventures of Cecil SmartSox, which teaches kids about banking and money, although it's a bit cumbersome and it's aimed primarily at schools.

There are several other sites, most of them based in the U.S., that enable kids to learn about money while having fun. These include:

www.BigChange.com This website teaches kids and parents how to set up and manage an allowance program that both of you can get excited about. It includes an interactive calculator that children can use to see how much of their allowance they need to put aside and for how long in order to reach whatever their goal happens to be.

www.kidsbank.com Remember I suggested that you begin by teaching your kids where money comes from? This site, developed by a bank to explain how money and banking work, can help you do exactly that. It features a step-by-step teaching tool you can use to teach your young children about where money comes from and what it is used for. What's more, it has a game room.

WHAT ABOUT PAYING FOR
UNIVERSITY OR COLLEGE?

While I have many concerns about how and what our schools teach our kids, I am still a strong proponent of education, teachers, and ultimately the value of a university or college education.

I just want your kids to know they have options. If you teach them the lessons you learn in this book, they can escape the rat race because they will know how to save, invest, and spend wisely.

This brings us to the most difficult financial challenge many parents face. How in the world are you going to pay for your children's post-secondary education?

Universities and Colleges Are Expensive . . . and Getting More So Every Year

Unlike the U.S., Canada still heavily subsidizes the cost of post-secondary education. Tuition accounts for one-third or less of the cost; government subsidies make up the rest. However, the share borne by students (and their parents) has risen faster than the consumer price index over the last 10 years. The CPI has gone up by about 2 percent a year; the cost of tuition has increased by 8.7 percent. Tuition fees range from $3,000 to $4,000 a year for undergraduates in a liberal arts program in Canada, more than twice as high as they were in 1990.

And it's getting worse every year. According to the experts, post-secondary education costs are expected to continue rising by at least 5 percent annually for the foreseeable future. So advance planning is important.

Fortunately, saving for your child's education does not need to be overly difficult or complicated, especially if you take advantage of the Registered Educational Savings Plan (RESP) program.

Registered Education Savings Plans

With an RESP, you can contribute up to $4,000 per child per year, with a lifetime limit of $42,000 per child. You get no tax deduction for contributing, and the money can come from any family member or friend.

Basically RESPs let you shelter investment income. Let's say you deposit $4,000 in a mutual fund within an RESP. It earns $250 in interest, which isn't taxed, but is reinvested. The accumulated savings within the plan grow tax-free.

The Canada Education Savings Grant (CESG)

The CESG provides a maximum $400 annual grant for children 17 and under. The grant is awarded as a percentage of RESP contributions

(20% to a maximum of $400 per year and a total lifetime maximum of $7,200). If you were to contribute $2,000 a year ($167 per month) beginning at the birth of a child and continuing till the child reaches 18, your total contribution would amount to $36,000. With the full CESG amount of $7,200, and an average annual return of 8 percent, your child's education fund will exceed $90,000.

You can't carry forward unused RESP contribution room from one year to the next. But you can carry forward the CESG. If you can't contribute anything one year, you can contribute up to $8,000 the next, and the CESG will be applied as if you had contributed $4,000 in each of two years, for a total grant of $800. (Maximum CESG credit is $400 a year, remember.)

Like an RRSP, an RESP can accommodate a variety of investments such as mutual funds, GICs, stocks, and bonds.

As long as the student is registered in a post-secondary program of more than 10 hours a week, RESP funds can be applied to tuition and living expenses.

If your child decides not to go to university or college, and the plan has been open for more than 10 years, you can transfer up to $50,000 to your RRSP, if you have the contribution room. You can also transfer the RESP plan to another child, or apply the funds to upgrading your own education. Contributions are returned without penalty or taxation, because they were made in after-tax dollars. If you register your child as both a contributor to and beneficiary of the RESP, the income can be transferred to his or her RRSP when he or she has built up contribution room. However, you must repay the CESG that you've received.

In other cases, the money withdrawn from an RESP is taxable. If your child is attending school, however, he or she will likely pay tax at a much lower rate than you would. If your child decides not to pursue a post-secondary education, and you withdraw the money, you pay tax at your regular rate.

SOME FINAL WORDS OF ADVICE ON
UNIVERSITY AND COLLEGE SAVINGS

Start a university savings account the year your child is born. If you do, you won't need to save more than $100 to $300 a month. On the other hand, if you wait until your kids are teenagers to start an educational fund, which is what many parents do, the exercise becomes extremely challenging. It's not too late, but you have to play huge catch-up.

In any case, while I am a big proponent of parents establishing savings programs for their kids' post-secondary educations, I don't think such efforts should come at the expense of the parents' own financial futures.

Your Security and Retirement Baskets come first. Educational funding comes second. I see too many parents sacrificing their financial security for the sake of their children's college education. That's a mistake. The greatest gift you can give your children is to ensure that you won't be a financial burden to them. Your kids can contribute to their own post-secondary education by getting a part-time job when they're in high school and starting to put aside their own money for university. There are also countless scholarships and loans programs for deserving students. Each year, millions of dollars in scholarships are available.

For an extensive listing of these scholarships and other sources of financial support, check out the Scholarships Canada website at *www.scholarshipscanada.com*.

Become a Mentor

I hope this chapter has motivated you to teach your kids about money—or, if you don't have any of your own, to mentor a child you care about. If you would like more information on mentoring and teaching kids, check out the Mentoring Canada website at *www.mentoringcanada.ca*, set up by the Big Brothers and Big Sisters of Canada.

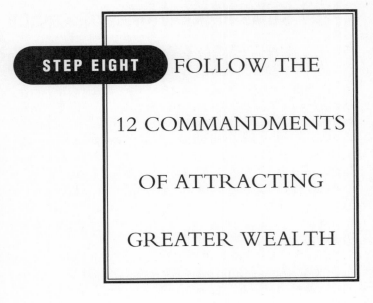

STEP EIGHT FOLLOW THE 12 COMMANDMENTS OF ATTRACTING GREATER WEALTH

So far on our journey to financial independence, we've concentrated primarily on how to make the most out of the financial resources you have—the best way, in other words, to slice up your financial pie. Now let's talk about how to bake a bigger pie.

The thing to keep in mind in this regard is that it's a mistake to separate your "money life" from your personal or professional life. It's not that your life should revolve around money. It's that your personal financial situation is inextricably linked to everything else that's important to you: your goals, your dreams, your health, your security, your freedom.

The fact is, the tools I hope you have acquired in the course of reading this book apply to much more than just money management. The good habits you should be developing as part of your journey to financial independence—things like focus and discipline and values-based behaviour—can reinforce success in every aspect of your life. Indeed, as you change your financial behaviour to match your values, you'll probably start noticing things happening in other areas of your life as well. At the very least, you're bound to become a lot more aware of the extent to which the choices you're making in your work life and personal life reflect (or *don't* reflect) your values. And that, in turn, will enable you to make more intelligent decisions about which professional and personal options make the most sense for you.

Remember, though, that it's not enough simply to understand intellectually the concepts we have discussed in this book. You have to apply what you've learned here. You have to go out and actually do it.

Now, that doesn't mean you have to climb Mount Everest. One of the most common misconceptions people have is the belief that in order to make massive changes in their lives, they have to do incredibly difficult and special things that require enormous effort and complicated skills. As a result of this misconception, most people get defeated—*they defeat themselves*—before they even get started. Don't let that happen to you! The point of this book is that you can make dramatic changes in your life—and ultimately help and support the people around you—just by using the simple tools I've provided.

But you have to use them.

GETTING PAID WHAT
YOU'RE WORTH

One of the defining characteristics of a Smart Woman is that she is paid what she is worth. But getting paid what you are worth doesn't just happen to you; you have to act to ensure that you get what should be yours.

With this in mind, the last tool I'm going to give you now may be the most powerful one of all. The tool I'm going to give you now will enable you to earn more money quickly, which will make it much easier for you to accomplish everything we've set out to do in the first seven steps of our journey.

Now, I know what you're thinking. Didn't I say that income didn't matter?

That's true; I did, and I still believe it. But as I said, the whole point of this book is that financial success is based on the cultivation of good habits—that to be financially secure and able to achieve your dreams, you need to have the right habits, tools, and beliefs. Now that you have them all, I want to make the process of getting where you want to go that much easier.

FIVE-STAR TIP: *Because the stories from readers have been so dramatic as a result of the commandments (in the 1999 edition) I am even more aggressive with these updated rules. Please keep an open mind as you read them. Many people are losing their jobs during this current recession, but the reality is that, if you are good at what you do, you deserve a raise! Don't let others convince you otherwise.*

TAKING CONTROL OF YOUR CAREER . . .
AND YOUR LIFE

I am convinced that most people earn 10 to 30 percent less than they could be earning if they just took control over their careers. Think about this for a second. What if you could easily increase your paycheque by 10 to 30 percent over the next few months? Before you read this book, you might have thought about rewarding yourself with a fancy vacation or some new clothes or maybe even a new car. But now, with your new insight, think what truly amazing things you could do with your extra income: go back to school, travel the world, have enough to retire on by the time you're 55. Rather than making onetime purchases that satisfy instant cravings, you will be making an investment in yourself that's permanent. It is these lasting contributions to your life that reflect a real, substantive change in you.

Now, how do you increase your wealth so that you can make these critical investments?

You don't have to get this extra money just through a paycheque, of course. Whether you are a career woman in a corporation, are self-employed, own your own business, or are managing an inheritance or alimony payments, there are certain behaviours and habits that will allow you to attract the wealth you deserve—as long as you decide to take control. These "rules"—which I call the 12 Commandments of Attracting Greater Wealth—aren't all about earning, however. One is even about giving it away! But, as you'll see, they are all about taking an active role in your life and making intelligent decisions rather than allowing fate to control you.

The 12 Commandments of Attracting Greater Wealth

Of all the stories I've heard over the years from women who have taken control of their lives, the most dramatic are about what happened when they went to work on improving their earning potential. That's because even a small increase in percentage terms—say, just 10 percent—can amount to thousands of dollars more a year in income.

Back in the introduction, I told you a story about a woman named Lauren whom I had coached on her personal finances and her career. As a result of my coaching, Lauren was able to double her income in less than six months. Today, she earns a six-figure salary and is significantly happier than she used to be.

The same thing happened with my wife, Michelle. Although she had a great job that she loved, Michelle was frustrated because she wasn't being paid what she knew she was worth. Finally, she reached what I call "maximum frustration" and took action. The result: In less than three months, by applying the principles contained in this chapter, she got herself a new job that literally doubled her pay.

The best thing about Michelle's new job wasn't the higher pay. It was that the new position allowed Michelle to grow as a person in a way that her old one hadn't. In just a year, she learned more about marketing and e-commerce than she had learned in five years on her previous job.

I'm not sharing her story to brag (okay, maybe a little . . . I *am* very proud of her) but to illustrate in advance the point of this chapter. The point is that by taking charge of your career, you can make sure that you're paid what you're worth—and by doing that, you can make sure you keep growing as a person!

The most important thing that happens when your income goes up is that your confidence goes up along with it. I'm not suggesting that your self-confidence should be based on your earnings. But I am a realist. If you think you are being underpaid, underappreciated, and underdeveloped in your current job, then you are being hurt as a human being—and that is unacceptable.

Chances are you are worth more than you are currently being paid. That's because you have abilities inside you that you haven't fully discovered yet, which are waiting to be brought out. By understanding and applying the following "commandments," you can bring these abilities out now.

> ### COMMANDMENT NO. 1
> DON'T ACCEPT LESS THAN YOU ARE WORTH.

When it comes to asking for a raise—whether you're dealing with a boss who signs your paycheque or a customer who has become used to paying a certain price for the product or service you provide—the biggest pitfall women face is their tendency to be "too nice."

Take my former client Lauren. She clearly had a serious case of "being too nice." Month after month, I listened to her complain about her 70-hour work weeks and the fact that she hadn't received a substantial raise in three years. Finally, after hearing one too many complaints, I asked Lauren why she thought she was worth more than the $65,000 a year her employer was paying her. She replied that there were people who did the same thing she did who were paid upward of $80,000 a year by a company that competed with hers.

"So why aren't you working for that company?" I asked her bluntly.

"Well, I like the people I work with," she said. "They're friends."

"Lauren," I explained, "friends are people you hang out with for free on the weekends. The people at your office are your coworkers and employers. Leave your job and you'll more than likely never hear from 90 percent of them again."

To make a long story short, I eventually persuaded Lauren to stop "being nice" and go talk to the competition. She did just that. A month later, they offered her more than $100,000 a year to come work for them. Her current boss (her good "friend") tried to get her to stay by offering her a big raise, but it was too little too late. Today, Lauren has new "friends" at her new job and earns almost twice what she was making a year ago.

The moral of Lauren's tale is simple.

You Earn What You Accept . . . So Decide Now to Accept More!

Are you thinking right now about your current situation? Are you being "too nice" about how much you are currently earn?

Having conducted more than a thousand Smart Women Finish Rich seminars over the past several years, I can tell you that one thing that really fires up the women who attend them is when I tell them it's time to stop being so nice when it comes to their earnings. You won't believe how many actually cheer when I say that. I remember a woman at a large seminar I did in Ohio, who yelled out, "Dammit, you're right. I *am* too nice. I'm going back to my office to demand a raise today." The other women in the room broke up laughing, but the outburst led to a powerful and meaningful conversation.

What came out of this particular conversation was not unusual. "How many of you are underpaid right now and know it?" I asked the audience. More than three-quarters of them raised their hands. "So," I continued, "what is keeping you from asking for a raise?"

Here is some of what they said—and I promise you: It's typical of how most people answer this question.

I don't ask for a raise because . . .

- I'm afraid my boss will say no.
- I know I can't get it.
- My company gives raises only once a year.
- I'm not "up for a raise" until next year.
- We are cutting back so I'm lucky to have a job.
- I don't want to rock the boat.
- I don't want to look greedy.
- If I raise my prices, my customers will take their business elsewhere.

This is negative thinking. The fact is, you deserve every dollar you can get your hands on. There is nothing greedy about it. You deserve a raise, and you're capable of getting one. You just have to believe in yourself and start asking for it.

There is plenty of documented proof that a big reason women earn less than men is that women don't negotiate hard enough when they get a job offer. In their recent book *The Shadow Negotiation,* Deborah M. Kolb and Judith Williams report studying similar groups of men and women who were offered similar jobs. The women, they found, tended to accept the first offer a prospective employer made. By contrast, the men generally held out for a higher salary and better perks— and they usually got them.

Women entrepreneurs tend to do the same thing. Studies show that women who leave the corporate world to start their own consulting

234 / SMART WOMEN FINISH RICH

firms often price their services as much as 20 to 30 percent lower than their male counterparts.

Don't do this to yourself. The reality of the working world is that you almost never get more than you ask for. Ask for a little and you will get a little. So be less nice, more aggressive, and go get the pay-cheque you deserve. Starting today, stop selling yourself short—refuse to accept anything less than you are worth!

COMMANDMENT NO. 2
ASK FOR A RAISE.

Has Commandment 1 got you fired up? I hope so. But now what?

The answer is simple. It's time to ask for a raise . . . now. (If you are self-employed, then it's time to raise what you charge for your goods or services.) You need to think of your income as a living thing—which is to say that like any other living thing, it is either growing or it is dying.

What is your income doing right now? Be honest. At a minimum, your goal should be to increase your income by 10 percent each and every year. Keep that up and your income will double just about every seven years.

Now, a 10 percent raise may sound like a lot, but it really isn't. If you ask for a 4 percent raise every six months, you'll effectively achieve your 10 percent goal every year, because the increases compound.

The nice thing about asking for a little raise on a regular basis is that it doesn't seem like such a big deal to your employer. An employer can rationalize letting you have a little extra money because the cost of re-placing you (provided you are a great employee) is extremely expen-sive. In many cases, the cost of replacing a trained employee often totals as much as twice the departing employee's annual salary!

Put yourself in your boss's shoes. You have a great employee who comes in and asks for a 4 percent raise. If this employee is earning, say, $40,000 a year, the cost of the raise she wants will be $1,600 a year— or just $133 a month. Now compare that to the cost of running a help-wanted ad in the newspaper to find a replacement. The ad alone for one week is going to cost your boss four times that amount. And there's no guarantee you'll be able to find a replacement in a week. And then there's the additional costs of downtime and training, not to mention the hassle of interviewing job applicants.

The bottom line is clear: It's not worth losing a good employee for the sake of a few dollars a month. If you add value on the job, this is how your boss will think about your request. It's something you should keep in mind when you ask for your raise.

The same logic applies if you are self-employed. Let's say you charge $35 an hour for your services. You have customers who have done business with you for years. If you raise your rates this week to $37 an hour, how likely is it that any of them will take their business elsewhere? Not very—not because of an extra $2 a hour. Face it, if you provide your customers with real value, it will be too much of a hassle for them to find a new "you."

Now, if you were to raise your rates every six months by a small amount—say, 5 percent—within a year, you'd have increased your annual earnings by 10 percent. This 10 percent increase could now go straight into your retirement basket and make you rich!

Many small businesses do exactly this sort of thing all the time, and you never even notice it. My dry cleaner raises its rates every six months like clockwork. Every six months, the cost of ironing a dress shirt goes up by 15 cents. What am I going to do—find a new dry cleaner I like as much as the old one just to save 15 cents a shirt? Of course not. And guess what? In this way, my dry cleaner has managed to double its prices over the last five years. And they haven't lost me as a customer. Because they do good work (they don't lose my clothes or ruin them), I just accept that they are in the business of making money.

Remember that phrase: the business of making money. This is what a business does and this is what an employee should keep in mind. You are in the business of making money. So go get that raise.

COMMANDMENT NO. 3
IF YOU DON'T LIKE YOUR JOB, QUIT.

When all else fails, there is a lot to be said for quitting your job. If you are currently being underpaid, underappreciated, or underdeveloped in your career or business, I suggest you consider finding someplace else to work or something else to do.

This may sound extreme. In fact, this commandment is bound to offend some of you. That's understandable. If you know in your heart that you really should quit your job, but you're afraid to follow your instincts, your gut reaction is going to be "Who does David think he is to tell me to quit my job? He doesn't have my bills, lack of savings, overhead, kids, mortgage payment, college costs [insert additional excuses here]. Anyway, you can't quit a job just because you don't like it. The fact is, most people don't like their jobs. That's why they call it a job."

If I've offended you, I apologize. By now I hope you trust me enough to know my goal here is to coach you to action. I'm being brutally honest here because I don't want you to rationalize accepting a bad career or job. You deserve better. Too many people rationalize their whole lives. They lead lives of quiet desperation. It's brutal and, worse, it's all a lie.

Here's how the lie works. People tell themselves it's okay to do the following:

It's okay . . .

- To work at a job you don't love.
- To work with people you don't like.
- To work for a company you don't respect.
- To work for a company that doesn't respect you.
- To work for less than you are worth.
- To suffer at a boring job because you need it.
- To spend time doing something you are not really interested in because you are paid well.
- To go for security, even though it's killing your spirit.
- To give up on your dreams because you are an adult.
- To put your life's energies into something you don't feel passionate about.

Well, I say it is NOT okay.

It's a truly terrible mistake to DECIDE to spend your life doing something you don't love because you believe that someday you will have enough money saved to be able to do what you really want.

In my book, this is too much of a gamble. What if "someday" never comes? What if you work another 20 years at something you don't love, what if you give up the best years of your life for a paycheque, and then it turns out to be too late for your dreams?

Here's what I want you to ask yourself right now. Are you one of those people who is putting off your dreams in the hope that someday you'll have the resources necessary to have the career or life you really want? *Is this really okay for you?*

If any of this rings true for you right now, if these ideas make you feel at all uncomfortable, then ask yourself this question: How would it really feel to quit your job? Imagine it. Might you ultimately feel better inside? Could this be a decision that's actually long overdue?

You'll know deep down inside if the answer is yes.

If it is, the time has come to make a decision.

Make a plan to quit your job and give it a deadline. Decide now that you will quit your job in six months. Or maybe a year from now. Whatever feels right, for your own sake, decide now. Create an "I Quit" date. Write it down and start planning your future today. Sure, you will feel nervous but, believe me, you may feel more energized by this decision than any you have made in years, maybe decades.

FIVE-STAR TIP: *To get started on this process, attend a job fair. (You can find a list of them in your local newspaper.) Even during economic downturns, companies are looking for employees. You should also harness the power of the Internet. The following websites are especially helpful.*

www.jobbus.com
jobsearch.monster.ca
www.careerclick.com
www.worksearch.gc.ca

COMMANDMENT NO. 4
START YOUR OWN BUSINESS.

Let's say you don't like your job. Who says you have to find yourself a new one? Did you know that most entrepreneurs today are women? Not only are women starting new businesses at a rate twice that of men, but according to Industry Canada, female-owned businesses, particularly small ones that employ less than 10 people, are also thriving at a rate higher than male-run businesses.

There are a lot reasons for this trend. Many women are fed up with corporate Canada and its invisible "glass ceiling." Others just want to be their own boss.

What about you? Each year, thousands of Canadians leave secure jobs to start their own businesses. Is it time for you to take the leap? Do you have an idea that you know would work if only you had the time? Do you have a dream of owning your own business?

If so, do what most entrepreneurs do. Start it on the side. Work extra hours, but get started. Maybe you'll need new job skills to make the transition. That's okay. The key is to figure out what you are passionate about that could earn you money.

Could you fail? Maybe. But maybe not. In Canada, most millionaires began as entrepreneurs. So think about it . . . what if you succeed beyond your wildest dreams? Here's my question to you:

What would you do if you knew you couldn't fail?

If the answer is "start my own business," then it's time to start doing some research.

FIVE-STAR TIP: *Be very wary of companies and websites offering "home-based business opportunities." There are too many people out there looking to take advantage of well-intentioned entrepreneurs. I suggest you start your research with a terrific book that has become a classic on the subject of starting your own business. It's called* The E-Myth Revisited: Why Most Small Businesses Don't Work and What to Do About It *by Michael E. Gerber.*

I also recommend the websites listed at *sbinfocanada.about.com.*

COMMANDMENT NO. 5
FOCUS ON BEING A "GO-TO GAL."

In sports, certain athletes are known as "go-to" guys. These are the players you can count on to deliver in a pinch. The idea is that when the game is on the line, you give the ball to the guy who can make the play—the "go-to guy."

These days, more and more women are making names for themselves in both sports and business. That's what a Smart Woman wants to do. She wants to become known as the type of woman who rises above the competition, who can make it happen. She wants to be a "go-to gal."

Whether you own your own business or work for someone else, you want to be someone other people can count on. What does it take to accomplish this? Fortunately, not a whole lot.

One of the amazing things about the business world today is that it is filled with people who are satisfied with being mediocre. As depressing as that may sound, it's also great news for Smart Women, because it means you don't have to do all that much to stand out. In fact, here's all it takes to make more money, earn the respect of your colleagues, and become known as a "go-to gal."

1. Show up on time.
2. Have a plan and implement it.
3. Always do what you say you will do.
4. Take total responsibility.
5. Be polite.
6. Smile.

These six things may not seem like much, but the fact is, most people don't bother to do them, either personally and professionally. So give it a try. How could it hurt to be a women who shows up early with a plan, always follows through on what she promises, takes responsibility, acts politely, and does it all with a smile? You may be stunned to discover how lavishly the world rewards such simple good manners and behaviour. Remember—simple is good, simple works!

COMMANDMENT NO. 6
KEEP YOUR OVERHEAD UNDER CONTROL.

Nothing will trap you faster in a job or career than needing the income. I know it should be obvious, but for many of us it's not until it's too late. Society is designed to get you to spend every penny you make and then some. The more you make, the more you are led to believe you should spend.

This is especially true as you become more successful. Advertisers want us to believe that when we succeed, we owe it to ourselves to buy their most expensive products. Open any magazine, listen to the radio, or watch TV and there they are: the beautiful people enjoying the good life—that is, the good life you get when you make lots of money and spend it on the advertisers' products.

In truth, most of us can't afford what they are selling. Lease a new BMW for $550 a month and you've just committed yourself to $6,600 a year in car payments. Add in taxes, gas, insurance, and registration, and that commitment has now grown to nearly $8,600 a year. And this is for a middle-of-the-road BMW. We're not talking about the big-time success (and expense) that requires you to lease the top-of-the-line BMW.

Now let's do the math. If you earn $50,000 a year after taxes, your take-home pay will be about $35,000. That means that 25 percent of your take-home pay is earmarked for car expenses! Sounds crazy, doesn't it? Yet there are hundreds of thousands of people out there driving fancy cars they can't afford. Why? Because they have focused on the "low" monthly payments.

Watch out for "low monthly payments"

The car industry created the concept of seducing customers by making luxury items available for "low monthly payments." Now nearly everything is sold on that basis. You can furnish your whole house and not pay a penny for 18 months. After that, it's just a matter of some low monthly payments. We North Americans are being "low monthly payment-ed" to death. People underestimate how these little things add up.

The fact is, we all need less than we think. Keep your overhead under control. Don't let it rise just because your income has gone up. If your overhead matches (or, worse, exceeds) your income, you can end up stuck in a job you don't want doing things with your life you'd rather not be doing.

COMMANDMENT NO. 7
WORK EACH DAY AS IF YOU WERE GOING ON
VACATION TOMORROW.

Remember the last time you went on vacation? Remember how much you got done right before you left? That last week at work and at home got you really organized, didn't it? You knew you had a lot to do, so you made a list of goals—a "to do" list—to get it all done. You were in what we call pre-vacation mode.

We all can relate to this. For most of us, the last several days before a vacation are some of the most productive days of the year.

I learned the power of this concept from the legendary motivational coach Zig Ziglar. Zig believes that the way to handle your life and your career is to live every day as if you were going to Hawaii tomorrow.

It's one of those things that make perfect sense when you think about it. Except that most of us never do.

For many employees, a typical work day is something like this: Get to the office on time around 9 A.M. (never early). Have coffee, check in with friends, talk about last night's episode of *Survivor*. Around 10 A.M. start to answer voice mail and e-mail. Fiddle around until 11 A.M. Work hard for a half hour because it's almost lunchtime. Get ready for lunch. Go to lunch. Get back at 1 P.M., tired from the big meal. Return some calls, maybe go to a few useless meetings, answer some e-mail, get ready to go home. Around 4 P.M., start winding down and prepare for another busy day at work tomorrow.

Exaggerated? Maybe, but it's more true than not. Even those people who say they are so busy that they work 60 to 80 hours a week are often kidding themselves.

Now, think about how much work you get done just before you go on vacation. That's a real work day. Okay, maybe you don't want to work that hard every day. I can accept that. But here's my suggestion. Get to the office early, work really hard for six to eight hours—and go home!

You might be thinking, *Wait a minute, David. There is no way I can do that. I've got a job where I have to punch the clock. I can't just go home early.* Fine, consider getting a new job. Find yourself the kind of career where you get rewarded for results instead of duration. There are millions of such results-based jobs out there.

The truth is that most of us can get very rich being very productive for no more than six to eight hours a day. Who wouldn't work hard if they knew that the reward included getting to have a life too?

Realizing this changed my life. When I go to my office these days, it's to work. It's to get the job done, achieve results, and go home. It's not to socialize. I'm not antisocial or rude, but I don't have time for chitchat. I come to work to work, and as soon as I am finished, I get out of the office. I have a life out of the office.

The point of business is to have a life, not the other way around. So start working like you are about to go on vacation—and then go on one. You deserve it!

FIVE-STAR TIP: *If you are not currently in a position to change your career, be honest with yourself. How much more productive can you really be at work? What would happen to your career if you "picked it up" a notch? What would happen if you came in to work an hour early every day just for 90 days and worked every day as if you were about to go on vacation? The truth is that your career would get a huge boost—and you would get noticed in a very positive way. Another truth is that when others (especially bosses) notice that you're getting to work early and are really working hard, they tend to be more open-minded about letting you leave early. Try it—the results may surprise you. I've now got friends who are working Monday through Thursday for 10 hard hours, but then they take Friday off completely. That's also a great approach.*

COMMANDMENT NO. 8
FOCUS ON WHAT MAKES YOU UNIQUE.

We are all blessed with special talents that make us unique. Some people discover their talent at a young age and from then on focus their lives on honing it until they are rewarded by society. We call the most successful of these people stars or "pros."

But I'm not just talking about sports or movie stars. Stars exist in every realm. There are star salespeople and star mothers and star teachers and so on. The question you need to ask yourself is, What makes you uniquely valuable? What is it that you have to offer? One of the saddest things I see as I get older are people I love who have given up on their dreams. When I see friends working at jobs I know they aren't passionate about, I realize they have forgotten what it is that makes them unique.

A few years back, a good friend of mine took a suit-and-tie job. Now, this is a guy who loves being outdoors and doing things with other people. But he had looked around at what his friends were doing, and feeling left behind, he took the path he saw others following.

Unfortunately, he was not uniquely valuable at a suit-and-tie job. In fact, he was uniquely bad at it. So instead of moving up, he went nowhere fast. In the process, he became increasingly unhappy. It took him years to figure out that he had taken a path to a destination he didn't really want.

What about you? Are you spending time at work doing something you are uniquely good at? Do you know what you are uniquely good at?

Here are a few life-changing questions you should ask yourself today.

- What is it that I am really good at?
- What do I enjoy so much that I would do it for free if I had $20 million?
- What would I stop doing tomorrow if I had $20 million?
- What would I do differently with my life if I only had just three years to live?
- What do others regularly tell me I am good at?

If you answer these questions honestly, the exercise can change your life. I know because it changed mine. This book and my seminars exist because in 1996 I had a heart-to-heart talk with myself in which I asked those questions. The answers surprised me.

The first thing I realized was that if I had three years left to live, I wouldn't spend it being a financial advisor. I realized I would want to write the book that you are holding in your hand today because I wanted to help thousands of people before I died.

The second thing I realized was that the one thing I really loved doing was coaching others. I love to speak on the topic of money, and if I had $20 million, I would still want to speak, write, and coach others about money (after I bought a Ferrari, and took a yearlong trip around the world with my wife).

This realization got me off my duff and forced me to focus on what I really wanted to do with my life. Ultimately, I realized that my unique talent wasn't just working as a personal financial advisor but exercising my ability to be a financial coach to thousands (and, hopefully, someday millions).

So how do you apply this to your own life? Here's what I recommend. Answer the above questions today. Write down your answers in longhand. (Don't type them; studies show that writing things in longhand embeds them in your subconscious faster and more deeply.) If you have trouble answering the questions, get help from your friends. Ask them what they think you're really good at, what they think makes you unique. Also ask your coworkers, customers, and (if you have one) your boss.

By doing this exercise, you will learn a great deal about yourself. You may find that you have a job at which you are uniquely talented—in other words, that you are already pursuing your life's passion. If so, what you need to do now is really buckle down and spend as much time as possible on it (and, as our next commandment says, delegate your weaknesses).

If it turns out you are not spending the majority of your time on your unique ability or talents, hopefully the realization will leave you motivated like I was to "get going."

I can tell you from firsthand experience that once you discover and start working on what you're uniquely talented at, your passion will take you to a place in life you can't even imagine right now. And chances are that your income will grow in a major, long-term way as result!

For more information about exploring your unique talents, visit *www.strategiccoach.com*. Dan Sullivan, the creator of Strategic Coach, has trained thousands of entrepreneurs to focus on their "Unique Ability." I highly recommend his audio program, *Focusing Your Unique Ability*™.

COMMANDMENT NO. 9
DELEGATE THE TASKS YOU SHOULDN'T BE DOING

First thing tomorrow, you should delegate one task you currently perform that you know you shouldn't be doing.

Here's a simple example. If you are a career woman who works or owns your own company, you should NOT be doing your own laundry, your family's laundry, or any cleaning at home. Forget it. I am telling you right now that your time and passion is too valuable to spend doing something you can delegate to a cleaning service or laundromat for less than $10 an hour.

If you earn $45,000 a year, you are making around $22.50 an hour. That's what your time is worth. So why waste it doing anything you can pay someone less than that to do? You are much better off spending an extra hour at work and really focusing on growing your business or career than you are doing menial chores around the house.

I am constantly amazed at how many women get excited by this idea when I share it with them. Women who are making more than $50,000 a year constantly come up to me at seminars, saying things like, "I spend the whole day Sunday doing the laundry and cleaning, which I hate, but I just never felt right hiring a cleaning lady."

Ladies, that is crazy. Stop now. If you hate cooking, stop doing it. If you hate cleaning, stop doing it. Delegate those jobs. Spend the extra time with your family or on your passion and grow your income so you can get more out of life.

The same goes for the way you handle tasks in the office. I meet women who have high-level careers, yet they still answer their own phones, do their own filing, and type their own letters.

Stop doing that. Stop doing anything that you can pay someone else to do for less than your time is worth. If you stop wasting time doing things others can help you with, you can then focus on the things that will get you results at work and make you more money!

Specifically, you can focus on what makes you unique. Many people spend half their time at work doing things that are "process oriented" rather than "result focused." The reality is that we get paid for results, not process.

What if you have the job that someone else is delegating to? What if you are the assistant being delegated the letter typing, the telephone answering, the coffee making? In that case, make sure your boss agrees that this is what you are really supposed to be doing. What does your boss regard as your unique ability? Are there ways in which your boss thinks you can do more to help him or her?

Often, what your boss really wants from you is something other than what you spend the majority of your time at work doing. If this happens to be the case, explain to your boss what you are actually being forced to spend time on. It's entirely possible that he or she may help you get these tasks off your plate.

If you're the boss, try this with your staff. You may be amazed at their responses.

Nothing will increase your productivity faster than delegating the nonessential tasks you currently perform yourself.

COMMANDMENT NO. 10
GET UP EARLY.

When I started writing the first edition of this book in 1997, I had a huge challenge on my hands. I had promised the publisher I'd deliver a full-length manuscript by a set date. But where would I find the time to write it? I had a full-time job to which I devoted an average of 10 to 12 hours a day, often six days a week, and I hadn't yet learned the power of Commandment 7 or Commandment 9.

I knew I had to come up with more time. But I faced the same challenge you face: There are only 24 hours in a day. Finally, I came to terms with what I knew I needed to do. I decided I would get up no later than 5:30 every morning and start writing. At first this was brutal. I would drag myself out of bed, brew myself some coffee, and struggle to stay awake at the computer. But then something unexpected happened. As the weeks and months passed, I began to love my early mornings. There was no one to bother me, no distractions or interruptions. It almost felt as if I were on a vacation, because the time was my own and it was so quiet and peaceful, and I was working on my passion.

Eventually, I fell into a comfortable rhythm, in which I rose at 5:30 and worked uninterrupted until 7:30. In this way, I could give myself two straight hours of writing time and still make it to the office before almost everyone else.

Doing the math, I discovered these two extra hours in the morning amounted to 14 hours a week, or 56 hours a month. That's 672 hours a year. Do you have any idea how much you can accomplish in 672 hours? You can go for your dreams "on the side," you can get your body in shape, you can organize your finances, you can clean out your house and garage, you can start a business on the side, you can change the world. The power of two extra hours a day is enormous. And it's yours for the taking.

Is it easy to do? In the beginning at least, it's not. But you adjust in a matter of weeks. For starters, you begin going to bed earlier. I'm now usually in bed by 9 P.M. I used to go to stay up until 11 or midnight. What have I given up? Two to three hours a night of useless channel surfing—which is to say, very little. These days, even when I'm not working on a book, I still get up early. I may write in my journal, or work out, or read the paper with a cup of coffee. I get time to think and time to begin my day in the most powerful way imaginable.

This book is filled with ideas and exercises that are meant to change your life. The only reason they won't work for you is if you don't go to work on them. The number-one reason most people have for not committing the time and effort to taking the kind of actions I suggest is that they are too busy. Well, what if you were to get up one hour earlier every day for a year and spend the extra time using this book as a tool to make your life better? I promise you, your future will be greater than you could have ever imagined.

> ## COMMANDMENT NO. 11
> ### FIND A PURPOSE GREATER THAN YOURSELF.

Recently, I've heard many stories about wonderful school teachers assigning their students to write their own epitaphs or eulogies. It's a powerful idea. What would you want people to say about you after you're gone? What will they say about you?

How we live our lives now determines how others will remember us. Will they say we left the world a better place? I know for a fact that not a single one of my friends or family members cares how much money I currently have in the bank. When I die they are not going to say, "Isn't it great that David had such a big retirement account. Isn't it great that he lived in such a nice home and had such a nice car."

Not that nice things aren't worth having, but they aren't what I want to be remembered for. What I hope is that when I die my friends and family will say that I touched their lives—that I made their lives better by being their friend, that I added value to their lives.

I find that the more I focus my energy on coaching others and helping strangers, the more abundant my life becomes. The greatest gift I get from writing a book like this one is that it allows me in a small way to help many strangers, and in time I hope these strangers will come to consider me a friend.

There are so many ways to help others. Recently, my wife Michelle and I trained for and completed a 575-mile AIDS Vaccine Ride across the state of Montana. The purpose of the ride was to raise money for AIDS Vaccine Research and to bring awareness to the world about why a vaccine for AIDS is critical. We shared our mission with hundreds of our friends, who supported us by helping us raise thousands of dollars for this great cause. The ride ended up being without a doubt one of the most physically and emotionally challenging things we ever did together. It is also one of our most cherished lifetime memories.

This is just one cause I care deeply about. Another is the need to provide kids with mandatory financial education programs. The reason I mention what Michelle and I are doing is not to toot our own horn. Rather, it's to get you thinking about what you might be doing. Have you ever wanted to give something back to your community but didn't feel you had the time to spare? Or maybe you weren't sure exactly how to go about it? Well, perhaps it's time you finally did something. You can make the time. You can get the information you need on the Internet.

The circle of life is truly amazing. Give to others and others will give back to you. Love others and you can feel that love come right back to you. Hold back your time, your energy, your wealth, and your love, and you ultimately lose it.

More than 6.5 million Canadians volunteer their time in one way or another. If you would like to start giving something back, check out *www.volunteer.ca*. You might also look at *www.pallottateamworks.com* (this is the AIDS ride Michelle and I did and the company that arranges these events worldwide).

COMMANDMENT NO. 12
BE GRATEFUL.

While I was trying to finish this chapter, I hit a brick wall. I knew there had to be one more commandment—the clincher—that would pull everything together. I just couldn't find the right words.

For two days, I suffered from writer's block, unable to figure out what the final commandment should be. It was so frustrating that on Sunday morning when I knew I had to finish the chapter, I didn't want to get out of bed. Then, while sitting there feeling sorry for myself, I decided to read a magazine. The magazine was O (Oprah Winfrey's magazine). I started reading an article in O about how to recover after a relationship breaks up.

The article had nothing to do with my life and nothing to do with what we're talking about here, but imbedded in it was something that struck a chord with me. It was a section entitled, "BE GRATEFUL."

Now, that's not exactly an original thought. In fact, when I was writing the first edition of *Smart Women Finish Rich,* I initially wanted to include a commandment to that effect in this chapter. The idea was to paraphrase what Sir John Templeton, the billionaire investor, said when Tony Robbins asked him to single out what he regarded as the most important lesson for people interested in pursuing wealth and happiness. "Learn to live with an attitude of gratitude," Templeton replied. I loved that advice and, as I say, I wanted to include it in the book. In the end, though, it was edited out of my manuscript—not original enough, someone said.

Well, original or not, there I was, three years later, updating this book and reading this magazine, and the concept of "BE GRATEFUL" hit me like a ton of bricks.

As a result, I got out of bed, took a shower, and started thinking about everything in the world that I had to be grateful for. In the end, I decided that rather than work on my book that day, I would make a list—a list of 50 things I felt grateful for. All at once, I went from being tired and depressed to motivated and passionate to feeling lucky to be alive.

How does this relate to you? Well, it hit me that no matter how motivated you are and no matter how much this book has inspired you to take action, there are going to be times when you get frustrated. There are going to be times when things won't go smoothly. You may ask for a raise and not get it (at least not not the first try). You may start buying stocks for your retirement account and the market will go down. You may decide to buy a home and then find out you can't afford the kind of house you want in the neighbourhood you want.

Stuff happens. Stuff has always happened. You can't let that throw you, for no matter how much stuff may get in your way, nothing determines your future more than your own internal drive to succeed in life and your willingness to take action.

The question is, What can you do to keep yourself motivated when the world seems determined to block your efforts to live and finish rich? As I see it, the answer is simple: You can be grateful. Be grateful for everything you have in your life that is gloriously right, starting with the fact that you happen to be alive.

Of course, just because the answer is simple doesn't mean doing it is easy. The fact is, when the going gets tough, our grateful muscles disappear fast. To protect yourself against that possibility, here's what I want you to do with this last commandment. It doesn't cost anything and it won't take much time, but it might just change your entire outlook on life.

What I want you to do is take a piece of paper and write down 50 things you are grateful for. Simply write down everything that comes to mind. Now, since many of the things you write down are bound to be about other people whom you love or appreciate, I suggest you share your list with your friends and loved ones. After you've done that, put this list in your purse, wallet, PalmPilot, or day planner. The next time you feel down, tired, or stressed because things aren't working out exactly the way you'd hoped they would, take out your list and BE GRATEFUL. Remember, there's only one you, and the simple fact that you exist makes this world a better place.

TAKE THE TIME TO
SMELL THE ROSES

We have now reached the end of our journey together—though your individual journey to financial security and independence is just beginning. I want to close this book with a reminder of something I myself am often guilty of neglecting. In our efforts to build a secure future and protect our financial destiny, we should never forget that the greatest asset we have is life. Unfortunately, life is of limited duration and not guaranteed. There is no insurance we can buy that will give us back our life or make it possible for us to bring back those we love.

My point is that you shouldn't get so consumed with your financial journey that you don't spend enough time sharing moments with the people you love. As you take control over your finances and your career, please remember to let those you really care about know how much they mean to you. Not only will it make you feel better but you will add more value to them spiritually than you will ever know.

Now that you've learned what it takes to become financially secure and reach your dreams, my final wish for you is that you enjoy the journey. The *Smart Women Finish Rich* process is not about pain or sacrifice. You don't have to give up the fun part of life to become a woman in total control of her financial future. You can become financially secure, reach your dreams, and still have time to smell the roses.

Live Your Life with No Regrets

Shortly before she passed away, I asked my Grandma Bach if she had any regrets in life. She said the only ones she had involved not things she did but the risks she didn't take. With that in mind, I'd like to suggest the following: If you believe you are going to be alive five years from now (and I hope you do), then there are really only two potential outcomes. You will either be five years older and have achieved your dreams (or at least be well on the way toward achieving them) because you have used the tools in this book and gone for it, or you will just be five years older.

As you go about your life, ask yourself regularly: Am I *making things happen* or am I watching things happen? Life is not a dress rehearsal. You get in life exactly what you go for. I say the heck with being a spectator. Go for it and jump in.

The choice is yours. Take the tools in this book and start now to begin your personal journey to the new woman you want to be in five years—more financially secure than you are now, more successful in your career, happier, even healthier. And remember, if you encounter a few setbacks along the way, don't let it deter you. You're not supposed to get everything right the first time. (And think about this: mistakes and failures are just market research for your future successes!)

As you grow and take greater control of your life, please know that my thoughts and prayers will be with you. This journey we call life is an incredible gift and I hope that in some small way this book has touched you for the better. I want you to know that I both respect you and admire your desire to be smart and finish rich—and that I look forward to meeting you some day along the journey.

FINISHRICH

SUCCESS

STORIES—

BE INSPIRED

Congratulations! You've completed the *Smart Women Finish Rich* journey. By now I am sure you have made tremendous movement toward your financial dreams, values, and goals.

Or maybe, you skipped ahead and you are reading this chapter first? Either way, you've come to my favourite chapter in this new edition of *Smart Women Finish Rich*. Since 1999, we've received thousands of e-mails and letters from women like those whose stories follow. These women read the book you hold in your hand, and they then helped themselves to a better life. Was it easy for them? Read their stories and find out.

One of the greatest things about reading others' success stories is that it should get your brain and "gut" to say to yourself "If they can do it, I can do it." And you are absolutely right to think that way. If they can do it, you can do it too! Maybe even better.

I hope that the stories of these women's real-life success will inspire you to take action in your own life. Please let us know what happens. It is your stories that inspire me to do what I do. I would love nothing more than to be able to include your personal FinishRich success story in a future book. Just think, maybe a year from now your life could be a life that inspires another woman to take action to go for her dreams to live and finish rich!

Rebecca Young—Hollywood, California

I was working at a radio station in Los Angeles, when a copy of *Smart Women Finish Rich* showed up on the desk next to mine. I was 27 years old, and had moved to L.A. (from Texas) about six months earlier. Ever since graduating from college three years before, I had been struggling desperately to figure out how to handle my money, make ends meet, and quit asking my parents for money each month.

I was overwhelmed with credit card debt, had zero retirement money, and no savings. Having just started the first job I ever had that paid more than $30,000 a year, I was determined to try to get my finances in some kind of working order, but I had no idea how or where to start.

I have a lot of books that I've never gotten around to reading, but as soon as I cracked open *Smart Women,* I couldn't put it down. I was so blown away that I was reading about money, investing, retirement funds, and the like—and I actually understood it! It was such an easy read while also being really informative.

I filled out all the worksheets, began thinking of my financial situation as manageable instead of overwhelming, and set goals.

The book made a huge impact on my life because it finally allowed me to put into perspective the big picture of my money and where I want to be down the road. Money was no longer this big, black cloud that I avoided because I didn't get it. *Smart Women* put the basics into terms that I understood.

After I read the book, I immediately went and changed my benefit choices with my employer. (My previous choices had been completely blind guesses I made the day the form was due.) In my conversations with the HR department and our benefits administrators, I was able to ask informed questions, get the answers I was looking for, and best of all understand what it all meant.

I signed up for my company's 401(k) plan, and invested the maximum. (In order to be able to afford this, I found other areas to cut back on.) For the first time, I was able to decide on my own exactly how I wanted to invest my funds, instead of asking my dad to take care of it. I also saved up some money and opened a Roth IRA.

I increased the size of my car payments, paid off my car, and then started focusing on paying off my credit card debt.

And even though the credit card debt is still a little unruly, it is slowly coming down, as a result of which I've been able to take some of the trips I've always wanted to make. I went to New York City for my first time, I'm going to Lake Tahoe next month, and I've applied for a passport so I can take a trip to Europe next year. All of this is possible because I now know my values and keep them in mind when I make spending choices.

Because of the recent dot.com downturn, I was laid off from my last job. Fortunately, thanks to *Smart Women,* I have sufficient savings to look for a job that I really want, instead of being forced to take the first thing that comes along.

I'm not yet where I want to be, but because of the habits and patterns I have learned from the book, I no longer feel like I'm in a hole that just keeps getting deeper. Instead, I really feel as if I'm headed in the right direction and that I'm in control of the outcome.

Gail Locklin—Tyngsborough, Massachusetts

When I first read *Smart Women Finish Rich,* it made me realize just how foolish my husband and I had been in planning for our future. Even though we'd been married for three years, owned a home, and had a two-year-old boy, we had no will, no life insurance, little savings, and minimal 401(k) contributions. One thing we had a lot of was credit card debt.

The foolish part was that all this was for no good reason. My husband and I are both successful in our careers and both earn comfortable incomes. We simply hadn't planned well.

Since reading the book, we have written a will, purchased life insurance, brought our debt under control, started a savings account for our son, begun making regular contributions to our own savings account, and "maxed out" our 401(k) contributions.

We've also automated all our savings contributions and signed up with an automatic bill-paying system, which gives us much more time to spend together as a family. (It also ensures that our bills are paid on time so our credit isn't at risk!)

I have always wanted to be able to live my own dream and not just help to run someone else's. With our new financial stability, I plan to start my own business. It's my hope that this will ultimately give me the flexibility to spend more time with my son and still feel successful as a career woman.

In my eyes, *Smart Women Finish Rich* gave me the knowledge I needed to be able to live my life according to my values. I can't tell you how much easier and under control my life is as a result.

Tonja L. Vallin—Hay, Kansas

I am 32-year-old single female who discovered by accident the power of paying myself first. I was working for the government and some older colleagues told me how important it was for me to begin saving. So at the age of 22, I began investing a small part of each paycheck.

At first it seemed to accrue very slowly. But then, one day, I remember opening my statement and seeing a balance of $20,000! Now, 10 years later, I have a $150,000 nest egg for retirement. I also own my own home and when I'm 42, my 15-year mortgage will be paid off and I'll be debt-free. What is truly amazing is that I've never earned more than $45,000 a year, and for a good part of my life so far I was making less than $30,000.

While I felt good about my retirement savings and my home purchase, I hadn't managed to save anything for my Dream Basket. Then I heard someone giving a Smart Women Finish Rich seminar at a trade show and I ordered the book from Amazon.com that day! Using the power of the Latté Factor, I have since saved an additional $6,000 over the last year and half. Over the next five years, I have set a goal of saving an additional $50,000. Sometimes I think I will use it to start my own business, or maybe buy a low-end Jaguar, or maybe take a year off from work and travel.

I can't even begin to tell you how exciting life is now that I have a Dream Basket. The greatest gift is that I have been able to teach four of my close girlfriends, ranging in age from 20 to 40 years old, the Smart Women Finish Rich principles. One friend began saving for her first house, another overcame bankruptcy, a third started contributions to her 401(k) for the first time, and the last negotiated a $10,000 raise from her employer.

Thank you, thank you, thank you so much for this book. Single and widowed women have been ignored for too long when it comes to money and finance.

Christina Bias—Elk Grove, California

You can't imagine how this book changed my life! For every one of the 12 years we'd been married, my husband and I had been having all-out battles over our financial situation. Then, for my last birthday, he gave me a copy of *Smart Women Finish Rich*.

My first thought was, Gee, thanks. Some more stuff I don't know anything about that he can use as ammunition against me next time one of our checks bounces!

All the same, I vowed to read and learn. Once and for all, I would get this figured out.

Within three days, I was creating files and asking questions and making phone calls. "I've created a monster," my husband said.

I read the book twice and completed every exercise and chart as honestly as I could. What had the greatest impact on me was learning how to create a values ladder; that's when I drew the battle lines. How could I list security and freedom as my most important values to live by when I was actually living in panic at the end of each month waiting for the credit card bills to arrive?

The reality of my life was that I felt like a financial prisoner. And the emotional toll on my marriage and family was just huge. What was I teaching my two children?

Following the book's advice, I made an action plan and a priority list of liabilities. Boy, was the list long! We had three credit cards, each with hefty balances and interest rates ranging as high as 19.99 percent! We had two truck payments. We had a 30-year mortgage. We also had a high-interest second mortgage that we were in complete denial about.

I made it my mission to pay off each and every debt on that liability list, one at a time. Using the techniques the book taught me, I saw for the first time where all our money was going—a latté here, a movie-rental late fee, and a bounced-check fee there. I never realized how much it was costing our family not only to be uninformed about money but also to be intimidated by something we could so easily have total control over. It's very expensive to live on the edge of bankruptcy; it's also unnecessary. *Smart Women Finish Rich* gave me both the perspective and the tools I needed to get the work done.

I had heard of the idea of "paying yourself first," but because of my overdraft fees and my spending, I never felt I had enough money to do it. Well, as soon as I finished reading about the Latté Factor, I marched down to the bank and opened a savings account. Now, every month, no matter what, I take a set amount of money off the top of my paycheck and deposit it in this account. I also use my savings account to automatically fund a Roth IRA I've set up.

So now I no longer feel panicked about my finances. And I no longer feel desperate to buy things I don't need. In fact, I get more emotional satisfaction these days out of depositing $20 into my account than I used to get spending it at a store. Who knew?

And it's not only my own habits that have changed. As a result of reading the book, I called the benefits department at my husband's office and found out we had no life insurance coverage and were putting only the minimum amount into his 401(k) account. Both these lapses were taken care of within the week.

Today, our credit card balances are nearly paid off, and those that remain carry much lower interest charges. Soon, we will only have one truck payment. I refinanced our house, combining the first and second mortgages into a new single mortgage that, if I have my way, will be paid off within 15 or 20 years. We have life insurance policies that we can understand and proper health insurance coverage. I pay the majority of our bills the first week of the month and have stopped playing the "when is the last possible moment I can put this in the mailbox?" game.

No one gets in the way of a mother protecting her family, and that's the approach I took. With the information to back up what I wanted and the values to validate what I needed to do, all the subjects that once seemed so intimidating to me are now easily manageable. As much as I hate using buzzwords, I have to say that *Smart Women Finish Rich* has made me feel empowered.

Unlike their mom, my children will not go through their first job interview in their 20s thinking—as I did—that IRAs and life insurance are the husband's job, or that stock options are just for 40-year-olds. They will be informed and well on their way to financial freedom. Just like I am now.

Brandi Klann—Anchorage, Alaska

Because of *Smart Women Finish Rich,* my dreams are coming true.

I bought the book just after finishing my first year of college, where I am majoring in finance. I had taken out $13,000 in loans to pay for the school year, owed another $3,500 in credit card debt, had just bought a new car, and was living on my own.

I knew I didn't want to travel the same financial road my parents had taken for the last 22 years. I read the book and was amazed; this was really good stuff!

I immediately started saving 8 percent of my paycheck, and kept raising the amount by 2 percent a month until I was "paying myself first" 12 percent of my gross income. I also opened a Roth IRA.

But the advice that really struck me the most was what David had to say about women getting paid only what they accept, not really what they deserve. At the time, I was working as a rental agent for a major national car rental company. Though it was just a summer job, I was their number-one rental agent. (That month alone, I earned the company $25,000 in extra revenue.) Given that I pay for my college and everything else, you can understand why I felt that the $7.50 an hour they were paying me was a lot less than I thought I should be getting.

So after reading what David had to say about this kind of situation, I woke up one Monday morning, got dressed, and went to the office of our biggest competitor, where I applied for a job opening they had advertised. Not only did they promptly offer me a job at $9.50 an hour, they also told me about their tuition program, in which after a year of employment they would pay 75 percent of my college costs, including books, fees, and tuition. The man who interviewed me made it clear he wanted me working for him, not my current employer, and he was prepared to do whatever it took to get me there.

When I told my manager that I would be leaving, she quickly relayed the news to our main office. Within 24 hours, I found myself having lunch with our Operations Manager, who offered me a job doing accounting in the main office at $10.25 an hour plus a guaranteed raise after three months.

I was shocked. The only accounting experience I have is one class I've taken in college. But David's advice was right on the money, and now that I've made them realize how valuable I am, they have faith that I will succeed in this job. I am determined, and I know I can do it. I will continue my education on top of my 40-hour work week. For the first time in my life, I have a job in an office, money in my savings and IRA accounts, and the momentum to keep going to make more of my dreams come true. Next stop, investing!

By the way, I have sent my sister a copy of *Smart Women Finish Rich* and given my parents a copy of *Smart Couples Finish Rich*. They love the books just as much as I do. Thank you for everything you have taught me.

Anne McGarry—Warrenton, Missouri

I am a single mother of two with my own exterminating business. *Smart Women Finish Rich* wasn't the first book I read on money management, but it was the only one that changed my life.

Reading it gave me the motivation I needed to get serious about my finances. By following all of David's exercises step by step, here's what I've accomplished so far:

1. I opened up a money market savings account.
2. I began making regular contributions into a mutual fund through an automatic withdrawal program.
3. I diversified my investments into large, medium, and high-risk funds.
4. I began contributing $2,000 a year to a Roth IRA.
5. I drew up a budget and took control of my credit cards so I would never be in debt.

As a result of all this, I'm in much greater control of my money, which gives me greater control over my life. My kids have always come first, and now I feel like I'm setting a positive example for them to follow in the future. What could be better than that?

Lisa Oliver—Aliso Viejo, California

I had worked for 15 years in the retail industry, gaining success but not happiness. Financially, I was doing okay, but I wasn't as disciplined as I should've been, considering I earned close to $100,000 a year. When I was unexpectedly laid off shortly after a personal tragedy (my father died suddenly), I was totally unprepared. Fortunately, I negotiated enough severance to give me a little breathing room. One week later, I found myself pregnant! This was my first pregnancy and, because of some health issues, I was a "high-risk" patient.

At that point, I decided that if I wasn't willing to try to change careers then, I never would. As a result, I took an entry-level job in an industry I'd always wanted to be in—computers—at one-third my old salary! Even with my husband working, with a brand-new house and two new cars, I really didn't know how we were going to make it financially.

It was quite amazing how resourceful we became, and on how much less income we could live. Fortunately, I enjoyed remarkable success at my new job, doubling my income within a year, even while bearing a beautiful, healthy baby. Still, my husband and I still were not where we wanted to be financially.

It was about this time that I discovered *Smart Women Finish Rich*. It was in October when I picked up the book, thinking it might help me to reformulate our financial plans for the following year.

I read the entire book in one sitting and followed all the steps immediately. I saw that although we were doing okay, there were some "holes" in our plan.

Here's what we've accomplished since then:

1. For the first time in our 15-year marriage, my husband and I completely paid off our credit card debt.
2. We created an emergency reserve fund, which we add to with every paycheck.
3. We increased our 401(k) contributions to the max for both of us.
4. We selected a lawyer, had wills created, and discussed living trusts.
5. We selected a financial planner to help with our daughter's educational funding and our own "Dream Basket."
6. I bought 15 copies of David's book and gave it to all of my friends for Christmas.

Smart Women Finish Rich has made us feel so much better about our financial health! The thing I like most about implementing its ideas is that now we have a complete and unified plan. Previously, my husband and I compartmentalized our finances—i.e., he took care of the insurance, I did the taxes, etc.—which left several "holes" in our strategy. But now we have a complete financial plan based solely on our values and goals as a family.

Nicole Ash—Valdez, Alaska

Growing up in a home with very little money, I was never taught how to handle my finances. In fact, I actually hated the subject and really didn't want anything to do with it.

When I first graduated from college, I had lots of bills—student loans, car payments, rent, you name it. On top of that, I had accumulated about $5,000 in credit card debt, on which I was only making the minimum monthly payment. Even though I was making about $30,000 a year working for a company, I was living paycheck to paycheck—barely. The only thing that kept me afloat was my boyfriend, who would send me some money every now and then so I could pay my bills.

A couple years later, I moved to Alaska and got a job making more than I ever could have imagined. (I am currently 27 and am earning $110,000 a year.) But I was still afraid of money and I didn't know how to handle it. Fortunately, my mother (who's like me with money) had read *Smart Women Finish Rich,* and LOVED it.

I loved it, too. It was easy to understand and taught me how to handle my own finances and enjoy it.

The first thing the book did was make me want to know where my money was going and how I could earn more. Not knowing any better, I had always put my money in a checking account that earned little or no interest. Now, I contribute the maximum amount allowable to my 401(k) plan and have taken some on-line investment classes to learn which stocks, bonds, or mutual funds might be good for me. I have also set up meetings with financial advisors to learn more about investing for retirement in other ways, such as IRAs and mutual funds.

I currently have no credit card debt and have very little left to pay on my student loans. In general, I have started taking an interest in the money I make and I have discovered that I enjoy learning new ways to invest. I'm sure there is more I could be doing, but I feel I have come a long way from where I was just a few years ago. Thank you, David—your book was a huge motivator for me.

Bobbi Geyer—Manassas, Virginia

The turning point for me came in October 2000, when I was facing back surgery and three weeks of recovery time away from work. I knew I needed to make some changes in my life. I'm a single mom of a special-needs child and was about to turn 50. I was commuting more than two hours each way to a job I enjoyed, but with no possibilities of promotion.

I originally bought *Smart Women Finish Rich* to read during my surgery recovery time. But then I started reading it on my commuter train ride home and couldn't put it down.

I've always been pretty resourceful with money. I own my own home. I don't have credit card debt. I contribute to my IRA and 401(k) accounts. I have savings for emergencies and creature comforts. But until I read David's book, my life didn't have any financial direction.

David's book helped me focus. The first thing it inspired me to do was immediately increase my 401(k) contribution from 3 percent to 11 percent. Then I started thinking about the future.

While I was recovering from my surgery, I dusted off my résumé and vowed to find a better job before June 2001. As it turned out, I was laid off before I had a chance to leave on my own. But because of the book, I was able to land on my feet immediately and find an incredible new job as an IT Applications Trainer for the state of Virginia. Even though I took an $11,000-a-year salary cut (with a son to support, I didn't feel I had much choice), my take-home pay turned out to be only $60 less a month than I had been earning in my old position. That's because as a state employee I get a number of benefits for free that I had to pay for myself when I worked in the private sector. And best of all, my commute was reduced to just 45 minutes a day, giving me much more personal time each day!

If I hadn't read *Smart Women Finish Rich,* I would have been blindsided by the layoff. The book helped me prioritize my life and approach things with a different focus. I now find it easier to make decisions and figure out what is best for my son and me. I've not only made a full recovery from my surgery, but I also feel as though I've been given a fresh start in life.

Reverend Donna Cassity—Hamden, Connecticut

Just a few months before reading *Smart Women Finish Rich,* I wasn't sure I'd finish anything in my life, much less come to believe that I might possibly get rich.

After a going through a divorce, a major career change, being a single mother, and moving three times, I was challenged to make ends meet for a long time. I had made some serious mistakes along the way and lost a great deal of money trying to survive and meet the demands of education and career changes. Five years after my divorce, I found myself financially and emotionally depleted. Finishing the track I was on toward ordination was important, but with my funds dwindling to almost nothing, I wasn't sure I would make it.

Reading David's book helped me see a glimmer of light for the first time. It seemed to offer a marvelous blueprint for the changes I needed to make. As I examined his ideas, I started to see that money was not an end in itself, but a means to an end. Whether I was saving money for retirement or for something special, money began to take on a new meaning for me. It was not something to fear, but something to respect. This understanding has been a key tool in my success, and I teach it to the finance committees at the churches I now serve when we review the budget.

In particular, I responded strongly to David's suggestion that you must "pay yourself first." This concept has made a huge difference in my life. I value myself, so why wouldn't I pay myself first? After practicing this for several months and making changes in my retirement and saving practices, I slowly began to develop a new sense of confidence. I feel much better about myself now. I have hope for the future and though I wish I had known these things in my twenties, I feel it is never to late to start.

Today, at the age of 49, I have a thriving ministry, I am happy, and my bank accounts are growing. I am seeking to write a book and looking for other ways to add to my financial success in the future. Paying myself first has paid off. Peace of mind and creativity, which are so central to my work, have increased—and along with them, so have my income and security. It is an incredible flow of energy!

Faith Hernandez—Tampa, Florida

As a result of reading *Smart Women Finish Rich,* I remind myself every day of the Latté Factor and how much it will cost me in the long run to keep spending $5 to $7 a day on coffee, muffins, and sodas! Now that I've got my Latté Factor under control by making coffee at home and buying sodas at the grocery store (instead of at the office), my checkbook balances AND my waistline has really improved!

Thanks to the book, I've also been able to discipline myself to keep an eye out for "ooh aah" purchases that end up costing too much for little value. I realized, for example, that I didn't need to spend an extra $200 to $300 on a really cool-looking refrigerator that actually has less cubic feet than a regular-priced one.

I've also been blown away by the astounding power of compound interest. It's really motivated me to save more! I increased my 401(k) contributions and didn't even notice that there was less money to take home, just that there is more money in my retirement account!

I have a wonderful husband who respects my desire to learn more and encourages me to share these principles with him. We've made it our goal to pay down what we owe and stay out of debt by saving for the things we want so we can pay for them the old-fashioned way—with cash.

Reading this book has made me feel smart—I'm making smarter money decisions and I'm also sharing my newfound knowledge with my family and friends in the hope that it will make a difference in their lives. David's work is not just for women, it's for anyone whose goal is to be financially independent.

Kristina Anderson—Seattle, Washington

I was a bookseller for 30 years and have struggled with finances for equally as long. Being a bookseller, I've read numerous books about finances, but *Smart Women Finish Rich* was the most effective.

Here's what I found particularly helpful.

Most money books explain how to invest what you have—not how to save enough so you have some to invest. *Smart Women* did that for me. It addressed simple and doable ways to save, which is exactly what I needed.

As a result of reading it, here's what I did.

1. I started tracking every penny I spent (well, almost every penny) and kept a spreadsheet on Excel.
2. I made a commitment to pay off my credit card debt by the end of September 2000. (I actually did it by that September 1.)
3. I enrolled in a voluntary investment program through work in which money is taken out of my paycheck and invested in the stock market. (In other words, I found ways to save money I didn't think I had.)

4. I financed a kitchen and bathroom remodel that fit into my budget. Doing this remodel has not only greatly increased the value of my home but also made me very happy! (I've lived in my current house for 14 years and always used to complain that I couldn't afford to remodel.)
5. I've passed the book on to others who have found it VERY helpful.

I've always been afraid of not having enough money. I've pretty much dispelled that fear now. Because of *Smart Women,* I now have the philosophy that I'll have enough money only when I decide that what I have is enough. I would love to have more, no doubt, but I manage very well on what I make. I don't feel deprived anymore. Life is great!

Elaine Murphy—Atlanta, Georgia

I am amazed at how different my life is now from what it was a year ago. As a result of David's advice in *Smart Women Finish Rich,* I have turned around my financial situation 180 degrees.

Before reading the book, I was in dire financial straits. I had declared bankruptcy after a long, depressing stint of trying to run my own business. I was borrowing constantly from family and friends, which really strained those relationships. My car had been repossessed, I was renting a $425-a-month basement apartment that I could barely afford, and creditors were hounding my roommate. It was beyond embarrassing. It was humiliating.

I didn't even open bills as they came in. I just let the envelopes sit there and gather dust. I was too depressed to think about how I was going to pay them. I didn't have a checking or savings account and lived paycheck to paycheck.

As I read *Smart Women Finish Rich,* a lightbulb went off in my head. I saw the financial mistakes I had made and how I could get out of the pit I had dug myself into.

The first thing I had to accept was that there wasn't going to be a quick fix. I estimated it would take me three years of steady work to get completely out of debt. I acknowledged that my business had failed and that it was time to get a full-time job, even if it was scrubbing toilets, so I could pay off my debts and begin to take care of myself!

That was a year ago. Since then, I've gone from having no savings, no steady income, and a $30,000 mountain of debt to having a full-time job, $6,000 in a 401(k) account, $1,000 in the bank (emergency money), a used car that I will soon own outright, and only $9,000 in debts. I now rent an apartment, on my own, in a secure neighbour-hood, for $680 a month. It's not ritzy but it's my own, in my name, with no co-signer, and I have no problems paying for it. Having repaid everything I owed my mother and brother, I'm now wading through a list of old creditors and paying them off. Now people call me to ask me to donate to charities, not to tell me my account is in Collections!

Best of all, I'm head of the volunteer committee and head of the United Way campaign at my job. People wonder why I always want to give clothing or time to charity. They don't understand. All I can think of whenever someone talks about the working poor is "That was me, that was me."

I guess most people have never been hungry or scared that they couldn't afford to pay for essentials. Or maybe they never had to walk everywhere (which, in the South, is hell). Or maybe they've never had to compromise their morals and beg for assistance. I have, and I swore if I ever got out of the situation I was in, I'd give back and give thanks.

Katie Killian—Bloomington, Indiana

After I read *Smart Women Finish Rich,* I realized I was unhappy with the way my financial future was looking—and I'm only 21! Even so, I knew I needed to do something about my future or I was going to end up like a lot of women I know. So I read the book twice, took notes, and started changing things.

First off, I got out of a bad credit card situation by paying off all my debt. I then got myself a new credit card that only has a $200 limit, so my monthly bill is never more than I can afford to pay in full. In addition, I write down every penny I spend on everything, and try to cut out anything I don't really need.

At the same time, I've started contributing to my 403(b) plan at work. I can only afford to put in 4 percent—but, still, it's something. I also put 12 percent of my take-home pay into my savings account each paycheck I get.

Paying myself first like this has really helped me to get all the other things in order. I want to go back to college (I had to quit for mone-tary reasons), but I want to get all of my debts paid off before I do.

Reading David's book has done more for me than just help with the money situation. When I was thinking about my values and goals, I realized that I haven't been doing a lot of the things I always wanted to do. I have always wanted to sing and learn to play the guitar so I could be in a band, but never thought I could. After reading *Smart Women,* I realized that just like I can't wait too long to start saving for the future, I can't put my happiness and the things that really matter to me on hold, either. So, I've started taking voice lessons, and just yesterday I bought myself a guitar.

I am finally happy doing the things I have always loved to do. What's more, after reading the book, I also realized that I wanted to become a financial advisor. Now, instead of being unsure about my professional future, I know exactly what I want to do!

Toni Hudson—Katy, Texas

Before I came across *Smart Women Finish Rich,* I had read other books on the subject and I would just get depressed. It just seemed too overwhelming to get started. I was confused about what exactly I needed to do, so I procrastinated.

When I read *Smart Women Finish Rich,* everything seemed to make sense. I read it all the way through and then went back and started writing down what I needed to do. It was so easy! Writing down my values and goals really gave me a reason to get my financial life in order. I started by setting up an emergency fund. I now have $100 taken out of my checking account each month and placed into a money market account.

Since I had already maxed out my retirement plan at work—and my husband doesn't have a retirement plan at his current job—I started Roth IRAs for both of us. I decided to go with a mutual fund for the IRAs. We have the money taken out of our bank account each month.

I also started a college fund for my son (he is nine months old). Based on what I learned in the book, I decided on a 529 college plan. I have $50 taken out each month through a mutual fund company, and I plan to increase the contribution as soon as I can.

Finally, I started a "Dream Basket" fund. We plan to buy a house within the next couple of years, so I have $200 transferred to a money market account each month.

It was such a relief to get each of these started. Honestly, before I read *Smart Women,* I didn't think I could ever afford to do this. But how could I afford not to? Now I feel so much more relaxed knowing I am automatically saving for everything. It is a wonderful feeling. Yes, I have had to learn to live on a smaller paycheck. But having money in the bank is so exciting that I want to save even more now.

By the way, one of my goals was to get a substantial raise. So following David's advice, I wrote down on my calendar when I would receive it and showed it to my boss. Sure enough, a few weeks later I was called into my boss's office and because of departmental reorganization, I was given a 15 percent raise! It really does make a difference when you write down your goals!

Smart Women Finish Rich really made an impact in my life. It helped me to understand, get organized, and finally get started with my financial planning.

Deb Holder—Greenwood, South Carolina

As a 37-year-old divorced mother of three (Mychael is 6, Kayla is 8, Lindsay is 11), I've lived a life of financial struggle. I divorced my abusive husband several years ago, moved from Arizona to West Virginia to be with my family, and then found myself labeled either "underqualified" or "overqualified" in my job search. Translation: No one would hire me. My bachelor's degree in psychology amounted to "too much" education for some jobs and "not enough" for others.

I am employed now, but it's not easy surviving on a $38,000 income while saving more than 15 percent of my pay. I still live from paycheck to paycheck, but I refuse to modify my savings habits.

Smart Women Finish Rich showed me that I wasn't going overboard by trying to save so much. Because of it, I now know that women who earn far more than I do may sometimes project the illusion of wealth, but in some ways I'm one step ahead of them. This makes me feel much better about myself.

Just a year ago, I had nothing. Today, I have a company-sponsored 401(k) account, a Roth IRA, a global mutual fund, and I buy U.S. Savings Bonds through automatic payroll deduction. Nearly all of my investments are made by automatic contributions that are deducted either from my paycheck or from my checking account.

In addition, I've recently started a House Fund to save for a home, and I've created an Emergency Fund, too. I actually put spare change in a couple of brightly painted flowerpots for my House Fund. I keep these pots in a conspicuous place—beside my bills—to remind me that I'm actually making progress toward buying a home.

While an outsider may laugh at me for being proud of my holdings—they total just a few thousand dollars—I feel incredibly empowered for the first time in my life.

Smart Women Finish Rich also helped me learn restraint. It's so easy to want to spend money when you get a tax refund. After all, when you're not used to having a healthy bank account, you think you deserve a "reward" for all the struggles you've endured. I had to make a paradigm shift because I've been guilty, in the past, of spending fast cash. This year, I didn't allow myself to get trapped in the fast-cash shopping spree. Instead, my income tax refunds were used entirely to pay off debts, and when I think about how many bills I've paid off in the past year, I can't help but smile. Step by step, I'm building a solid financial future for my family.

Most important, I'm teaching my children investment strategies. I give them their allowances twice a month on my paydays, and I have rules for the distribution of their money: Tithe, Invest, Save, and Enjoy. They must tithe at least one dollar to a family-selected charity; they must invest a portion of their money for future wealth; they must save for something they'd like to buy; and whatever's left after all these, they can enjoy.

I keep our charity money in a family "kitty," and each child has two bank accounts: one for savings and one for investments. Once they earn enough money to invest in a stock or mutual fund, we deduct the money from their investment account for that purchase. My middle child, Kayla, is especially excited about mutual funds and dividend reinvestment plans. (She can't remember the names; she just knows that the money goes up, down, and up again!)

I encourage other women I know to give a small portion of their income to charity on a regular basis and to teach their children to do the same. Even on a tight budget, you can send something each payday. Instead of focusing on the small amount, see what you'll contribute over a year's time. I think it's important for children to experience the act of charitable giving. After all, people have been there for us when we've needed help.

You can do the same with your savings accounts and investments. When my children and I started talking about buying a home, I showed them how little purchases can add up to large amounts over time. I made saving a family project, and I got the children actively involved.

We started listing things we could cut from our lives, and we were amazed at how much "found" money was in our small budget. I was spending close to $100 a year on bags of ice. Frozen water! Now I make my own ice.

My children now weigh the need for things before they buy something with their allowances. The struggle is not over, but we're on the right track. I teach my children that ordinary people can achieve extraordinary results, even when the odds are seemingly against them. I'm proud of my success thus far, and I know that the future holds many more rewards.

WHERE DOES YOUR MONEY *REALLY* GO?

One of the most important parts of getting your financial life together is having a solid grasp on exactly what your current cash flow is. To do this, use the worksheet below.

First, determine how much you earn . . .

Your Income

Wages, salary, tips, commissions, self-employment income	$_____
Dividends from stocks, bonds, mutual funds, savings accounts, GICs, etc.	$_____
Income from rental property	$_____
Income from trust accounts (usually death benefits from an estate)	$_____
Alimony, child support, Old Age Security	$_____
Canada Pension Plan benefits	$_____
Other income	$_____
TOTAL MONTHLY INCOME	**$_____**

Second, determine what you spend

Your Expenses

Taxes

Federal income taxes	$_____
Provincial income taxes	$_____
CPP/OAS	$_____
Property taxes	$_____

TOTAL TAXES $_____

Housing

Mortgage payments or rent on primary residence	$_____
Mortgage payment on rental or income property	$_____
Utilities	$_____
Homeowner's or tenant's insurance	$_____
Repairs or home maintenance	$_____
Cleaning service	$_____
Television cable	$_____
Home phone	$_____
Landscaping and pool service	$_____
Internet service	$_____
Condo or association dues	$_____

TOTAL HOUSING $_____

Auto

Car loan or lease	$_____
Gas	$_____
Car insurance	$_____
Car phone	$_____
Repairs or service	$_____
Parking	$_____
Tolls	$_____

TOTAL AUTO $_____

Insurance

Life insurance $_____

Disability insurance $_____

Long-term care insurance $_____

Liability insurance (umbrella policy) $_____

TOTAL INSURANCE $_____

Food

Groceries $_____

Other food $_____

TOTAL FOOD $_____

Personal Care

Clothing $_____

Cleaning/dry cleaning $_____

Cosmetics $_____

Health club dues and/or personal trainer $_____

Entertainment $_____

Club dues $_____

Association memberships $_____

Vacations $_____

Hobbies $_____

Education $_____

Magazines $_____

Gifts $_____

TOTAL PERSONAL CARE $_____

Medical

Extended health care insurance $_____

Prescriptions, over-the-counter medicine, vitamins, etc. $_____

Dental expenses $_____

Chiropractic, massage therapy, etc. $_____

TOTAL MEDICAL $_____

Miscellaneous

Credit card expenses $_____

Loan payments $_____

Alimony or child support payments $_____

Anything you can think of that I missed! $_____

TOTAL MISCELLANEOUS EXPENSES $_____

TOTAL MONTHLY EXPENSES $_____

Murphy's Law Factor

Take the total expenses and increase by 10 percent $_____

Total Income

Minus total monthly expenses $_____

Net cash flow (available for savings or investments) $_____

FINISHRICH INVENTORY PLANNER™

DETERMINING YOUR NET WORTH

STEP ONE: FAMILY INFORMATION

Client Name _____ Date of Birth _____ Age _____
Nickname _____
Spouse's Name _____ Date of Birth _____ Age _____
Nickname _____
Mailing Address _____
City _____ Province _____ Postal Code _____
Home Phone # _____
Work Phone # _____ Fax # _____
Spouse's Work # _____ Spouse's Fax # _____
E-mail _____ Spouse's E-mail _____
SIN _____ Spouse's SIN _____
Employer _____ Job Title _____
Spouse's Employer _____ Job Title _____
Are You Retired? Yes _____ Date Retired _____ No _____ Planned Retirement Date _____
Is Your Spouse Retired? Yes _____ Date Retired _____ No _____ Planned Retirement Date _____
Marital Status: Single ____ Married ____ Divorced ____ Separated ____ Widowed ____

Children

		Date of Birth	SIN
Name	1) _____	_____	_____
	2) _____	_____	_____
	3) _____	_____	_____
	4) _____	_____	_____
	5) _____	_____	_____

Dependents

Do You Have Any Family Members Who Are Financially Dependent Upon You or Could Be in the Future?
(i.e., Parents, Grandparents, Adult Children, etc.)

Yes _____ No _____

Name 1) _____ Age _____ Relationship _____
2) _____ Age _____ Relationship _____
3) _____ Age _____ Relationship _____

STEP TWO: PERSONAL INVESTMENTS
(DO NOT INCLUDE RETIREMENT ACCOUNTS HERE)

Cash Reserves

List Amount in Banks and Credit Unions

Name of Bank	Type of Account	Current Balance	Interest Rate
Example: CIBC	Chequing/Savings/Money Market	$10,000.00	2%
1)			
2)			
3)			
4)			
5)			

Fixed Income

List Fixed-Income Investments

Example: GICs, Treasury Bills, Notes, Bonds	Dollar Amount	Current %	Maturity Date
1)			
2)			
3)			
4)			

Stocks

Name of Company	Number of Shares	Price Purchased	Approximate Market Value	Date Purchased
1)				
2)				
3)				
4)				
5)				

Do You Have Stock Certificates in a Security Deposit Box? Yes ———— No ————

Mutual Funds

Name of Mutual Fund	Number of Shares	Cost Basis	Approximate Market Value	Date Purchased
1)				
2)				
3)				
4)				
5)				
6)				

Annuities

Company	Annuitant/Owner	Interest Rate	Approximate Market Value	Date Purchased
1)				
2)				
3)				

Other Assets (i.e., Business Ownership, etc.)   Approximate Market Value

1)	$	
2)	$	
3)	$	

STEP THREE: RETIREMENT ACCOUNTS

Are You Participating in an Employer-Sponsored Retirement Plan?

Yes _____ No _____

Name of Company Where Your Money Is	Type of Plan	Approximate Value	% You Contribute

You:

1) _____ _____ _____ _____

2) _____ _____ _____ _____

3) _____ _____ _____ _____

Spouse:

1) _____ _____ _____ _____

2) _____ _____ _____ _____

3) _____ _____ _____ _____

Do You Have Money Sitting in a Company Plan Where You No Longer Work?

Yes _____ No _____ Balance _____ When Did You Leave the Company? _____

Spouse:

Yes _____ No _____ Balance _____ When Did He/She Leave the Company? _____

Self-Directed Retirement Plans

Are You Participating in a Retirement Plan?

(RRSP, for example)

Name of Institution Where Your Money Is	Type of Plan	Approximate Value

You:

1) _____ _____ _____

2) _____ _____ _____

3) _____ _____ _____

4) _____ _____ _____

5) _____ _____ _____

Spouse:

1) _____ _____ _____

2) _____ _____ _____

3) _____ _____ _____

4) _____ _____ _____

5) _____ _____ _____

STEP FOUR: REAL ESTATE

Do You Rent or Own Your Home?

Own _____ /Monthly Mortgage Is _____

Rent _____ /Monthly Rent Is _____

Approximate Value of Primary Home $ _____

—Mortgage Balance $ _____

= Equity in Home _____

Length of Loan _____

Interest Rate of Loan _____ Is Loan Fixed or Variable? _____

Do You Own A Second Home?

Approximate Value of Second Home $ _____

—Mortgage Balance $ _____

= Equity in Home _____

Length of Loan _____

Interest Rate of Loan _____ Is Loan Fixed or Variable? _____

Any Other Real Estate Owned? _____

Approximate Value $ _____

—Mortgage Balance $ _____

= Equity In Home _____

Length of Loan _____

Interest Rate of Loan _____ Is Loan Fixed or Variable? _____

STEP FIVE: ESTATE PLANNING

Do You Have a Will in Place? Yes _____ No _____

Date It Was Last Reviewed _____

Who Helped You Create It? Lawyer's Name _____

Address _____

Phone Number _____ Fax _____

Is Your Home Held in Your Name Alone or

Do You Own It with Someone as Joint Tenants or Tenants in Common? _____

Risk Management/Insurance

Do You Have a Protection Plan In Place for Your Family? Yes _____ No _____

Life Insurance Company   Type of Insurance (i.e., Whole Life, Term, Variable, etc.)   Death Benefit   Cash Value   Annual Premium

1) _____ _____ _____ _____ _____

2) _____ _____ _____ _____ _____

3) _____ _____ _____ _____ _____

Tax Planning

Do You Have Your Taxes Professionally Prepared? Yes _____ No _____

Name of Accountant _____

Address _____

Phone Number _____ Fax _____

What Was Your Last Year's Taxable Income? _____

Estimated Tax Bracket? _____ %

STEP SIX: CASH FLOW

Income

Your Est. Monthly Income _____ Estimated Annual Income _____

Spouse's Estimated Monthly Income _____ Estimated Annual Income _____

Rental Property Income: Monthly _____ Annually _____

Other Income (Partnerships, CPP, OAS, Pension, Dividend Cheques, etc.)

Type of Income	Monthly	Annually
1) _____	_____	_____
2) _____	_____	_____
3) _____	_____	_____
_____	_____	_____

Expenses

Use the "Where Does Your Money *Really* Go" Form (on page 271) to Figure Your Estimate

Monthly Estimated Expenses _____ Annual Estimated Expenses _____

STEP SEVEN: NET CASH FLOW

What Do You Earn a Month After Taxes? $ _____

What Do You Estimate You Spend? – $ _____

Net Cash Flow = $ _____

STEP EIGHT: NET WORTH

Net Worth

Total Assets $ _____

– Total Liabilities – $ _____

= **Estimated Net Worth** $ _____

STEP NINE: FINANCIAL OBJECTIVES

What Are Your Current Financial Goals and Objectives? _____

Is There Anything in Particular That You Are Currently Concerned With Regarding Your Financial Situation?

Are You Anticipating Any Major Life Style Changes That Could Require Money (i.e., Retirement, Divorce, Inheritance, Children Going to College, etc.)? _____

What Is the Best Financial Decision You Have Ever Made? _____

Have You Made Any Financial Decisions That You Regret? _____

Do You Own Any Investments or Real Estate That You Are Planning to Sell or Want to Sell in the Near Future?

If You Were to Hire a Financial Advisor, What Are the Three Most Important Things You Would Want Your Advisor to Do for You? _____

Any Additional Comments? _____

SUGGESTED PROGRAMS AND READINGS

I have read literally hundreds of books on motivation and investing. I believe no one person or company has the monopoly on good ideas, and I would like to share with you some of my favourite authors and the coaches who have influenced me. I highly recommend the following authors' and speakers' books and programs.

ANTHONY ROBBINS Tony Robbins is currently regarded as one of the world's greatest motivational speakers and peak-performance coaches. I have read all of his books, listened to all of his audio programs (more than once), and attended all of his seminar programs. I have also had the privilege of teaching at his Financial Mastery program three times. You have not experienced a motivational seminar until you've attended one of Tony's programs. They are awesome. I highly recommend his books and programs to anyone who wants to improve the quality of his or her life. To learn more about the programs, books, and audio products, you can reach Robbins Research directly by calling (800) 445-8183. *www.tonyrobbins.com*.

DAN SULLIVAN Dan Sullivan runs a three-year coaching program for entrepreneurs called Strategic Coach, which I attend every 90 days. This program is designed for entrepreneurs who want to clean out the messes in their lives and focus on what their unique abilities really are.

This program teaches you how to increase your business while having more free time to appreciate and enjoy your life. The simplicity of his program and the focus it can give you is truly life changing. To learn more about the program and the products, call Strategic Coach at (800) 387-3206. *www.strategiccoach.com.*

BILL BACHRACH Bill Bachrach is one of the leading coaches in the financial advisor industry. His books, *Values-Based Selling* and *Values-Based Financial Planning,* and his Trusted Advisor Program teach financial advisors how to help their clients tap into their values about money. I have attended his program and believe strongly that if you are a financial advisor, you owe it to yourself and your clients to read his book and learn about his products and seminars. Bachrach & Associates can be reached toll-free at (800) 347-3707. *www.bill-bachrach.com.*

BILL PHILLIPS Bill Phillips's book *Body for Life* has changed my life and my health. After reading it and doing his workout program, I lost 20 pounds and three inches of waist size in 12 weeks. It's been over a year now since I used his program, and not only have I kept the weight off, but I'm in the best physical shape of my life. I love this program and highly recommend it. Visit Phillips's website at *www.bodyforlife.com.*

I would also like to recommend the following books:

A Short Guide to a Happy Life, Anna Quindlen (Random House, 2000)

Awaken the Giant Within: How to Take Immediate Control of Your Mental, Emotional, Physical & Financial Destiny! Anthony Robbins (Fireside, 1991)

Beating the Street: How to Use What You Already Know to Make Money in the Market, Peter Lynch and John Rothchild (Fireside, 1993)

Don't Sweat the Small Stuff . . . and It's All Small Stuff: Simple Ways to Keep the Little Things from Taking Over Your Life, Richard Carlson (Hyperion Press, 1997).

Don't Sweat the Small Stuff for Women, Richard and Kristine Carlson (Hyperion Press, 2001)

Jesus CEO: Using Ancient Wisdom for Visionary Leadership, Laurie Beth Jones (Hyperion Press, 1995)

How to Win Friends and Influence People, Dale Carnegie (Pocket Books, 1990)

One Up on Wall Street, Peter Lynch and John Rothchild (Penguin, 1990)

Rich Dad, Poor Dad, Robert Kiyosaki and Sharon Lechter (Warner Books, 1999)

Swim with the Sharks Without Being Eaten Alive: Outsell, Outmanage, Outmotivate, and Outnegotiate Your Competition, Harvey Mackay (Ballantine Books, 1988)

Take Time for Your Life and Life Makeovers, Cheryl Richardson (Broadway Books, 1999 and 2001)

Ten Things I Wish I Had Known Before I Went into the Real World, Maria Shriver (Warner Books, 2000)

The Millionaire Next Door: The Surprising Secrets of America's Wealthy, Thomas J. Stanley and William S. Danko (Longstreet Press, 1996)

The Richest Man in Babylon, George S. Clason (New American Library, 1988)

The Wealthy Barber: Everyone's Commonsense Guide to Becoming Financially Independent, David Chilton (Stoddart, 1997)

The Truth About Money: Because Money Doesn't Come with Instructions, Ric Edelman and Cal Thomas (Georgetown University Press, 1996)

Think and Grow Rich, Napoleon Hill (Ballantine Books, 1998)

Values-Based Financial Planning, Bill Bachrach (Aim High Publishing, 2000)

Who Moved My Cheese? Spencer Johnson (Penguin Putnam, 1998)

INDEX

accountant(s), 67, 126, 175, 177

action, importance of, xxi, 74, 236, 249, 252–53

actively trading. *See* stocks, actively trading

age and compound savings charts, 101–2, 196, 217

allowance money, children and, 213–15

Amazon.com, 198

Anderson, Kristina, 264–65

annual renewable term insurance, 116–18

Ash, Nicole, 261

asset(s)
  allocation when investing, 141
  keeping track of, 57–58
  life as the greatest, 250–51
  automatic bill paying, 255
  automatic chequing account transfers, 153, 161, 166, 195

automatic payroll deductions, 100, 104, 127, 153, 195

Bach, Rose ("Grandma"), xii, 2, 36, 208, 250

Bachrach, Bill, 42n, 282

bankruptcy, spending and, 88

bank statements, filing the papers concerning, 63

Barclay's iUnits, 163

"baskets." *See* financial planning, "three-basket" approach to

Bias, Christina, 256–57

Body for Life (book), 282

bonds, 3
  buying into a fund of, 158
  Canada Savings, 156
  corporate & municipal, 157
  defined, 156
  interest rates and, 158
  investment grades of, 157
  "junk," 156
  maturities on, 158
  ratings of, 157

books, Bach recommended, 282–83

borrowing. *See* debt; RRSPs, borrowing for; RRSPs, borrowing from

brokerage account(s), filing the papers concerning, 63

Buffett, Warren, 200, 210

business owners. *See also* employment, self; entrepreneurs
  female, 5, 237
  overhead of, 239–40

Canada Customs and Revenue Agency (CCRA), 63, 65, 199
audits by, 63
Canada Pension Plan, 26–27, 130
disability benefits of, 123
filing the papers concerning, 63
Canada Savings Bonds (CSBs), 156
Canadian Association of Financial Planners, 177, 183
Canadian Deposit Insurance Corporation (CDIC), 155
Canadian Education Savings Grant (CESG), xxi, 225–26
Canadian Marketing Association, 190
Canadian Securities Administrators, 178
Carrey, Jim, 70–71
cash, helpful nature of paying with, 69, 73, 97, 190
cash flow, worksheets for, 271–74
"cash value" insurance. See insurance, "cash value"
Cassity, Reverend Donna, 262–63
CCRA. See Canada Customs and Revenue Agency
chequing accounts, 109–10
filing the papers concerning, 63
children. See also dreams, children and
filing the papers concerning, 65
financial education of, xxi, 208–27
parental life insurance and, 113–116
retirement accounts for, 216–18
weekly allowance and, 213
"churning." See financial advisor(s), churning by
college savings programs. See Canadian Education Savings Grant; Registered Educational Savings Plans
commissions. See also financial advisor(s), the payment of, 166, 168, 172
commitment, financial, 6, 16
company retirement accounts, 100
filing the papers concerning, 63
compliance departments, 178
compound interest. See interest, compound
consistency in financial matters, importance of, 17
corporate bonds, 157
couples, joint financial efforts of, 65–67
CPP. See Canada Pension Plan

credit card(s). See also cash, helpful nature of paying with
destructiveness of debt from, 187, 190
filing the papers concerning, 64
stopping offers of, 190–91
teaching children about, 219–21
vacationing from, 97–98
Credit Counselling Canada, 189
credit reporting companies, 188–89

"Date with Destiny" (seminars), 74
Davis, Ken, 214
debt. See also credit card(s), 64
proportion of disposable income and, 21
defined-benefit pension plans, 129–31
defined-contribution pension plans, 129, 131
dependents. See children
deposit accounts, defined, 154
disability insurance. See insurance, disability
diversification
importance of, 201–2
in your RRSPs, 147
Dividend Reinvestment Program(s) (DRIP), 168
divorce, financial effects of, 4, 27–28, 31–32, 263
Dominion Bond Rating Service, 157
downsizing, effects of, 18
Dream Basket. See financial planning, "three-basket" approach to
dreams, 148–49, 152
children and, 221
funding of, 153–54
goals and, 68–69, 107
long-term, 160–70
mid-term, 156–59
short-term, 153–55
values ladder and, 48
worksheets for, 150–51

earnings. See income
the "Earnings Outlook Chart," 22
education (higher), costs of, 65, 83, 114, 223–24, 226–27
the elderly, care of, 18
The Eleven Commandments of Wildly Successful Women (book), 68
emotions, finance and, 11, 15–16
employment. See also jobs

episodic nature of, 18
part time, 18
when to quit, 235–36
women's role in creating, 5
empowerment, Smart Women and, 257, 268
The E-Myth Revisited (book), 238
entrepreneurs. *See* business owners; self-employment
Equifax Canada Inc., 188
estate planning, 110–13
ETFs. *See* Exchange Traded Funds
exchange rate (foreign), 147
Exchange Traded Funds (ETFs), 163
expenses. *See also* spending; "Murphy's law and
emergency, 108

filing, the FinishRich system for, 62–65
final-average pension plans, 130–31
finances (family), the general ignorance of, 31–35
financial advisor(s), xx, xix, 67, 135, 139, 141, 166
background checking of, 177–78
churning by, 174–75
investment philosophy of, 173
selection/hiring of, 170–83
the payment of, 173–74
financial documents (organizing). *See also* filing, 58–67, 172, 186–87
financial education, xxi, 16
of children. *See* children's financial education
financial goals. *See* goals
financial knowledge
lack of, 16
quiz on, 33–35
financial literacy. *See* children's financial education
financial management, nine steps in. *See also* financial planning, 9
financial objectives worksheet, 280
Financial Planners Standards Council, 178
financial planning. *See also* retirement planning
importance of, 18
long-term, 10
"three-basket" approach to, 2, 106–8, 127–28, 148, 153, 169, 186

websites for help with. *See* website(s)
financial security
five elements of, 108–27
personal values and, 38
steps to achieving, 59–67
values and, 44
FinishRich File Folder System. *See* filing
FinishRich Inventory Planner, 58, 60–62, 65
worksheet, 275–80
Focusing Your Unique Ability (audio program), 244

gambling, dangers of, 197
GARP (Growth at Reasonable Prices) funds, 165
Gerber, Michael E., 237
Geyer, Bobbi, 261–62
GICs. *See* Guaranteed Investment Certificates
Gilberd, Pamela, 68
Gimbel's, 3
Global/International funds, 165
goals. *See also* women, success stories of, 186
achievement of. *See also* "Latté factor," 70
challenges and impediments to, 82–85
dreams and, 68–69
frequent reviewing of, 74, 76–77
immediate action toward, 73–74
public sharing of, 74–75
importance they be put in writing, 70–72, 85
"quantum leap system" for attaining, 72–77
specific and clear, 72–73
typical examples of, 53
values and, 40–41, 50–51, 53, 76
worksheets for, 78–79
gratitude, importance of expressing, 176–77, 248–49
Guaranteed Income Supplement (Canada), 27
Guaranteed Investment Certificates (GICs), 135, 155

Hammer, M.C. , 87–89
Hernandez, Faith, 263–64
Hill, Napoleon, 68–69, 71
Holder, Deb, 268–70
home improvements, filing the papers

concerning, 64
homes, financial value and importance of, 193–94
"hot tips," unreliability of, 6
household accounts, filing the papers concerning, 64
HRDC. See Human Resources Development Canada
Hudson, Toni, 267–68
Human Resources Development Canada (HRDC), 27, 63
husbands/partners, cooperation from, 65–67

illiquid investments. See investments, liquidity of; liquidity, importance of
income
  disability insurance and, 121–23
  "earned" defined, 134
  lifetime, 21–22
  myths about, 20–21, 25
  problems with, 20–21
  of women. See women, income of
index (mutual) funds, 162
Individual Pension Plan (IPP), 136
inflation
  insurance and, 118, 126
  myths about, 29–31
  pensions and, 130–31
  RRSPs and, 139–40
  truth about, 30–31
insurance
  of bank deposits & GICs, 155
  "cash value" and, 118
  disability, 65, 120–23
  filing the papers concerning, 64
  health, 120, 125
  the importance of, 107–8
  level term, 116–18
  life, 28–29, 33, 113–20, 124, 135
  long-term care, 124–27
  portability of, 118, 122
  tax-deductible aspects of, 126
  universal life, 118–19
  variable universal life, 119
  whole life, 118
interest
  on bank accounts, 109–10
  compound, 99–103, 212–13, 217
  rates on bonds, 158
  reduced payments of, 191–93

Internet. See stocks, Internet-related; website(s)
Inventory Planner. See FinishRich Inventory Planner
investment(s), 3
  advice and guidance for. See financial advisor(s)
  by children, 215
  for children, 65
  diversification of portfolios, 201–2
  for growth vs. capital preservation, 139–41
  inflation and, 139–40
  the "Latté Factor" and. See "Latté Factor"
  liquidity of, 203, 205–6
  by millionaires, 23
  in options, 197
  "pretax," 89–90
  risks and rewards (chart), 181
  serious mistakes made in, 186–207
  speculation in. See gambling
  systematic, 161, 166, 168
  women's greater success at, 6
investment accounts, filing the papers concerning, 63
Investment Dealers Association of Canada, 178

jobs, unique talents and, 242–44

Kids and Cash (book), 214
Killian, Katie, 266–67
Klann, Brandi, 258–59
knowledge, of what you don't know, 19
Kolb, Deborah M., 233

large capitalization funds, 164–65
the "Latté Factor," 2, 86, 93–95, 99, 215, 263
  compound interest and, 102–5
liabilities
  keeping track of, 57–58
  filing the papers concerning, 64
life
  living your, 250–51
  proactive design for your, 78–81
life expectancies, for women and men, 18
lifetime work and income, 21–22
limited partnership(s), 205
liquidity, importance of, 203, 205–6

living trusts, 111–12
loans. *See also* borrowing
    filing the papers concerning, 64
locked-in retirement account (LIRA), 132
Locklin, Gail, 254
long-term care (LTC) insurance. *See*
    insurance, long-term care

managed money portfolio, 160
Markowitz, Harry, 141
McDonald's, 3, 106
McGarry, Anne, 259
mentoring, 227
Microsoft Corp., 68, 198
Microsoft Money software, 59
The Millionaire Next Door (book), 21
millionaires, 23, 87
million-dollar savings chart, 101
money
    attitudes concerning, 6–7, 9, 38
    children and. *See* children's financial
        education
    emotions concerning, 11
    goals and. *See* goals
    human worth and, 211–12
    importance of, 1
    management of. *See* financial
        management; financial planning
    myths about, 20–21, 25
    as a tool not a goal, 41–42
    values and. *See* values
money market accounts, 109–10
money market funds, defined, 154
money purchase pension plans. *See*
    defined contribution pension plan
monsters, the creation of, 256
Moody's, 157
mortgages
    debt and, 187
    filing the papers concerning, 64
    importance of reducing, 191–93
    secondary, 206
municipal bonds, 157
Murphy, Elaine, 265–66
"Murphy's law"
    disasters and, 89
    expenses and, 96
mutual funds
    average performance of, 167
    choosing among, 162–67
    "core" type, 164

filing the papers concerning, 63
great diversity of, 160–67
load charges and, 166

National Association of Realtors, 194
National Association of Securities Dealers
    (NASD), 177
net worth
    of an average millionaire, 23
    computations of, 62, 65
    worksheets for, 275–79
nursing-home care, 125

Old Age Security, 26–27, 47, 63, 130
Oliver, Lisa, 259–60
OneShare.com, 219
options, speculation and, 197

partnership, limited. *See* limited
    partnership(s)
"Pay Yourself First" principle, 89–91, 95,
    100, 104–5, 135, 161, 215, 263
pensions, 26–27
    women and, 18
pension plans, 129–47
    portability of, 34, 132
    profit sharing and, 132
    rollover of, 136
    vesting of, 132
permanent insurance. *See* insurance, "cash
    value"
"Personal Plan for Success," 82–84
Phillips, Bill, 282
planning. *See* financial planning
portfolios. *See* investment portfolios
power of attorney, 64
pretax retirement accounts, 128
Pritchard, J.J., 213
probate, 110–13
procrastination, how to overcome, 103–4
profit-sharing plans, 132
publicly held companies, 3

Quest for the Pillars of Wealth (book), 213
Quicken financial software, 59, 143

raises (salary). *See* salary, maximizing your
real estate. *See* homes
Registered Educational Savings Plans
    (RESPs), xxi, 65, 225–26
Registered Pension Plans (RPPs), xx

Registered Retirement Savings Plans
(RRSPs). *See also* retirement
accounts, xx
in addition to company retirement
accounts, 133–34
beneficiaries of, 145–46
borrowing for, 143
borrowing from, 144
for children, 216–18
choosing investments for your, 139–43
consolidation of, 144–45
diversification in, 147
filing the papers concerning, 63
foreign content in, 146–47
importance of contributions to,
136–37, 147
managed vs. self-directed, 135
maximum permitted contributions to,
130, 136
pretax advantages of, 89–90
rollover of, 136
spousal, 145
wills and, 110
withdrawals from, 144
retirement, as a key financial goal, 107
retirement accounts. *See also* Registered
Retirement Savings Plans (RRSPs)
employer-sponsored, 129–32
filing the papers concerning, 63
"maxing out," 13
Retirement Basket. *See* financial
planning, "three-basket" approach to
retirement planning. *See also* financial
planning, 127–47
delay of, 195–96
for women, 90–91
Old Age Security and, 26–27
Revenue Canada. *See* Canada Customs
and Revenue Agency
risk, 250–51
control of, 198
importance of accepting some, 222–23
Robbins, Tony, 74–75, 248, 281
ROB TV, 218
Rockefeller, Nelson, 214–15

safety deposit box(es), 112
salary, maximizing your, 232–35
saving(s)
compound interest on, 99–101
by gentle degrees, 91

recommended proportion of disposable
income for, 21
tax-deferred. *See* Registered Savings
Plans
12 percent rule, 90–91
savings account(s)
filing the papers concerning, 63
interest on, 109
schooling, financial basics and, 209
security, as a key financial goal, 107–8
Security Basket. *See* financial planning,
"three-basket" approach to
self-employment. *See also* business
owners; entrepreneurs
disability insurance and, 121–23
retirement accounts for, 135–36
the "Seven-Day Financial Challenge," 96
The Shadow Negotiation (book), 233
small capitalization funds, 165
Smart Couples Finish Rich (book), 67, 259
Smart Women Finish Rich (seminars),
20, 39, 41, 80, 233, 255, 294
speculating. *See* gambling
spending. *See also* bankruptcy, spending
and; expenses
control of, 21, 24–25, 91–99
delaying large impulse outlays, 98
by teenagers, 214
tracking of, 96–97
using only cash for, 97–98
values and, 45, 100
spousal RRSPs. *See* Registered
Retirement Savings Plans (RRSPs),
spousal
St. George, Vicki, 75
Standard & Poor (S&P), 157, 167
S&P/TSX Composite Index Fund, 162,
164, 167
S&P/TSX 60 ("blue chip") index fund, 162
Stanley, Tom, 21, 23
State Street (ETF), 163
Statistics Canada, 5
stocks. *See also* mutual funds, 3
actively trading, 199
defined, 160
DRIP, 168
filing the papers concerning, 63
"growth," 165
Internet-related, 198, 200
taxes and, 199
"value," 164

"Strategic Coach" (program), 281–82
Streep, Meryl, 170
Streisand, Barbra, 169
success. *See also* women, success stories of
  goals and, 68–69, 80–81
  stories of, 12–13, 253–70
  worksheet for, 84
Sullivan, Dan, 244, 281–82
systematic investment plan. *See*
  investment(s), systematic

taxes
  filing the papers concerning, 63
  saving of, 89–90, 203–4
  stocks and, 199
Taylor, Tom, 214
TD Bank (ETFs), 163
Templeton, Sir John, 248
term deposits, defined, 154
thanking. *See* gratitude
Think and Grow Rich (book), 68
"three baskets." *See* financial planning,
  "three-basket" approach to
time, gaining extra, 245–46
Treasury bills, defined, 155
Trusted Advisor Program, 282
trusts, 111–13
TSE. *See* S&P/TSX
tuition fees, increases in, 225

university/college costs. *See* education
  (higher), costs of; tuition fees

Vallin, Tonja L., 255–56
values. *See also* women, success stories of,
  9–10, 186, 243–44, 247–48
  defined and illustrated, 39–41
  financial implications of, 44–45
  goals and, 40–41, 76
  "ladder," 42–44, 46–49
  of money, 38–55
  typical examples of, 51
vesting. *See* pensions plans

wealth
  "Latté Factor" in the creation of. *See*
    "Latté Factor"
  12 commandments and, 231–49
website(s). *See also* Internet

for bank fee comparisons, 109
for Bank of Canada rate, 110
for business startups, 238
for buying one share of stock, 219
for college scholarship information, 227
for contacting MPs, 210
for CPP statements, 63
for credit rating reports, 188–89
for data about potential investments,
  142–43
for disability insurance, 124
for DRIP companies, 168–69
financial advisors and, 178, 183
for "giving back," 248
home buying and, 194
for HRDC, 27, 124
for index funds, 162–63
for job finding, 237
for life insurance, 120
for long-term care information, 125
for mortgage calculations, 192
for mutual funds, 166–67
for teaching children, 223–24
widowhood, financial effects of, 4, 28,
  113–115
Williams, Judith, 233
wills, 110–13
  filing the papers concerning, 64
  importance of, 28–29
  RRSPs and, 146
Winfrey, Oprah, 215, 248
women. *See also* divorce; success;
  widowhood
  "bag lady" fears and, 11
  and Canada's workforce, 5
  Canadian businesses owned by, 5
  "Cinderella myth" and, 25–26
  as entrepreneurs, 237
  financial education of, 4–5
  income of, 17–18, 26–27
  poverty rate of, 18
  retirement needs of, 90–91
  single, 114, 116
  success stories of, xxi, 252–69
Woods, Tiger, 169

Young, Rebecca, 253–54

Ziglar, Zig, 241

Attend a FinishRich™ Seminar

My grandmother taught me anyone could be rich if they had the right tools and the right motivation. Now I want to teach you! Come to a Smart Women Finish Rich™ or Smart Couples Finish Rich™ seminar—or both!

They have been taught to thousands of people who have learned—just as you can—that improving their financial lives can be easy and fun. You will also learn how to focus on your values so that the money you do spend enhances the life you always dreamed of living.

Both seminars are usually offered at no cost and include a free workbook.

To see David live or attend a FinishRich™ seminar in your area, please visit:

www.finishrich.com

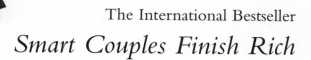

ALSO BY DAVID BACH

The International Bestseller
Smart Couples Finish Rich

The ultimate 9-step system to live and finish rich—
for couples.

Currently published in six languages and distributed around the world, *Smart Couples Finish Rich* is helping couples everywhere achieve financial security.

Join the tens of thousands of couples who are implementing the remarkable FinishRich™ strategy in their own relationships. Strengthen communication, create a financial plan that reflects your dreams and desires as a team, and build a foundation for a lifetime of wealth . . .

Together.

"*Smart Couples Finish Rich* teaches women and men to work together as a team when it comes to money. Bach's 9 steps are powerful, yet easy to understand and fun to implement. The entire family can benefit from this great book."

—Robert T. Kiyosaki, author *Rich Dad, Poor Dad*

David Bach

is the author of the phenomenal bestsellers *Smart Women Finish Rich* and *Smart Couples Finish Rich* and the recently released *Finish Rich Workbook*. The host of his own PBS special, "Smart Women Finish Rich," Bach is an internationally recognized financial advisor, author, and educator.

Mr. Bach is the creator of the FinishRich™ book and seminar series. Millions of people have benefited from his quick and easy-to-use financial strategies. In just the last few years, nearly a half million people have attended his Smart Women Finish Rich™ and Smart Couples Finish Rich™ seminars, which have been taught throughout North America by thousands of financial advisors in over 1,500 cities. Each month, through these seminars, men and women continue to learn firsthand how to take smart financial action to live a life in line with their values.

David Bach is regularly featured on television and radio, as well as in newspapers and magazines as a financial expert who makes money and financial planning easy to understand. Mr. Bach has appeared as a regular on ABC's *The View*, as well as on NBC's *Weekend Today*, CBS's *Early Show*, Fox News Channel's *The O'Reilly Factor*, CNBC, CNN and MSNBC. Mr. Bach has been profiled in major publications, including *BusinessWeek, USA Today, People, Financial Times, Washington*

Post, Wall Street Journal, Los Angeles Times, San Francisco Chronicle, Working Women, Bottom Line Personal, and *Family Circle.* Bestseller lists that have featured *Smart Women Finish Rich* include the *New York Times* and *Wall Street Journal* business lists, *Business Week, Washington Post, Boston Globe,* and *San Francisco Chronicle. Smart Couples Finish Rich* has also appeared on the *New York Times* business, *Business Week, USA Today, Denver Post* and *San Francisco Chronicle* bestseller lists. Bach's books are currently available in six languages.

A renowned financial speaker, Bach each year presents seminars and keynotes to the world's leading financial-services firms, *Fortune* 500 companies, universities, and national conferences. David Bach is the founder and CEO of FinishRich™ Inc., a company dedicated to revolutionizing the way people learn about money. Prior to founding FinishRich™ Inc., Bach was a senior vice president of Morgan Stanley and a partner of The Bach Group (1993 to 2001), which during his tenure managed over a half billion dollars for individual investors.

David Bach lives in New York with his wife, Michelle. He is currently working on his next two books, *The Automatic Millionaire* (2003, Broadway Books; Canadian edition: Doubleday Canada) and *Start Young, Finish Rich* (2004, Broadway Books; Canadian edition: Doubleday Canada) and is a contributing editor to *Smart Money* magazine. Please visit his website at *www.finishrich.com.*

(How to Reach Us)   . . . go to *FinishRich.com*

If you would like more information about *Smart Women Finish Rich* or other financial-management products and services we have developed, please contact us at *www.finishrich.com*. There you will find information on:

- My free online FinishRich™ newsletter
- How to attend a Smart Couples Finish Rich™ and/or Smart Women Finish Rich™ seminar
- How to hire David Bach to speak at your next event
- Books
- Audiotapes
- Videos
- Interactive CD-rom
- FinishRich™ QuickStart Program
- For financial advisors: How to become licensed to teach FinishRich™ seminars
- Coming soon . . . information on new books, including the *Finish Rich Workbook*, *The Automatic Millionaire*, and *Start Young, Finish Rich*.

To everyone who has written and e-mailed me . . . THANK YOU from the bottom of my heart . . . I am incredibly grateful and humbled by the amount of letters and e-mails I have received thus far. If this book has made a significant impact on you, please know that I would like to hear about your successes!

Maybe your personal story (if you give us permission) will become part of a future edition. To share success stories, visit *www.finishrich.com*.

Lastly, I am no longer taking financial planning clients, and due to legal liabilities, I unfortunately cannot answer personal financial questions. If you have specific financial questions, I strongly recommend meeting with a professional. Visit our website resource center, where we have created a section on how to find a financial advisor.